1949 Ross Macdonald's first Lew Archer book, *The Moving Target*, is published.

1949 "Man Against Crime" and "Martin Kane, Private Eye," the first television detective series, go on the air.

1951 *Black Mask* goes out of business.

1952 Hillary Waugh writes *Last Seen Wearing . . .*, a pioneering police procedural.

1952 "Dragnet" moves to television.

1956 Ed McBain's first 87th Precinct novel, *Cop Hater*, is published.

1957 The Perry Mason television show debuts.

1959 NBC cancels "Dragnet."

1959 Raymond Chandler dies.

1959 Coffin Ed Johnson and Grave Digger Jones appear for the first time as minor characters in Chester Himes' *A Rage in Harlem (For Love of Imabelle)*.

1961 Dashiell Hammett dies.

1961 Wall Street banker John Putnam Thatcher solves his first case in Emma Lathen's *Banking on Death*.

1964 Travis McGee colors his first page in John D. MacDonald's *The Deep Blue Good-Bye*.

1964 Rabbi David Small's first appearance, *Friday the Rabbi Slept Late*, is written by Harry Kemelman.

1964 The literary professor-detective, Kate Fansler, solves her first case in Amanda Cross' *In the Final Analysis*.

1966 CBS cancels "Perry Mason."

1969 *Blind Man With a Pistol*, the final Coffin Ed Johnson/Grave Digger Jones novel, is published.

1970 Erle Stanley Gardner dies.

1970 Hard-boiled insurance investigator Dave Brandstetter, who is gay, debuts in *Fadeout*.

1971 Manfred Lee, one half of the Ellery Queen pseudonym, dies. The final Queen novel, *A Fine and Private Place*, is published.

1973 *The Case of the Postponed Murder*, the final Perry Mason novel, is published posthumously.

1974 Robert Parker's first Spenser novel, *The Godwulf Manuscript*, appears.

1975 Rex Stout dies. *A Family Affair*, the final Wolfe book, is published.

1976 *The Blue Hammer*, the final Lew Archer book, is published.

1982 V. I. Warshawski debuts in Sara Paretsky's *Indemnity Only*.

1982 Sue Grafton writes the first Kinsey Millhone novel, *A is for Alibi*.

1982 Frederic Dannay, the other half of the Ellery Queen pseudonym, dies.

1983 Ross Macdonald dies.

1984 Chester Himes dies.

1986 John D. MacDonald dies.

THE AMERICAN DETECTIVE

Also by Jeff Siegel:
The Casablanca Companion

THE AMERICAN DETECTIVE

AN ILLUSTRATED HISTORY

Jeff Siegel

Taylor Publishing Company
Dallas, Texas

Published by Taylor Publishing Company
1550 West Mockingbird Lane
Dallas, Texas 75235

Designed by Hespenheide Design

Library of Congress Cataloging-in-Publication Data
Siegel, Jeff, 1958–
The American detective : an illustrated history / by Jeff Siegel.
p. cm.
Includes bibliographical references and index.
ISBN 0-87833-829-2
1. Detective and mystery stories, American—History and criticism. 2. Detectives in literature. I. Title.
PS374.D4S53 1993 93-7189
813'.087209—dc20 CIP

Printed in the United States of America
10 9 8 7 6 5 4 3 2 1

To the worst damned sports desk in the world, wherever they may be and whatever they may be doing.

Contents

Introduction

When I was in the sixth grade, I missed a couple of days of school with the flu. My mother, in her desire to keep me occupied, brought home a couple of books from the library. One of them was the *Raymond Chandler Omnibus,* a collection of Philip Marlowe novels and the only original Marlowe short story, "The Pencil."

My life hasn't been the same since.

Chandler and Marlowe started me on the road that led to this book. I hope it will be a guided tour of the place that is part of what novelist Fay Weldon calls the City of Invention, and of the Houses of Imagination that make up that city. This is the city where Marlowe and Sam Spade and Lew Archer and Spenser live, in a part of town where the streets are mean but where the heroes are not. Near them, but in a much nicer neighborhood, are Ellery Queen and Philo Vance, who favor mind over muscle. The 87th Precinct is in this particular City of Invention, as are "The Streets of San Francisco," and it's where Sgt. Joe Friday walked his first beat. Perry Mason works in the city's courthouse, while two policemen named Coffin Ed Johnson and Grave Digger Jones patrol its ghetto and Rabbi Small watches over the city's spiritual needs. The City of Invention's borders even include those who work outside its borders, like Alexander Scott and Kelly Robinson and Mr. Moto.

Do not be alarmed, however, by all of this rhetoric. This is not an attempt to explain the American fictional detective in terms decipherable only to graduate students working on theses. I plan to write this in English.

In fact, one of the most amazing contradictions in the entire field of mystery criticism in this country is that there is little middle ground between those who claim the American fictional detective is as much a part of American literature as Walden Pond and F. Scott

Fitzgerald (just wait until I explain what they claim James Fenimore Cooper and Joe Mannix have in common) and those who dismiss the genre as a bunch of oversexed male stereotypes (including the women detectives) who are little better than the characters who people romance novels.

I want to find the middle ground. There is no doubt that Mike Hammer, the Mickey Spillane–created hard guy's hard guy, is a parody of a parody. The violence is comic-book brutal, and Hammer never met a firm, young breast that wasn't pouting. But it's equally true that anyone who wants to get an idea of what the paranoia and repressed sexuality of the McCarthy-era 1950s felt like could do a lot worse than to read Spillane's *I, the Jury* or *My Gun Is Quick*, where there's a Commie under every bed—and a floozie on top.

It's that sort of perspective that I hope to bring to the subject. The fictional detective is a lot like the musical comedy, another distinctly American form of entertainment. Both are of American origin, and although both are created and performed elsewhere in the world, the best practitioners are still found in the United States (Andrew Lloyd Webber and Georges Simenon notwithstanding). Another point in common: It's difficult to find the best approach to discuss them. On the one hand, it's hard to take seriously as an art form anything in which two actors suddenly burst into song for no particular reason. On the other hand, it's hard not to take an art form seriously that produced George Gershwin.

That is the dilemma facing anyone writing about the American fictional detective. For every Raymond Chandler or Dashiell Hammett or Edgar Allan Poe, there are thousands of penny-a-word hacks whose characters are forgotten as soon as the page is turned. The trick, again, is to maintain perspective during the tour of this particular part of the City of Invention. Just because a character started in the pulp magazines doesn't mean it has been unjustly overlooked for six decades (as anyone who has plowed through a Raoul Whitfield novel will testify). And just because a character has known only a television existence doesn't mean it can be dismissed without a second thought. The original "Dragnet," for instance, is not only the most influential cop show in the history of television, but is one of the most influential works in the history of detective fiction—whether printed, spoken or viewed.

That's the tour offered in this book, beginning with Poe's invention of the detective in 1841, through the detective's appearance in the dime novels of the late nineteenth century, and its move to books and short stories in the early twentieth. It's a tour that will spend time in the pages of magazines—both slicks and pulps—and on the television and movie screens, as well as on radio. It's a tour that will introduce a variety of American detectives, from the best known, like Poe's Dupin and Hammett's Sam Spade, to those long forgotten, like Robert Leslie Bellem's Dan Turner, and Randolph Mason, a distant cousin of Perry. The tour will visit the American City of Invention, although certain stops will have to be made elsewhere—in England and France, for instance—to flesh out the genre's history.

Finally, the process to determine what makes a character a detective must remain necessarily flexible. To paraphrase former Supreme Court Justice Potter Stewart (who was discussing pornography), it's hard to explain what a detective is—but I recognize one when I see one.

It's easy enough to realize that a character like Dave Brandstetter, who may be atypical because he's gay, is still a detective in the fullest sense of the American tradition. It's also easy enough to realize that the psychotics who sprang from the imagination of Jim Thompson are not detectives, no matter how morbidly fascinating they may be. What's harder to figure out is whether the characters devised by writers such as Elmore Leonard and George Higgins, whose thrillers have been especially popular in the past decade, or James M. Cain and Cornell Woolrich, whose works have been popular for a lot longer, fit into this niche. I tend to doubt it. The protagonists in these stories are rarely detectives, certainly not of the sort that the writer and critic H. R. F. Keating calls The Great Detective. Cain's *Double Indemnity*, for example, is the story of what happens when a Great Detective decides not to detect, much as all of Cain's books are the stories of strong men being seduced by sex or money or both. Higgins, too, disdains the detective label. In fact, he once told Keating he didn't even consider himself a crime writer.

These attitudes contrast with even the bleakest visions of the hard-boiled detectives, whose cynicism all too often hides a romanticism as sickly sweet as the smell of burning sugarcane. Take, for instance, Dave Robicheaux, a reformed alcoholic and failed Catholic (which gives him two strikes in a world where three strikes is a luxury). Yet even Robicheaux, while realizing that there is no order in the world, battles to provide some sort of order in his part of the world (based in large part on his near-fanatical adherence to the twelve steps outlined by Alcoholics Anonymous for staying sober). This contrasts even more vividly with the attitude of the traditional detectives, fellows like Queen and Vance, where order is always part of the equation, and is always restored to the world after all of the suspects have been brought into the drawing room and the culprit is bundled over to the police.

I'm also going to exclude any detective who wasn't created by an American. This not only excludes the obvious—like Sherlock Holmes and Hercule Poirot—but any number of detectives who work in America or take a distinctly American approach to their work. Peter Cheyney's Slim Callaghan, one of the few examples of a hard-boiled British private eye, is one of the latter. He has not only an American approach to violence, liquor and women (God only knows what Dorothy L. Sayers thought of Slim), but also a reverence for Hammett and Chandler that is shocking in a British detective writer of his era. But despite all of these characteristics, he still isn't an American.

Know, then, that for the purposes of this book, a detective is someone who tries to discover some sort of truth, and is around at the end to reflect on his search and his discovery. It may be the truth about the case he is working on, whether in an official or unofficial capacity. He may be a hard-boiled detective, a traditional detective, a policeman, a lawyer or a spy. This truth may be about himself or about some higher calling. He may even arrest someone, but that is not the most important thing. The most important thing is that the detective searched and discovered some truth, and that because of that, one person will always be a witness to the truth. This may not be much, but it's all the detective wants, whether it's C. Auguste Dupin or V. I. Warshawski. Paul Newman (playing Ross MacDonald's Lew Archer, renamed Harper to suit Hollywood) put it best. He told Joanne Woodward in *The Drowning Pool* that "I'm not all that interested in justice. It's the truth I'm interested in."

There are dozens and dozens of people who deserve thanks for helping me write this book, far too many than I can mention here. I owe a special debt to each of the writers and critics who answered my questions and helped to compile the Hall of Fame lists in this book, and who did so with patience and perseverance—especially Jon Tuska, Sue Grafton, Robert B. Parker, Loren Estleman, Bill Pronzini, William F. Nolan, Jim Siegel, and Willam Ruehlmann. Priscilla Ridgeway, the executive director of the Mystery Writers of America, rifled her files and forwarded a number of letters to help make my job easier. Kathy Hoke at Bowling Green State University was the epitome of public relations professionalism. Big Max Lakin shared his mystery collection and words of wisdom, while Holly McGuire, his colleague at Taylor Publishing Company, edited the book with a firm hand and a gentle touch. Amy Fikes, the owner, and her colleagues June Leftwich and Carol Ann Luby at Dallas's Mystery Book Store, answered every question I took to them with patience and perseverance. And, as always, I'd like to thank Lynne Kleinpeter, who better have learned by now that I can't write anything without her help.

Finally, if you disagree with any of the sentiments, comments, wisecracks, or lists outlined in this book, don't get angry at any of the people mentioned here. Get angry at me. The opinions are entirely mine, based on my research and on my twenty years in this particular City of Invention.

150 Years of Gumshoes

1

"Hammett gave murder back to the people who commit it for reasons; not just to provide a corpse. . . . He put these people down on paper as they were, and he made them talk and think in the language they customarily used for these purposes."

—Raymond Chandler

Raymond Chandler, who was as acutely aware of his position as the litterateur of the American detective as he was of his flair for metaphors and similes, was never one to throw superlatives around just to get his name on the dust jackets of books. He was, as he was the first to admit, a snob.

Yet in his ground-breaking essay, "The Simple Art of Murder," Chandler spends almost as much time writing about Dashiell Hammett as he does writing about himself.

This is no accident. Three writers made the American fictional detective what it is today, and Hammett—a former Pinkerton operative, unreformed alcoholic, convicted perjurer, decorated Army hero, and longtime companion to Lillian Hellman—was the third of them. The first, Edgar Allan Poe, invented the detective in 1841 when he wrote about an eccentric Frenchman named C. Auguste Dupin who solved the murders in the Rue Morgue (and along the way, invented almost every convention used in the mystery story in the past 150 years).

The second, Ellery Queen, shepherded the detective across the Atlantic Ocean, where it had resided since Arthur Conan Doyle turned Poe's invention into Sherlock Holmes. Queen (who was actually two men, the cousins Manfred B. Lee and Frederic Dannay) was, in many ways, as English in style as the Battle of Waterloo. The early Queen is too often insufferable, and he solves entirely too many locked-room puzzles. But Queen, who was not only the author but the detective of the stories, had something working for him that none of his English contemporaries did. He was an American, and he almost single-handedly—as a detective, author, editor, and anthologist—twisted all of the accent out of the English detective until he sounded wholly American. He made it respectable for an American writer to write about an American

(Courtesy Bob Lakin Books)

(Courtesy Bob Lakin Books)

detective. Without Queen, it's difficult to imagine Nero Wolfe; it's even harder to imagine that Perry Mason would have become anything more than another one of Erle Stanley Gardner's hard-boiled pulp characters.[1]

Then Hammett took the detective and finished the process Queen started. It's all but impossible to find a detective who has appeared since Hammett's first Continental Op stories who hasn't been influenced by Hammett, regardless of whether the detective was a hard-boiled tough guy or the most traditional English-style, prying old lady. The key, as Chandler pointed out in "The Simple Art of Murder," was Hammett's use of language. Hammett, whose contemporaries included literary icons like Ernest Hemingway and F. Scott Fitzgerald, doesn't always get the credit he deserves for this—after all, anyone competing against Hemingway is usually overlooked (although there is one of those wonderfully academic debates raging as to whether Hammett influenced Hemingway or vice versa). But, as Chandler realized, Hammett was one of the first writers to discover that spoken American English was a legitimate form of literary expression. "I believe this style," wrote Chandler, "can say things [the writer] did not know how to say, or feel the need of saying. In [Hammett's] hands it had no overtones, left no echo, evoked no image beyond a distant hill. . . . He wrote scenes that never seemed to have been written before."

Hammett's masterpiece is *The Maltese Falcon,* which is not only the finest accomplishment in the history of detective fiction but a landmark in the history of American literature as well. It

[1]Do not be too confused by dates here. Hammett's work actually predates Queen's. The first Hammett Op stories appeared in 1923, six years before Queen's first appearance in *The Roman Hat Mystery*. The first Hammett novel, *Red Harvest,* came out in 1929, too. But while Queen was an instant hit (both in terms of sales and in critical acclaim), Hammett remained little known save for the pulp magazine audience that bought his short stories. Queen, for instance, wrote fourteen novels between 1929 and 1938. Hammett wrote only five in his lifetime. Queen's influence was immediate and has faded over time, while Hammett's influence was gradual, and shows no indication of leveling off. In fact, as Queen's character changed over the next half-century, it took on many of the characteristics pioneered by Hammett.

ranks with anything ever accorded this status, thanks to Hammett's skill in using it to transform the fictional detective. Still, it was another decade before anyone fully realized what Hammett had done. In 1930, the critics knew *The Maltese Falcon* was an outstanding, if slightly different, sort of mystery novel. Later, others (including Chandler), would discover that it was a novel first, and that the mystery in it was just one part of the novel. Howard Haycraft dominated mystery criticism in the United States between the two world wars, but for all of his critical skill and acumen he saw little that was redeeming in either the hard-boiled novel, hard-boiled detective, or the hard-boiled writer. Still, he recognized Hammett's ability: "No other author of modern times—certainly no other American—has basically changed and influenced the form."

Dashiell Hammett.
(Photograph by Azarnick, courtesy Alfred A. Knopf)

That form, in fact, had changed little in the eighty years since Poe had written "The Murders in the Rue Morgue." Someone once analyzed "Rue Morgue," and discovered that Poe invented thirty-two conventions of the mystery story, ranging from the creation of the haughty amateur detective to the locked-room puzzle to the devoted (if slightly bubbleheaded) assistant to the even more hapless policeman. Without Poe's C. Auguste Dupin, there would have been no Sherlock Holmes; without Holmes, there's serious doubt as to whether the detective as it exists today would exist, in either the United States or Britain. Every detective owes something to Holmes, and Holmes is nothing more than Arthur Conan Doyle's vision of an Englishman who started life as a Frenchman created by an American.

This is not to denigrate Holmes, who has suffered enough at the hands of the genre's revisionists. Rather, it's an attempt to put Holmes in perspective, and to give Poe the credit he deserves. Consider just two things: First, Dupin exhibits a disregard for the police and their methods, similar to Holmes's reaction every time he meets Inspector Lestrade. Second, Dupin can deduce the most obscure facts about a person's background after a brief meeting, which he does at the beginning of "Rue Morgue." Compare this to what Holmes does to his visitor at the beginning of the classic Holmes story, "The Hound of the Baskervilles." Those two points alone should establish the historical and literary connection between the two characters.

Edgar Allan Poe.

Dozens more of these similarities abound, and they are not hard to see. Anyone can go through "The Murders in the Rue Morgue" and play literary detective, and it's not only the Holmesian connections that are noticeable. Just remember that every cliché in the story was brand new when Poe wrote it. Today, even the most casual reader of mysteries might scoff at Dupin's solution to the murders—an ape crawled through an opening too small for a human—but a century and a half ago, it was a novel answer to a unique puzzle.

Poe himself is as much of a mystery as any of his stories. Today, he is as well known for being an alcoholic and drug addict as he is for being a writer (and to tastes 150 years ago, his behavior was even more disreputable). Poe's reputation as a writer of horror and fantasy—"The Raven," "The Masque of the Red Death"—far outweighs his renown for the trio of detective stories—"The Murders in the Rue Morgue," "The Purloined Letter," and "The Mystery of Marie Roget"—he wrote. He stumbled into writing only because he could find no other way to support himself. His adoptive parents had cut him off after his first, scandal-plagued year at the University of Virginia, and a three-year stint in the army (including three months at West Point) was no more productive.

Poe was editing a magazine in Philadelphia in 1841, then popular and now defunct, called *Graham's*. He earned $800 a year, and it was one of the best jobs he was to have in the forty-one years of his life. Both he and his wife, who also died young, were in good health during this period for one of the few times in their life together. Whether this financial and physical affluence influenced Poe's writing at the time, and whether he set out to invent a new literary form, or was merely mining the ground he had uncovered when he wrote earlier stories such as "The Tell-Tale Heart," is for earnest college students to decide. What's certain is that Dupin was as completely different from any other previous literary character as baseball is from ice hockey. They are both sports, but that's about where the comparison ends.

There are, of course, dissenters who claim Poe no more invented the detective story than Dr. Seuss did. They point to Poe's failure to use the word "detective" in describing Dupin—the closest he comes is in calling him a "ratiocinist." They point to a number of other things, as well, but this is all academic quibbling.[2] So is the attitude of a sizable school of English critics, which credits the redoubtable Charles Dickens, in his unfinished *The Mystery of Edwin Drood* (1870), for inventing the detective story. They seem to overlook one important fact, though: Poe wrote his story twenty-nine years before Dickens wrote his.

In fact, this form of detective carbon-dating can be taken back indefinitely. An English writer, William Godwin, included a detective in a book he wrote in 1794, although the detective's role is not part of the main plot. Haycraft lists Voltaire's *Zadig* (1748) as

---

[2]Among those credited with inventing the detective story are Wilkie Collins in *The Moonstone* (1868) and Daniel Defoe in a number of works, including *Moll Flanders* (1722) and *Roxana* (1724). Collins at least wrote about a policeman; the tie to Defoe is even more tenuous.

the great-grandfather of the detective story (it's about a fellow who specializes in abstract reasoning, and isn't about crime so much as it is about this fellow's plight in society), and there are even critical references that go back farther than that. Didn't Hamlet have to solve a murder? Didn't Iago try to gaslight Othello? Didn't Cordelia try to uncover a plot against her father? But before someone tries to make a case for Shakespeare as the daddy of the whodunit, remember this: Solomon had to do a little spade work to find out who was the real mother of the baby.

This reasoning is as fruitless as it is unnecessary. Poe invented the detective story, if only because he was the first writer to present it in the form as it is known today. Poe wrote a story that revolved around a detective trying to solve a crime. There were no ghosts, no subplots, nothing to detract from the focus of the plot. No one before Poe had written a story quite this way.

Poe almost surely based Dupin on a Frenchman named François-Eugène Vidocq, a criminal turned informer turned

Universal—Hollywood horror capital of the thirties—put out Murders in the Rue Morgue *in 1932 after the success of* Dracula. *Bela Lugosi was the star/villain, which is an indication of how closely this film adheres to the Poe story—note gorilla in the background.*

policeman turned private detective. Vidocq's memoirs, published in 1832, are of doubtful historical authenticity. But whether fact or fiction, they gave Poe the idea that reached fruition in "Murders in the Rue Morgue." In his memoirs, Vidocq recounts a career as a petty thief that began when France was still ruled by a king. Vidocq claims he was not only the greatest criminal in the world, but the greatest detective once he set his mind to it. The change came, he says, after Napoleon—yes, that one—recruited him as some sort of secret agent.

What's important is that before Vidocq retired in 1827, he had been chief of the fledgling Sûreté, the French crime bureau that is considered the first national police agency in world history. Before the Sûreté, founded in the aftermath of the French Revolution, few countries had any sort of municipal law enforcement. In the mostly rural and highly structured class systems that dominated pre-Revolutionary society in France and throughout the rest of the Western world, there was little need for a cop. It wouldn't have done any good for a serf to call one against the lord of the manor, since the serf had few civil rights (including the right to own property that could be taxed to pay for a cop). And if the lord of the manor wanted to settle a score, he had armed troops at his disposal to take care of the matter. Even in enlightened Britain, the Metropolitan Police in London didn't establish a detective force until 1842—one year after the first appearance of Dupin. A decade previous to this, there had been a furious debate as to whether or not to establish a regular police force. The landed gentry were afraid it would infringe on their rights, while the poor were convinced it would be used to oppress them.

It is no coincidence that the first detective story appeared after the first detective made an appearance, and it also helps to explain why Poe made Dupin a Frenchman. Since the only detective Poe knew about was Vidocq, it was that much easier to make Dupin a Frenchman. Poe couldn't very easily have made Dupin an Englishman or an American, since those countries didn't have detectives. If this sounds overly literal, consider that Poe even went so far as to transfer the factual disappearance of a New York woman, Mary Rogers, into the fictional disappearance of a French woman in "The Mystery of Marie Roget."

That is Vidocq's contribution to the genre. He may not have been the best or even the first detective, but he was the first and the best at publicizing himself. His memoirs take up sixteen hundred pages and four volumes, and include enough material about the alleged twenty thousand crimes he allegedly solved to give authors story material for another century or two. Which, in France, they did, as the work of Émile Gaboriau and the *feuilletonists* testifies. Gaboriau and his contemporaries, named after the

French phrase for leaflet, *feuilleton*, wrote detective stories for newspapers (often based on the crimes Vidocq wrote about), and they were extremely popular in France in the middle decades of the nineteenth century before becoming as obscure as most of the rest of Second Republic and Second Empire France. Gaboriau's character Monsieur Lecoq regularly appears in discussions of the most important pre-Holmesian detectives.

The decade or so between Vidocq's memoirs and the first Dupin story not only coincides with a phenomenal growth in literacy rates (no one is going to buy a book if they can't read), but also with the beginning of the Industrial Revolution. This is neither the time nor the place for a long, dull discussion of the impact of the Industrial Revolution on world history. What's important here is that the Industrial Revolution helped to generate several changes in society that made it possible for the detective to exist, both in fact and in fiction.

First, people stopped living mostly in rural areas and moved to cities. The overcrowding and lack of community structure led to an increase in crime, and to the public's perception of crime and its fascination with crime. Hence, the need for someone to solve crime. Second, science and the scientific method became, as many scholars have phrased it, a religion as powerful as any previously established. Science would provide all of the answers for the problems of life, from guaranteeing food and shelter to prolonging life. This scientific progress touched detectives, too. There was no longer any need for torture or trial by combat when a detective could solve a crime with science: taking fingerprints, making ballistics tests and the like.

Third, the Industrial Revolution created entirely new economic, social and political classes centered around the newly prosperous cities. This led to any number of political reforms, especially in the United States and Britain, to guarantee civil rights such as voting to these urban classes. Most previous political systems with any sort of democratic process—such as Parliament—based the process on owning property. These new urban classes didn't own property, but also didn't feel they should be excluded for that reason. The Reform Act in Britain in 1840 expanded that country's suffrage, and the gradual abolition of the property test in the individual states before the Civil War in the United States did an even better job of allowing more people to vote and spreading the growth of democracy.

The relationship between these political developments and the first appearance of the detective is not as obscure as it seems. Keep in mind that the fictional detective is an extraordinarily democratic character who doesn't care who commits a crime—whether they are rich or poor, noble or peasant, men or women,

EXAMINING THE CLUES

Hammett taught a mystery-writing class in New York City for a decade after World War II, which gave him an opportunity to preach what he practiced. "He taught us that tempo is the vital thing in fiction, and that you've got to keep things moving, and that character can be drawn within the action," one of his students told Hammett biographer William F. Nolan. Another student had submitted a story in the English garden party tradition, and Hammett told her the story wasn't very good. What do you do for a living? he asked her. She said she worked in a factory, on the assembly line. Then write about that, he said—write about what you know. Put a body on the conveyor belt in the factory and go from there. That theory was a crucial part of Hammett's success. He claimed that each of the characters in *The Maltese Falcon* was based on someone he knew: He had followed Gutman's original in Washington for the Pinkertons; Dundy was a cop in North Carolina; Cairo had been picked up on a forgery charge; Wilmer had robbed gas stations in California; Effie, the good-girl secretary, had asked Hammett to help her smuggle drugs; and Brigid was a woman who had hired Hammett to fire her housekeeper.

black or white. The important thing for the detective—the only important thing—is to uncover the truth. This contrasts with society's attitude before the Industrial Revolution: the rich and powerful were always right, even when they weren't. One reason why there have been few great detective stories written by Russians or Germans is that their political processes have been traditionally undemocratic, and thus have not been fertile ground for fictional detectives.[3]

These new urban classes, which could read, and were faced with crime unlike anything society had seen before, were ready to accept a literary hero who would fight crime in a new, scientific and democratic way. This accounted for the great popularity of the *feuilletonists,* even though their stories were poorly written (even by the standard of the day). Crime was running rampant in the rapidly growing cities, and Lecoq and his colleagues seemed to be the only ones who could stop it.

But Lecoq is gone, and the American fictional detective is not. It's not hard to find a reason. What is, for all of its flaws, the most democratic country in the world? The United States, where voters elect not only presidents and legislators, but also law enforcement officials. This astonishes visitors, even from countries like Britain with a long history of elected officials. This attitude goes a long way toward explaining why Americans love detectives in a way none of the rest of the world does. Thousands of new titles are published each year, ranging from paperback originals to erudite works of literary criticism. Hollywood loves detectives, and always has, both on the screen and on television. These days, for instance, up to one-third of a network prime-time television schedule is made up of detective programs. What Poe did, with his particular genius, was to seize on this opportunity. The debate should not be whether an American invented the detective, but why it took as long as it did for an American to do it.

So why did it take so long for an American detective to have that much influence again? Some eighty years passed between Poe and the first stories by Hammett and Queen, eighty years that Haycraft dismisses with hardly a notice. American writers and especially American writers of that era, he says, were consistently lagging behind their English counterparts. This period makes up the shortest chapter of his book, and the most barren. Save for Mary Roberts Rinehart, who more or less invented the "lonely

---

[3]The detective is so democratic, in fact, that a couple of Marxists invented one just to show how decadent and corrupt the democratic, capitalist system is. He is the Swedish policeman Martin Beck, whose creators—Maj Sjowall and Per Wahloo—wanted to use Beck to expose the ills in Swedish (and by implication, Western) society.

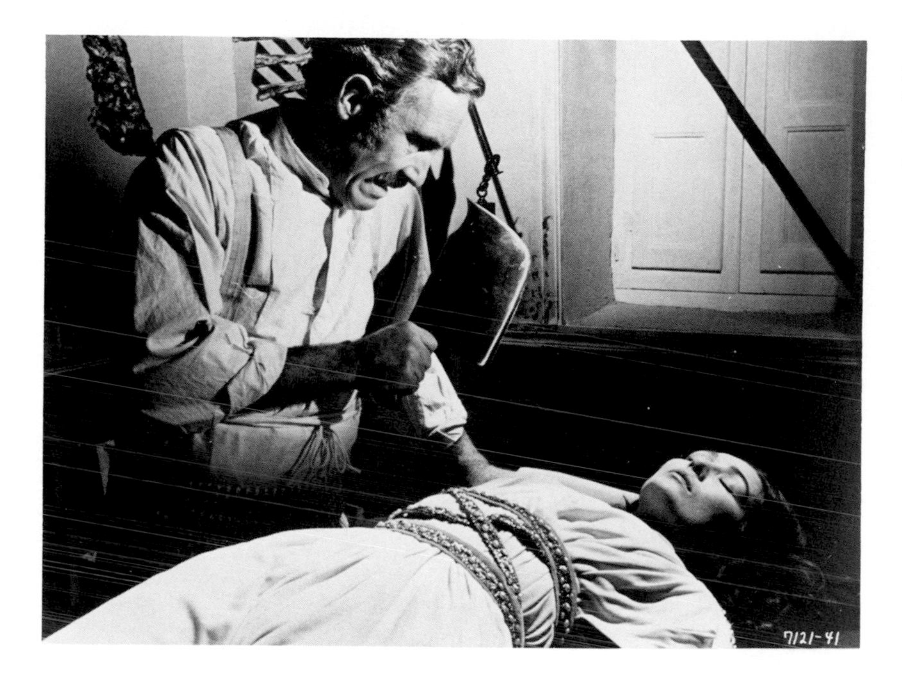

Jason Robards in the 1971 Murders in the Rue Morgue. *Neither of Hollywood's versions had anything to do with the story.*

woman trapped in an old house who opens one door too many" book, few writers from that era have withstood the scrutiny of time. Critic H. R. F. Keating's 100 all-time best crime and mystery list includes eleven works between Poe and Hammett/Queen; only three of them are American and one of them is Rinehart's masterpiece (for those who like that sort of thing), *The Circular Staircase.*

Most of the few successful American detectives of that era were English in all but name. Professor S. F. X. Van Dusen, "The Thinking Machine," seems to be little more than a knockoff of the English detective Dr. Thorndyke. This is clear in stories like "An Absence of Air" and "The Problem of Cell 13." Jacques Futrelle, who created Van Dusen, wrote complicated, involved stories that included very little in the way of character. They were all puzzle. The Van Dusen stories aren't particularly dated, just cold and distant. "The Problem of Cell 13" is supposed to be one of the great locked-room mysteries of the genre, yet any discriminating reader will hope Van Dusen, who is obnoxious beyond belief, rots in the cell. Whether Futrelle, an ex-newspaperman, realized any of this is unclear. He was thirty-seven when he died in 1912, a passenger on the *Titanic,* and he left

(Courtesy Bob Lakin Books)

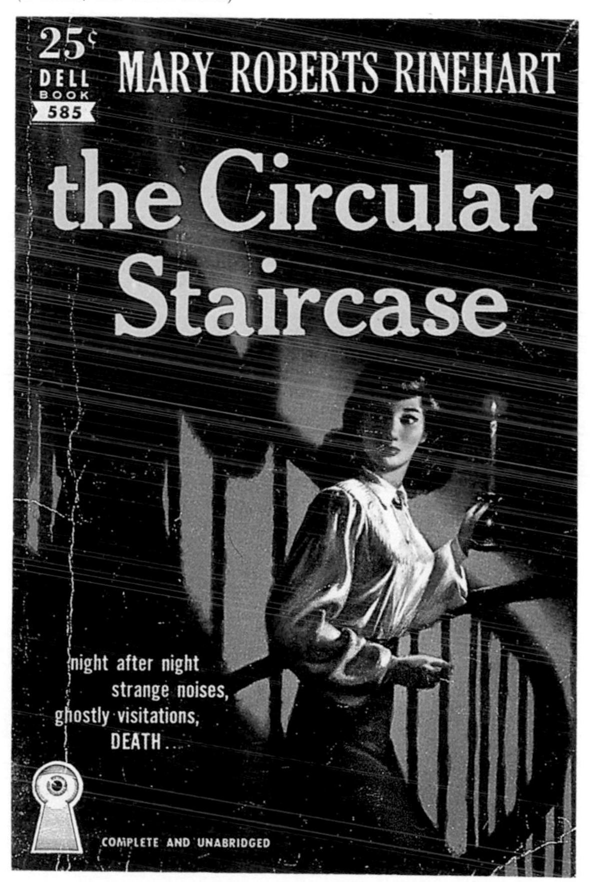

Walter Pidgeon was Nick Carter in three films, starting with *Nick Carter, Master Detective.*

behind only a handful of Van Dusen stories (one account says four), and no novels.

Holmes's influence certainly had a lot to do with retarding the growth of American detectives created by American authors. The situation was much the same then as it had been with Poe and Vidocq. If the only successful detective anyone has heard about is an eccentric Englishman, it's natural to make every new detective just like that eccentric Englishman. That same pattern showed up again after Hammett pioneered the hard-boiled subgenre; his successors each possess the same attitude toward language, women, violence and crime, though, like those who came after Holmes, few who followed Hammett possessed the Hammett touch.

One sort of American detective from this period refused to follow this English road. He is Nick Carter, who made his first appearance in the dime novels of the late nineteenth century (and who still exists today in paperback originals as a sort of avenging-angel-like Mack Bolan). Carter's exploits were based on the supposedly autobiographic tales of Allan Pinkerton, who founded America's first private detective agency, in much the same way the French *feuilletonists* borrowed from Vidocq. Carter is one of the first dime novel heroes to leave the frontier for the city, and did so at the time when the American nation was transforming itself from a rural to an urban society. In this, Carter is a necessary step between Poe/Dupin and Queen/Hammett. His exploits helped to move the character of the frontier cowboy—a staple of American pop culture since James Fenimore Cooper had written his Leatherstocking tales in the first couple of decades of the nineteenth century—to the city, where the American detective would eventually roam. Note that few American fictional detectives spend much time out of the city, whether they are hard-boiled or not. This is an important difference between the U.S. detective and his British counterpart. How many places could Miss Marple exist in this country?

The city even influences the exceptions to this rule. Tony Hillerman's Navajo policemen, who spend most of their time in the barren New Mexico desert, must solve crimes such as grave robbing and desecration. These are crimes that the rural Indian society that they protect doesn't commit, but that are foisted upon them by Anglos from the city. The archaeologists and academics who are the villains in Hillerman's books are from the city; the Navajos and Zunis who are the victims in the stories are not. This is a theme that is common to all of American literature, from Cooper to Herman Melville to Mark Twain to Fitzgerald. Huck Finn lights out for the frontier because he doesn't want to go to school and wear starched collars, and it doesn't take a glance at the Cliff Notes to know that those two things represent society's ills.

Nick Carter also had a comic book career.

(© 1948 Street & Smith Publications, courtesy Mike Benton)

(Courtesy Bob Lakin Books)

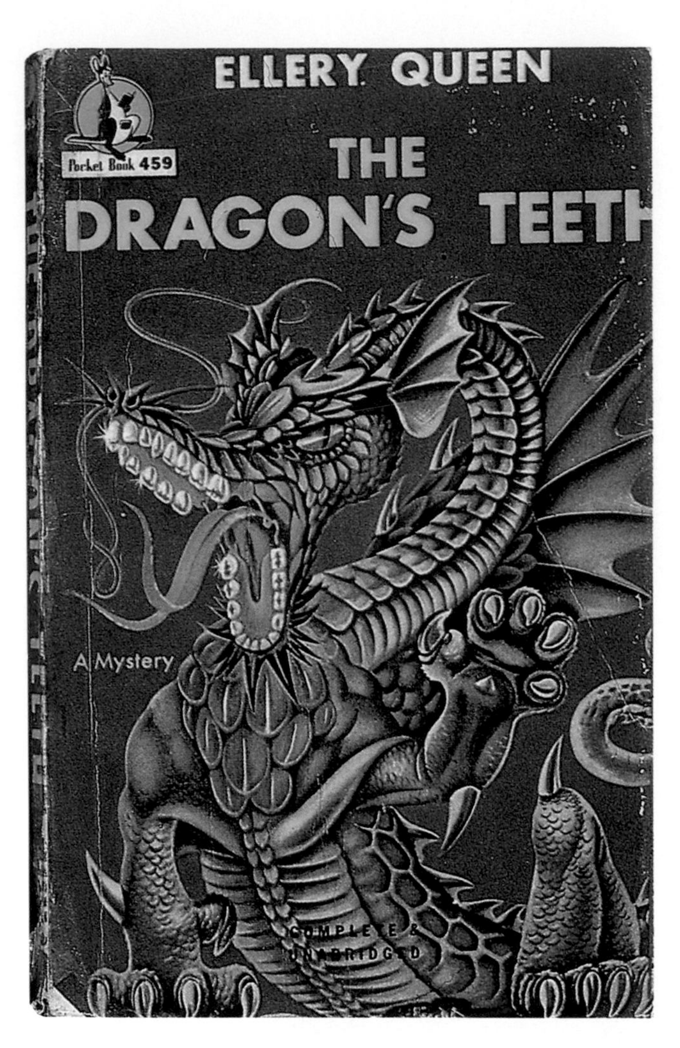

Yet not everyone thinks Nick Carter and his dime novel contemporaries qualify as detectives. Haycraft didn't (and makes the point viciously), and the dime novel detectives often don't appear in any of the standard reference works. The objection to them revolves around the lack of classical puzzles in these stories; Nick Carter isn't presented with a traditional, English-style puzzle to solve by traditional, English-style methods. Instead, Nick spends his time doing what Wyatt Earp would have done if the Earp stories had placed him in New York City instead of Wild West Tombstone—bluff, bluster and shoot his way to a solution. But this is not a drawback. Rather, it is the future, as anyone who reads Hammett will discover. Consider Melville Davisson Post's Uncle Abner, who appeared in magazines and short stories in the decade or so before World War I. Uncle Abner solved any number of unsolvable cases, aiding a bumbling county magistrate in backwoods Western Virginia during the Jeffersonian era. It's true Uncle Abner solves classical puzzles in these stories, but it is equally as true that the stories are a part of the tradition of American frontier literature. All of the signs are there: the theme of purity versus corruption, the emphasis on individualism, and the value of common sense over book learning.

The most successful of the pre-Queen detectives, S. S. Van Dine's Philo Vance, was also the last of the American detectives who would have been as at home in Belgravia as he was in Manhattan. This isn't the place for a detailed discussion of Vance (more of that in chapter 3); it's sufficient to know that between 1926 and 1939, Van Dine wrote twelve Vance novels, and that Hollywood used Vance fifteen times between 1929 and 1947. He was a popular and critical success: Vance was the first of the great detectives to make the best-seller list, and Van Dine's editor at

Ralph Bellamy was Ellery Queen in four movies of the early forties, beginning with Ellery Queen, Master Detective *(1940).*

Scribner's, which published the books, was the immortal Maxwell Perkins, who also discovered Hemingway and Fitzgerald.

The early Queen is not unlike Vance. But Vance disappeared within a decade, while Queen's success continued past the death of his creators, and included movies, radio shows, a television series, more than forty novels, and one of the few remaining crime magazines that publish short stories. Queen was able to do something that Vance, Van Dusen and the rest could not. He was able to change as the times changed. More important, the Queen novels were examples of the reward waiting for American authors who wrote detective stories about American detectives, and not about fellows who pretended they were the English gentry in an American accent. Queen, after the first few novels, bears more than a passing resemblance to a grown-up Andy Hardy—cheerful, well-scrubbed and with a healthy appetite for girls. Vance doesn't get a girlfriend until almost a decade into the series, and even then it's a younger woman he can only admire from afar. Queen is entirely middle class, and while he doesn't work for a living, his father (a New York City cop) does. Try to imagine Lord Peter Wimsey taking time out from snooping to get a job; it's enough to make the entire concept of the aristo-sleuth unimaginable.[4]

Queen is not unimaginable. That is one of his strengths, if not his greatest strength. He is no different from any other fellow walking down the street, even though he is the greatest detective in the world. Queen was so ordinary that he should have been played by Gary Cooper in the movies (instead, Hollywood used B actors like William Gargan). Consider this scene from a typical Queen novel, *Double, Double* (1950), in which Ellery gets into a cab in the small town where he regularly vacations:

> "Where to?" said Ed.
> "You don't remember me, do you?" asked Ellery with a smile.
> Ed Hotchkiss scratched his nose. He was heavier; he had another chin. "I hacked you years ago. Say!"
> "You do remember."
> "Green. . . . No, Queen! By Christmas, Mr. Queen!"

EXAMINING THE CLUES

Marketing motivated the cousins Dannay and Lee to not only choose one pen name for the two of them, but to use that pen name for the name of the detective. They reasoned that readers would have trouble remembering the names of two authors, and that they would have little trouble remembering it if the author and detective had the same name. So Queen is a pseudonym not only for the real-life authors, but for Queen the detective. In *The Roman Hat Mystery,* a Queen family friend reveals that although Ellery decided to tell his story, he changed all of the names—including his own—to protect everyone's privacy. This device, also used by S. S. Van Dine's Vance character, was dropped shortly thereafter as Ellery's character became more human.

This anonymity is a distinctly American attitude. Would a London cab driver have failed to recognize Sherlock Holmes or Hercule Poirot? Would either man have even had a conversation with the cabbie? Of course not. Each man would have been offended if he had not been greeted with the deference required to the greatest detective in the world. Queen's cases are often just as esoteric (in *Double, Double,* the characters quote from *Paradise Lost*) as anything in the stories of Holmes or Poirot, and usually revolve around a clue so obtuse only the world's greatest detective would notice it. But it doesn't matter, because Queen always manages to retain the reader's affection.

In the short story "The Adventure of the Mad Tea-Party," the solution to a disappearance and murder revolves around a series of seemingly unrelated clues that represent a line not from *Alice in Wonderland*—the Lewis Carroll book most people know—but from Carroll's other book, *Through the Looking Glass.* Yet all of this arrogance is redeemed immediately after Ellery unmasks the murderer.

[4]One of the silliest of Dorothy L. Sayers's Wimsey stories is "The Adventurous Exploit of the Cave of Ali Baba," which has nothing to do with the Arabian Nights. In it, Lord Peter fakes his death and goes undercover as a member of the working class to infiltrate a gang of thieves. This, undoubtedly, is another example of why there will always be an England.

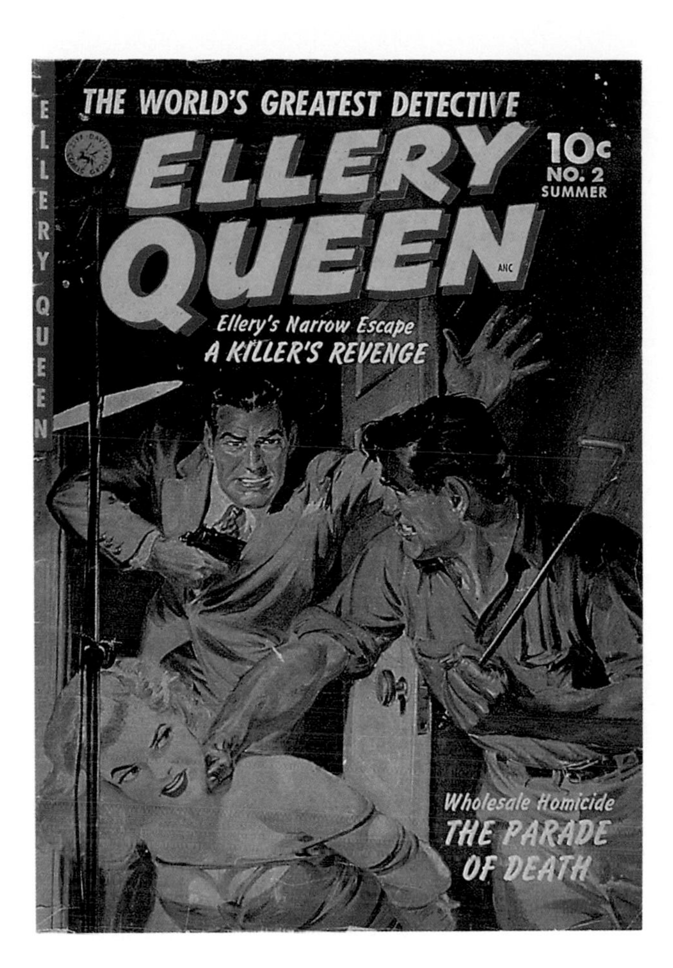

Ellery Queen made it to the comic books, looking very energetic here in 1952.

(© Ziff-Davis Publishing Company, courtesy Mike Benton)

He returns to New York City from the country house where the crime took place, traveling with the attractive actress who was also on hand for the weekend. Their scene in the train restores the reader's faith in Ellery: He may be the world's greatest detective, but he also knows what to do with a pretty girl. "'. . . How do you feel?' he asked. 'As Alice would say,' she said softly, leaning a little toward him, 'curiouser and curiouser.'" Pretty steamy for *Redbook* in 1934, eh?

The other Queen asset is his readability. This may be fiction written by two men who picked it up as they went along, but their technique is far from shoddy. Lee and Dannay didn't have Hammett's genius, but they knew enough to develop a style that was light, tight and bright. There are few purple adjectives in the Queen stories and novels, and the narrative is firmly in the post–World War I tradition pioneered by Hemingway and his peers. Compare the Queen style with the stuff that made up the Vance stories, like this from 1935's *The Garden Murder Case*: "He had

John Huston's The Maltese Falcon *(1941) starred (left to right) Humphrey Bogart, Peter Lorre, Mary Astor, and Sydney Greenstreet.*

always impressed me as a man so highly mentalized, so cynical and impersonal in his attitude toward life, that an irrational human weakness like romance would be alien to his nature." Not much room for girls in that sentence, is there?

In Hammett's sentences, there was room for girls and a lot more. A myth has grown up that Hammett was a careless writer. This is based on his excessive drinking and his world-record case of writer's block. When he died in 1961, he had written nothing but a comic strip, some newspaper stories and several movie treatments in three decades. Nothing, however, could be farther from the truth. Hammett knew what he was doing with every word, just as Hemingway and Fitzgerald did. Hammett's next-to-last novel, *The Glass Key,* is as vibrant as anything he wrote, but contains as much symbolism as any Italian movie—starting with the title. It refers to a key that can only be used once before it breaks. Once it unlocks knowledge, the knowledge can never be locked up again. Hammett always considered this his best work, and he makes a good argument for it. *The Glass Key* has a murder in it, but it is not so much about solving the murder as it is about the people who are involved in the murder. It wouldn't be going too far to say that *The Glass Key* is about people in the same way a Jane Austen novel is about people. Hammett's people are just a little more hard-boiled.

And quite a bit more American.

The Gumshoe Hall of Fame

Detective: Sam Spade
Creator: Dashiell Hammett
Classic appearance: *The Maltese Falcon*

Spade appears in only one novel and three short stories, but no one else—not Dupin, not Queen, not Chandler—has had more influence in making the American fictional detective what it is today. Much of that can be traced to his film appearance in *The Maltese Falcon* (1941), which was as influential among writers as it was among filmmakers. Before Spade, every American detective on film and in books was like Sherlock Holmes; after Spade, every detective was like Spade. Spade (as well as Hammett's other important creation, the Continental Op) was the first detective who dealt with crime as the business that it was, and not as something to provide diversion during a weekend in the country. His adventures are the stories of a man negotiating his way through the treachery of a corrupt society, who is neither as treacherous nor as corrupt as he appears to be.

Detective: C. Auguste Dupin
Creator: Edgar Allan Poe
Classic appearance: Short story, "The Murders in the Rue Morgue"

It's hard to believe, in these days of creative writing schools, that a character created by a college dropout could have shaped the direction of American letters. And Dupin is just one part of Poe's ground-breaking canon. Dupin is arrogant, eccentric, bizarre and quite possibly a candidate for institutionalization. Even Poe admits this: "Had the routine of our life at this place been known to the world," he writes in "Rue Morgue," "we would have been regarded as madmen." Yet this condition is part of Dupin's attraction. Poe's skill allowed his characters to tread the line between fantasy and reality, a line that so many other authors fail to find. This is just one reason why Dupin is indispensable.

(Courtesy Bob Lakin Books)

Detective: Ellery Queen
Creator: Ellery Queen
Classic appearance: Novel, *Calamity Town*

Ellery Queen is always credited for his work as an anthologist, editor and critic. Sometimes, it seems as if his books are included in these discussions only because there were so many of them. This does not give Queen enough credit. The books show that Queen was truly different from the English traditional detectives who preceded him, whether Americans or Englishmen. There's a joke in the publishing business about how editors reject manuscripts. They tell aspiring authors one of two things: either their idea is so new and so different that no one would buy it, or their idea is so old and so trite that no one would buy it. The catch, then, is to find an old idea that is new. That's precisely what Queen did. In form he is little different from the eighty years of detectives who preceded him. In substance, he is a revelation.

Detective: The Continental Op
Creator: Dashiell Hammett
Classic appearance: Novel, *Red Harvest*

(Courtesy Bob Lakin Books)

One of the most revealing moments in the history of the American detective comes in the much-collected Op story, "The Gutting of Couffignal," one of the three dozen short stories and two novels about the nameless operative from the Continental Detective Agency. In "Couffignal," the Op is guarding the presents at an exclusive wedding when the lights go out on the island of the same name, a gang starts to raid the island's homes and shops, and mayhem begins. The Op spends the next couple of thousand words chasing the bad guys, and finally comes face to face with the woman who is part of the gang that pulled the job. The Op has been wounded in the leg, and is hobbling on a makeshift cane. The woman refuses to believe he will shoot her. She starts to make her escape when "I put a bullet in the calf of her left leg. She sat down—plump! Utter surprise stretched her white face. It was too soon for pain. . . . 'You ought to have known I'd do it!' My voice sounded harsh and savage and like a stranger's in my ears. 'Didn't I steal a crutch from a cripple?'" This moment is just as important as the more widely quoted passage earlier in the story, when the Op explains his Code, or when Spade tells Brigid O'Shaughnessy that he is giving her to the cops in *The Maltese Falcon*. The passage re-emphasizes that it's not enough to talk about professionalism. Action is always required to prove the point.

Detective: Philip Marlowe
Creator: Raymond Chandler
Classic appearance: Novel, *The Big Sleep*

Marlowe, the hero of all six of Chandler's novels (but only one short story), has had an impact far beyond his few literary appearances. Each of his novels has been made into a movie (many more than once), and Robert Altman chose a Marlowe book in his attempt to make the definitive anti-detective film. Only Spade among the hard-boiled detectives has been more influential in determining what came next. This is because Marlowe, while as much of a fantasy figure as any other detective, carries a sheen of believability that few others have. Marlowe is a lousy detective, if classical sleuths like Holmes, Poirot and Vance are the standards. He spends a lot of time in jail, he is always one step behind the bad guys, and his clients always seem to be getting killed or arrested. He would have as much luck figuring out that Colonel Mustard committed the murder with the candlestick in the drawing room as any of his readers would. This doesn't matter, though. None of his readers care about Colonel Mustard, either, and don't see any reason why they should.

Detective: Joe Friday
Creator: Jack Webb
Classic appearance: Television series, "Dragnet"

Anyone who knows Friday only through his late-1960s television incarnation could not possibly realize that the Friday of radio and early-1950s television is a pivotal figure in the police procedural. He was one of the first characters to play a cop as a cop—not as a Sir Galahad or as a wise-cracking smart aleck or as a fashion plate. Friday was so dull and uninteresting that he was fascinating. He took the professionalism of characters like the Op and Sam Spade to new levels, so that there was nothing to the character but his professionalism. In fact, when Los Angeles police were videotaped beating a motorist a couple of years ago, more than one newspaper columnist blamed "Dragnet" for the abuses of the system. Their logic: Friday was so convincing that no one paid enough attention to what the real cops were doing. Everyone, they wrote, assumed that L.A.'s cops were just like Joe Friday. Although a couple of literary police procedurals had appeared before "Dragnet" (Hillary Waugh's *Last Seen Wearing . . .* and Lawrence Treat's *V as in Victim*), the television series propelled the genre to a popularity it retains today. Don't kid yourself. Without Joe Friday and "Dragnet," it might not have been possible for Ed McBain to publish his eighty-seventh Precinct novels, let alone for television to bombard viewers with everything from "Car 54" to "Cops."

"Isn't it true . . .": Television's enormously popular Perry Mason (Raymond Burr) with ever-helpful Della Street (Barbara Hale).

Detective: Perry Mason
Creator: Erle Stanley Gardner
Classic appearance: TV series, "Perry Mason"

There isn't a trial lawyer in the United States who hasn't apologized to a jury for not being Perry Mason, and it's easy to see why. In the long-running television series (still seen regularly in most of the country) and in eighty-two books from 1933 to 1973, Mason is remarkably consistent: He never loses. He doesn't even have to go to trial. His clients are always acquitted during the preliminary hearing, when everyone else's clients are being fitted for their jail outfits. This has done more than make it hard for real lawyers to follow his act; it has made it equally as difficult for fictional lawyers to follow his act. The Mason stories are so entertaining that few other attorneys have been successful. Even Erle Stanley Gardner, the lawyer who created Mason, ran afoul of the character's popularity. None of his other characters—including two lawyers—came close to matching Mason's success.

Detective: Lew Archer
Creator: Ross Macdonald
Classic appearance: Novel, *Sleeping Beauty*

(Courtesy Bob Lakin Books)

Archer is the last of the great hard-boiled detectives; in fact, he did as much as anyone to kill the hard-boiled mystique. When Archer first appeared in 1949, he was one of hundreds of post-war hard-boiled dicks. When he appears for the final time in *The Blue Hammer* in 1976, he is more like a character in an Ingmar Bergman movie. Macdonald abandoned many of the traditional components of the hard-boiled subgenre over the last two decades of his career, eschewing action for contemplation. Little happens physically in the latter Archer books; instead, Archer gets a case (usually involving a broken family), interviews a lot of people, drives a lot of places, and eventually leaves the family completely shattered, but with a chance to build again. There is more therapy in the plots than detection. Yet this sort of story, which could easily turn into parody in less talented hands, does not. Macdonald may not be as good as Eudora Welty once claimed in a front-page article in *The New York Times Book Review,* but he's good enough.

Detective: Nero Wolfe
Creator: Rex Stout
Classic appearance: Novel, *The League of Frightened Men*

Why is Wolfe so popular, as well as so important? In some eighty literary outings (evenly divided between novels and short stories), a couple of movies and a television series, he is fat, arrogant and overbearing. Yet the Wolfe stories are as charming and as necessary as Wolfe is obnoxious. Much of the credit must go to Stout for coming up with Archie Goodwin, one of the few sidekicks in the genre who is not a buffoon, and who is a legitimate character in his own right. It's also hard not to feel a little sorry for and a little envious of Wolfe, who is terrified to leave his Manhattan brownstone and who spends his time eating, drinking beer, tending his orchids and making Archie's life miserable. Wolfe manages to live everyone's fantasy despite residing in the middle of the world's greatest city—he can close his door on the world and (except when he needs to take a case for the money) the world can't bother him.

Detectives: Coffin Ed Johnson, Grave Digger Jones
Creator: Chester Himes
Classic appearance: Novel, *Cotton Comes to Harlem*

Himes's black police detectives, featured in seven novels and a couple of movies, are so underrated that they haven't even become trendy. Save for a paperback reissue by Vintage in the late 1980s, Coffin Ed and Grave Digger are almost as unknown today as they were when Himes wrote about them thirty years ago. Poor Himes. While similarly neglected writers (Jim Thompson, Cornell Woolrich) were being reprinted and reissued by wealthy and prestigious publishers in the past decade, all Himes got for a collection of his short stories was a small house with limited distribution. This is wrong. If this book accomplishes anything, it should be to help the world realize just how good Himes was. There are three guidelines to earn admission to this Hall of Fame, and Coffin Ed

EXAMINING THE CLUES

Sleuth had a meaning long before it meant detective. The modern English word can trace its roots back some six hundred years to the Middle English term *sleuth,* which meant the track of a man or animal. A dog that followed a sleuth was a sleuth-hound. There are any number of references throughout English literature to the dog as sleuth; Charlotte Brontë makes them in her novels. It's not entirely clear when and how the meaning of the word made the transition to detective. The *Oxford English Dictionary* says it is an Americanism, and leaves it at that. Melville Davisson Post created Sir Henry Marquis, "the sleuth of St. James's Square," in 1920, and there almost surely has to be an earlier reference than that. The origin of private eye is much clearer. It dates from the founding of Allan Pinkerton's detective agency in the mid-nineteenth century. Pinkerton's slogan was "We never sleep," and his symbol was a wide-open eye.

(Courtesy Bob Lakin Books)

and Grave Digger meet all three. Their exploits have endured and have not become dated; they have influenced other writers and characters; and their stories are told in a compelling manner. The two men are not only fascinating detectives, but they may very well be Literature. Anyone who wants to learn what it was like to be black in America three decades ago will learn a lot more by reading *Cotton Comes to Harlem* or *The Real Cool Killers* than they will by checking out a news magazine or a learned journal. Chandler talked about mean streets, but Himes lived them. He served eight years during the Depression in the Ohio penitentiary for armed robbery. This is where he began writing, and no one was spared from his razorlike vision. Coffin Ed and Grave Digger are not only the toughest characters in American detective fiction ("You've got to be tough to be a colored cop up in Harlem," says their boss), but they may be the most honest. They can trust no one but each other—not their colleagues, who hate them because they are black, and not Harlem, which fears them because they enforce the white man's law. This is something most critics haven't paid proper attention to. Too many black critics have taken Himes to task for his unflattering portraits of Harlem life, while too many white critics have dismissed Himes as a genre writer. What they don't see is that Himes, like Hemingway, wrote truly. Every writer should be so fortunate.

THE THIRD DEGREE:
The American vs. the British Detective

In the late 1970s, Robert Mitchum played Philip Marlowe in a film version of Chandler's *The Big Sleep*. The producers, however, had one of those things that pass for great ideas in Hollywood and transplanted Marlowe from Chandler's Los Angeles to post–World War II London. In a newspaper interview, the director said London would make a great city for a hard-boiled detective film. It's got all of that fog, all of that atmosphere, he said.

That may be true. But it didn't make it the appropriate place to stage a hard-boiled detective story. For the past seventy years, detectives on this side of the Atlantic Ocean have evolved in a completely different direction from their counterparts on the other side of the ocean. Marlowe seemed as out of place in London (he couldn't even carry a gun) as Hercule Poirot would have been in Los Angeles. Some cop would just as soon sap Poirot with a blackjack as listen to him exercise his "little gray cells."

(Courtesy Bob Lakin Books)

The differences between the two types of detectives are more than the amount of violence in each society, of course—although that's a good starting point. There is very little violence in the typical English story, just as England is a less violent society than America. More people are killed in New York City annually than in all of Britain, and guns are not nearly as common as they are in the United States. Most British police still don't carry firearms. Once the crime is committed, the English fictional detective rarely faces danger again. The cops do not threaten to beat him up, the client doesn't double-cross him with a kick to the head, the bad guys do not torture him to add a little excitement to the climax. In England, the cops aren't crooked, the criminals have manners and murder is only committed, to paraphrase Chandler, by people who think it is a plot device, and not an act of infinite cruelty.

Second, Britain's class system, as hard as it may be for Americans to believe, plays a crucial role in preventing crime, and hence influencing the English detective story. British society is much more structured, so it's going to be much less violent. Someone whose family has had their place in the world drummed into him for generations is a lot less likely to shoot the lord of the manor if the lord is caught in bed with the Englishman's wife. This also goes a long way toward explaining why there are so few working-class detectives in British fiction. The typical detective is wealthy (even if he works for Scotland Yard), and usually an amateur whose personality makes Holmes seem like a man of the people. After all, how can the proletariat be trusted to preserve order for the aristocracy? On the other hand, American authors since Queen have gone out of their way to make their characters as down to earth as

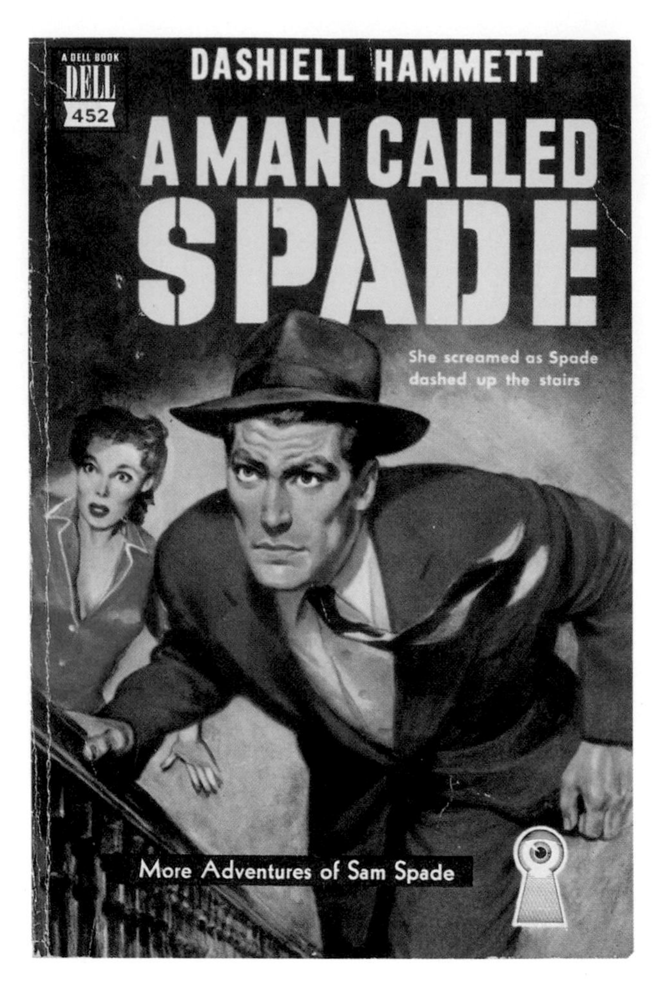

(Courtesy Bob Lakin Books)

politicians at election time. A television show like "Mannix" doesn't last nine seasons on its artistic merit, but because its hero is someone viewers can identify with.

Certainly there have been changes in the English detective since Sayers wrote about Wimsey, changes that have been influenced by the Americans. But the English detective has retained his essential Wimsey-ness. How else to explain that two of the most popular detectives in British history are a nosy old lady from an English village and a meek, quiet Catholic priest. There are exceptions to this pattern, but they have not shown the staying power of characters like Miss Marple and Father Brown. In their society, there are no doors to kick down with guns blazing. In the United States, and especially the United States during Prohibition and the Depression, violence was as common as whiskey and unemployment. So it is entirely plausible that the detectives conceived during this period would be characters like the Op and Sam Spade, and that they would do their thinking with their guns instead of with long sentences full of words where the final "g" has been dropped. The birth of the American detective was shaped by its surroundings and was a reaction against a society in which Al Capone was an honored and respected man. In this world, little old ladies didn't solve crimes; they got beat up and killed (see Chandler's *Farewell, My Lovely*). Its hardness demands a harder man than Lord Peter, and its amorality demands a man whose morality was not formed on the playing fields of Eton. If the cops are crooked and the politicians are crooked, then someone was needed who would do their work, but who was not, as Spade pointed out, "as crooked as I'm supposed to be."

This moral ambiguity shows up again in the endings of the two types of stories. The British detective assembles the cast in the drawing room for the denouement of the story after observing the suspects and gathering his clues. Then, he brilliantly dissects the crime, eliminating the red herrings among the clues and the suspects before unmasking the murderer. The murderer then gives a shrug and turns himself over to the police, who have been just as baffled, amazed and bewildered throughout the detective's narrative as everyone else in the room. All is once again right in the world, which has been cleansed of evil as if by a surgeon taking out an appendix. By contrast, crime is like a cancer in an American story. It can't be cut out quickly or easily, and there is no guarantee it won't grow back. The solution is rarely neat and clean. There are usually bodies lying around, and if the suspect gives up without a fight it's because he is often already dead.

Finally, there is the puzzle itself. Haycraft rates the puzzle above everything else—before writing ability, before characterization, before plot. To someone like Haycraft, the solution in *Murder on the Orient Express* is not an insult to the reader, but a compliment to the author. Chandler, on the other hand, could not care less about the puzzle. Supposedly, when Howard Hawks was filming his version of *The Big Sleep* with Humphrey Bogart and Lauren Bacall, he was stumped about one of the murders in the book. He sent Chandler a wire, asking to clear up the mystery of who killed the Sternwood chauffeur. The reply from Chandler: "I don't know."

This is not Chandler being flip, either. In the American story, character is all. No one reads a Mike Hammer book to see how he elegantly solves the puzzle; that's why they read P. D. James. It's almost impossible for instance, to be halfway through one of James's Adam Dalgliesh books without wondering how he is possibly going to solve the crime. With Hammer, the crime is irrelevant. What matters is the number of women he seduces, the number of toughs he beats up, and the venom with which he kills the criminal. That's why Mike Hammer, the character, is memorable in a way that Mike Hammer books are not. A reader may remember specific Dalgliesh plots and solutions, but it's almost impossible to keep track of Hammer in the same way. *Kiss Me, Deadly* is little different from *I, the Jury.* Hammer hates Commies, pinko politicians, and lefty women who refuse to acknowledge they should be barefoot and pregnant. This pattern is equally as discernible even when the detective is less hard-boiled. Television audiences didn't watch "Columbo" to see how the criminal committed the crime; that was shown in the first couple of minutes of the program. They watched it to see Peter Falk go through his paces, waiting patiently for the moment when Falk as Columbo would walk out the door, turn around, and say, "Excuse me, but I have one more question."

(Courtesy Bob Lakin Books)

THE SOLUTION: The Electronic Pulps

The pulps are not dead.

This may seem to fly in the face of the documentary evidence, since there are only two mystery magazines still published in the United States, and the final pulp is generally acknowledged to have gone out of business in 1957.

But the pulps these days are not printed, and they are not magazines.

It's no coincidence that the pulps died in the late 1940s and early 1950s, when the television first became the most important piece of furniture in the American living room. Television didn't kill the pulps all by itself, but it played a crucial role in the demise of the cheap magazines by replacing it in the public's affections. Not only did it offer the same sort of formulaic, crude, fascinating, and popular entertainment that the pulps did, but it reached a wider audience with a more easily accessible product. The viewer didn't have to make a trip to the newsstand to buy a copy of a magazine: All he had to do was flip a switch in the comfort of his home.

(Photograph by Michael Keller Photography, courtesy John Wooley)

This may very well turn out to be a controversial statement. The pulps, thanks to the work of authors and critics like Bill Pronzini and E. R. Hagemann, have enjoyed a renaissance in the past couple of decades. They may well be more popular today as objects of popular history than they were during their heyday between the two world wars. The pulps (so called because of the cheap, wood pulp paper they were printed on) covered dozens of categories. There were sports pulps, crime pulps (hard-boiled and traditional), Western pulps, adventure pulps, fantasy pulps, and science fiction pulps. There were pulps for kids and pulps for adults. The latter included sexually oriented stories, especially from the infamous Spicy line. Its titles—*Spicy Detective, Spicy Western,* and *Spicy Adventure,* among others—featured detective or western or adventure stories larded with plenty of naughty bits.

That lineup isn't all that different from a weekly prime time television schedule—especially the adult fare, which came in for as much criticism in its day as shows like "Dynasty" and "Charlie's Angels" did in their's. It's one reason why it isn't difficult to draw a parallel between the pulps and television. And don't be fooled by those who claim the pulps hold some sort of intellectual or cultural superiority over the boob tube. That is not true. Each medium had its artists, but each medium was also geared toward the lowest common denominator, and that is never art.

The vast, overwhelming majority of the stories that appeared in the pulps—from those lucky enough to appear in the legendary *Black Mask* to those that were gobbled up by magazines that lasted only one or two issues—weren't even worth the penny a word their authors were paid. In this respect, the stories that appeared in *Sure-Fire Detective* are no different than one-shot television series like "Lady Blue" and "Downtown" (although they were probably a lot cheaper to produce). Even Pronzini, who almost singlehandedly brought the pulps to the public's attention, acknowledges this: "To be sure, most pulp fiction was of poor quality. . . . the bulk of them should be allowed to lie undisturbed in their mouldering pulp graves."

(Photograph by Michael Keller Photography, courtesy John Wooley)

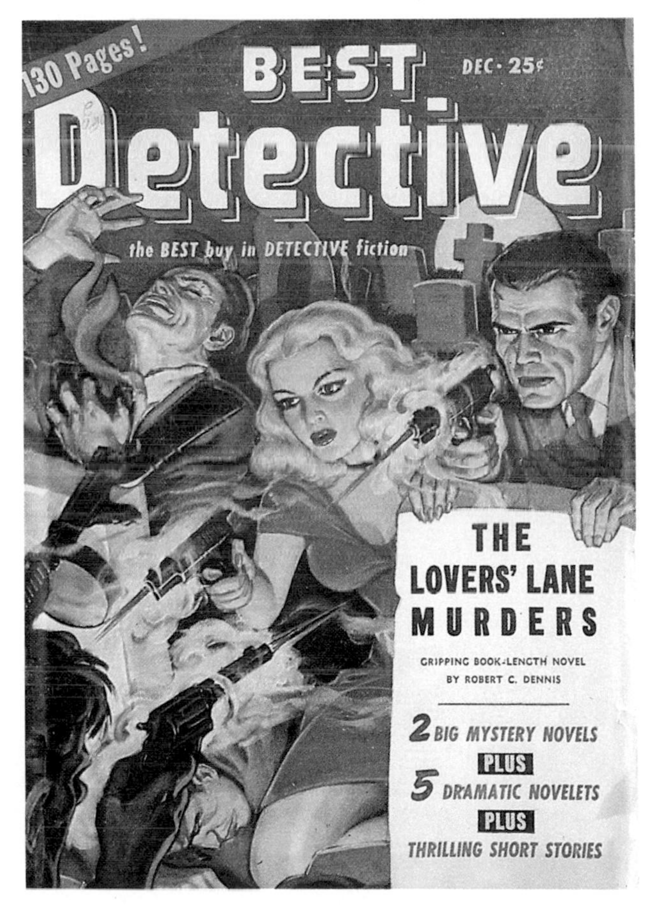

The pulp universe—and this was especially true of the fictional detective portion—was a triangle with a narrow tip and fat bottom. At the pinnacle were a handful of writers like Hammett and Chandler, who started in the pulps and soon left because they were too good to stay. Then came a slightly larger second tier, writers like Erle Stanley Gardner, John D. MacDonald and Frederick Nebel, who weren't as talented as the first group, but were still good enough to make a living as writers. Many of them graduated from the pulps to the slick magazines that printed fiction, and from there to books and Hollywood. This is the group that benefitted the most from the upsurge in interest in the pulps. A writer like Raoul Whitfield, for instance, whose hard-boiled exterior is actually as brittle as a freshly laid egg, has actually been compared favorably to Hammett. This is as silly

Ed Jenkins was one of Erle Stanley Gardner's most popular pulp characters.
(Courtesy John Wooley)

An Ed Jenkins Novelette
By
ERLE STANLEY GARDNER

as comparing "Mr. Ed" to *King Lear.* Certainly, some previously unappreciated writers like Nebel, Lester Dent and Paul Cain got their due. Nebel's "Rough Justice," a short story featuring Tough Dick Donahue, does for summer in St. Louis what *Dr. Zhivago* did for winter in Russia. Cain's "Fast One," featuring Gerry Kells, ranks among the best work from this second-level group, as do Dent's stories about the hard-bitten Oscar Sail.

But most of the rest of the pulpsters, as they are so quaintly called, were forgettable. They were writers like Lew Merrill, E. Hoffman Price, Mark Plum, and Arnold Duncan—all of whom published detective stories in pulps and then vanished into literary thin air. The following line from Martin Wolson's "When a Man Murders" (*Dime Detective,* 1947, and courtesy of Pronzini's remarkable accumulation of bad taste, *Gun in Cheek*) should more than explain why: "'OK,' I told him when his words ran out, 'I'm a rat, a louse, my feet stink and you won't play marbles with me anymore.'"

Given that, it's not too much of a leap of faith to "Starsky and Hutch," is it?

The two mediums also need immense amounts of material. At their height, the two hundred pulps that published once or twice a month needed hundreds of millions of words' worth of stories a year—the equivalent of 3,300 novels. This is no different from a typical television season, where writers must come up with plots for twenty-five or so weekly episodes, often an hour long. It's no wonder that it's hard to remember the plots of so many hour-long television detective shows. A show that lasts three seasons requires seventy-five or so original scripts. That's a lot of murders, written and conceived on deadline to meet not only a budget but the whims of a director, star and cast.

This incredible demand for material means formula is always going to be more important than content. It's difficult to devote too much time to art when a writer has a deadline hanging over his head. In the typical pulp detective story, there are certain set pieces that always appear. The femme fatale, for instance, always tries to seduce the hero in the hard-boiled story, while there is always a formal affair of some sort in the traditional story. Throw in assorted gun play, various wisecracking (or very stilted) dialogue, and a story has written itself. This used to infuriate Chandler, who kept insisting to his editors at *Black Mask* and *Dime Detective* that the audience was much more intelligent than the editors gave them credit for being.

(Photograph by Michael Keller Photography, courtesy John Wooley)

This creative process has carried over to television. The producers make sure Jessica Fletcher, the author-turned-sleuth of "Murder, She Wrote," is surrounded by once well-known guest stars and wears expensive clothes as she solves cases every week. It doesn't make quite as big a difference if the plot creaks, after all, when the audience is trying to recognize who's who in the supporting cast. In cop shows, the format may be different, but the formula is just as rigid. There is always a car chase in the final few minutes, for example, and the boss is always an understanding, sympathetic sort who is constantly going to bat for his men with the police bureaucracy. "Miami Vice," despite its flashy stars and pastel backgrounds, was no different from the black-and-white shadows of "The Untouchables."

What it comes down to in the end is that the pulps and television shows were and are equally disposable. Readers spent their nickels and dimes, read the pulps, and then threw them out. Is this any different from the viewers who taped "Simon & Simon" over "In the Heat of the Night," which had been taped over "Wiseguy"?

THE RAP SHEET: The Hard-boiled Detective

M.O.: The hard-boiled detective is distinctly American. He (usually, but sometimes a she) is a professional who is usually, but not always, unaffiliated with any sort of official agency. He is usually a loner. He is usually broke; in fact, every hard-boiled story seems to start with the detective accepting the case because his bank account is "low enough to kiss the stoop." There is rarely anything elegant about his stories; he solves cases with his fists, and asks questions later. This means that some policemen, such as Chester Himes's Coffin Ed Johnson and Grave Digger Jones, fit into this category. These sorts of cops are, for some reason, outcasts on their force, and so must solve crimes without the assistance that their colleagues receive. The key to the hard-boiled detective, whether official or unofficial, is The Code, as best outlined by Raymond Chandler: "Down these mean streets must go a man who is not himself mean." Not all hard-boiled detectives interpret this as literally as Chandler does, but all agree that those streets are pretty mean, and act accordingly.

Perpetrators: Chandler's Philip Marlowe, Dashiell Hammett's Sam Spade and the Continental Op, Mickey Spillane's Mike Hammer, Lawrence Block's Matt Scudder, Robert Parker's Spenser, and Sue Grafton's Kinsey Millhone.

Aliases: Sleuth, shamus, private eye, operative, investigator, hawkshaw, private dick, private richard, sherlock.

The Shamuses

2

"[It] must be confessed that in its pristine form, the hard-boiled tale of detection—once so vigorous and refreshing—is beginning to become just a little tedious from too much repetition of its rather limited themes. . . . The mode seems to be receding today."

—Howard Haycraft, 1941

Somewhere, wherever it is esteemed literary critics spend eternity, Howard Haycraft must finally be breathing a sigh of relief. More than fifty years after he predicted and hoped for the demise of the hard-boiled hero, it may be happening.

The subgenre that started with a story in *Black Mask* magazine more than seventy years ago, and that has shaped the character of the American fictional detective with its vibrancy, violence and never-ending action, both physical and verbal, may have finally reached a dead end. There have been a number of developments, many of them significant, in the hard-boiled form since Lew Archer's final appearance in 1976, but none of them have transcended the genre in the way the characters invented by Dashiell Hammett, Raymond Chandler and Ross Macdonald did. The modern heirs of these traditional hard-boiled heroes have broken little new ground—whether the hard-boiled detectives were black, homosexual or women. There is nothing disreputable about this, and Dave Brandstetter and Kinsey Millhone are as compelling in their own way as any of their hard-boiled predecessors. But they are not breakthroughs, and they have not taken the hard-boiled detective to another level. Brandstetter may be gay and Millhone and her sisters may be women, but they are still walking Marlowe's mean streets in much the same way Marlowe did. It's no coincidence that the blurbs on the paperback editions of the Millhone books each have the same quote: "Tough but compassionate." That's as applicable to Millhone as it was to Archer as it was to Marlowe as it was to Spade.

This has left today's hard-boiled detective in the position of offering little that is new, and letting Haycraft be a prophet after his time. The question is not whether authors will keep writing about hard-boiled detectives or whether publishers will continue to

(Courtesy Bob Lakin Books)

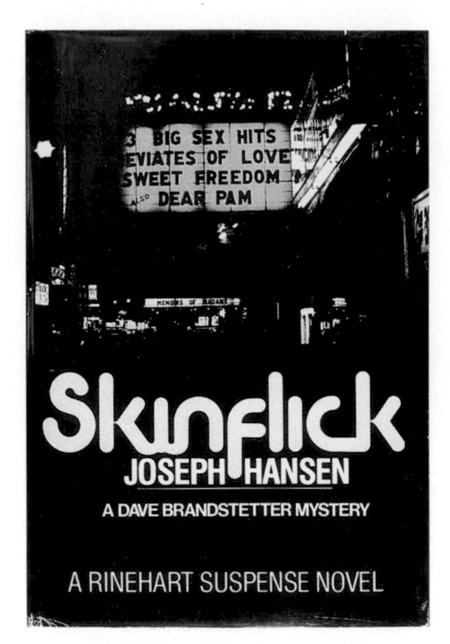

(Courtesy Bob Lakin Books)

print them or whether producers will persist in making television shows and movies about hard-boiled detectives. There seems little doubt of that. What's questionable is whether the hard-boiled detective will continue to be an appropriate hero as the United States enters the twenty-first century. Or will it become an interesting pop cultural sidelight, passed over by time and history and taste in much the same way big band music was replaced by rock 'n' roll? Edward Margolies, whose specialty is not pop fiction but English and American literature, points out that "from time to time, a plethora of new hard-boiled detectives appear on the horizon chiefly to exploit the current interest—but on the whole they quietly fade as it becomes clear they are simply intruders on the zeitgeist."

Even in the best hands, such as Joseph Hansen, Loren Estleman and Jonathan Valin, the traditional hard-boiled hero is an anachronism, as out of place as a fedora in the wardrobe of a '90s kind of guy. Besides, as talented as Estleman and his colleagues are, they are not Hammett and Chandler. A talented craftsman can not find gold in a played-out mine, no matter how talented the craftsman is. And this mine is almost certainly played out. Estleman's Amos Walker fulfills all of the Chandlerian requirements for a hard-boiled hero, but these days that doesn't seem to be enough. Perhaps the world is no more cynical than it was when Philip Marlowe roamed the streets of Los Angeles, but it sure seems like it is. The appeal of Marlowe, Sam Spade, the Continental Op, Archer and the thousands who followed them was that they offered a vision that wasn't corrupt in a world that was overwhelmingly corrupt. Their vision offered hope. These days, it's hard to believe in hope.

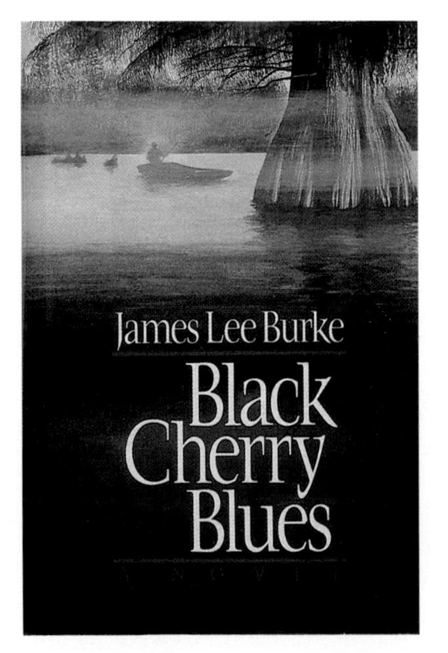

(Courtesy Bob Lakin Books)

None of the current batch of hard-boiled detectives demonstrates this better than Dave Robicheaux, the Cajun detective created by James Lee Burke. Robicheaux has appeared in six well-received novels—both critically and commercially—in the past several years, and Burke won an Edgar award for his first adventure, *Black Cherry Blues*. He is not only typical of the current group of hard-boiled authors, but he is a little better than most. Burke writes with skill (he started writing literary fiction, which didn't ruin him), and his characters fulfill the first rule of the American fictional detective—they're memorable. Yet there is no hope in the Robicheaux novels, and this seems alien to the entire concept of the past seventy years of the hard-boiled hero. They are as bleak and as desolate as a suicide note. Robicheaux is a former New Orleans policeman who left the department in a scandal, a neat trick in a department that has never been known for its rectitude. His wife was killed in an especially brutal attack ("The sheet is twisted in her hands; she holds it against her breasts as though it could protect her from 12-gauge deer slugs and double-aught buckshot"). His mother ran off with another man when he was a child. He is a recovering alcoholic who clings to AA's twelve steps in much the same way a drunk clings to a bottle. He has adopted a Central American orphan, whose life was even bleaker before she came to live with Robicheaux. Compounding this atmosphere is the violence and viciousness of the novels, on a level with anything Mickey Spillane ever wrote. There is no redemption, only the opportunity for Robicheaux to live another day. This, not coincidentally, is something he knows from AA: Take every day one day at a time.

(Courtesy Bob Lakin Books)

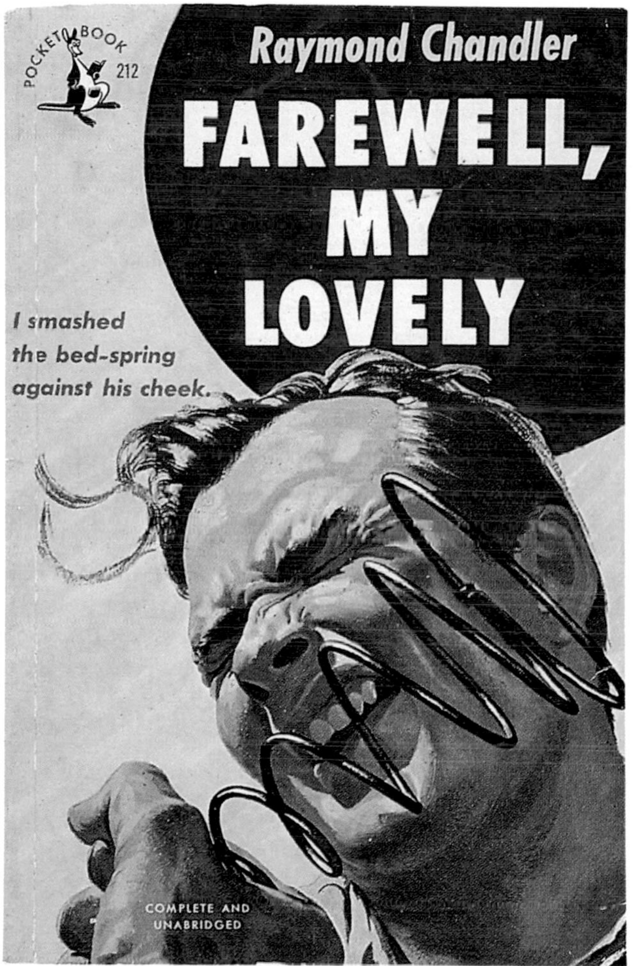

Contrast this with Marlowe, or any of the others who are firmly part of his tradition. The reader knows almost nothing about Marlowe's personal life from the five and a half novels and one short story, save for what he tells General Sternwood in the opening pages of the first novel, *The Big Sleep*, and in another scene in *The Long Goodbye*. Marlowe has no family, no home, no roots, no connections, no friends. All the reader ever finds out is that Marlowe went to college for a while, used to work for the district attorney, plays chess, and moves every couple of years. There is little other material to work with because Chandler wanted it that way: The emphasis is never on Marlowe's life, but on the people he comes across. Consider Paul Pine, the little-known but well-regarded Chicago detective created by Howard Browne. Pine, whose supporters rate him as highly as everyone else rates Marlowe, appeared in four novels after World War II. Save for a couple of obvious facts that would apply to any detective from that era—he thinks movie private eyes are phonies, he is loyal to a fault, especially to clients, and he lives in dingy apartments and works in dingy office buildings—it's almost impossible to learn anything about Pine. He has no family, no background, no prospects and few friends. But that sort of information isn't important, because the reader learns about Pine in another way. David Geherin pointed out in *The American Private Eye* that "Pine is, like Philip Marlowe, the type of first-person narrator who can be judged by the language he uses and by the distinctive way he observes and describes what he sees." This is, after all, what Chandler praised Hammett for in "The Simple Art of Murder"—and it is a sort of subtlety that is missing from the life of the modern hard-boiled detective such as Robicheaux and Robert B. Parker's Spenser. The focus has shifted in these characters, from the world around the detective to the detective itself. This is not an improvement. If anything, the detective has become too self-absorbed.

It is this subtlety that has always been crucial in transcending the subgenre. The Op novels and stories are violent, but they are not crude, and the Op is not a simple man. Hammett did not invent the hard-boiled story; he was the first to make it something more than it was. Chandler then improved on Hammett, and Macdonald then took Chandler in a different direction. Credit for inventing the hard-boiled detective, however, goes to Carroll John Daly, who wrote a story called "The False Burton Combs" for the December 1922 issue of *Black Mask*. The detective, who is nameless, describes himself as a gentleman adventurer, and he kills people as easily and as calmly as he splits infinitives (dialogue was never Daly's strong suit during his more than thirty years in the business). Daly followed this nameless detective[1] with another before creating Three Gun Terry Mack, Race Williams and Satan Hall, the trio who would be Daly's most memorable contribution to the subgenre. Almost to a bullet, they are Mike Hammer without the sex and sadism. (Spillane reportedly said his inspiration came from Daly, while Daly never got over how much money Spillane made from Daly's formula.)

DETECTIVE FICTION WEEKLY

Satan's Kill

A Novelette

By Carroll John Daly

Satan Hall Stalks the Denizens of the Underworld to Rout Out the Two-legged Jackals Who Prey on Human Lives

CHAPTER I

(Courtesy John Wooley)

"Oh, I ain't a killer," Race says in the first Williams story, "The Knights of the Open Palm" (*Black Mask*, June 1923), "but remember, there were four of them, that left two more to be accounted for yet; it wouldn't do to wound a lad and then to have him pop up again when you least wanted to see him." That pretty much sums up Daly's credo: Shoot the crooks before they shoot you. Each of his stories was an excuse for Three Gun Terry or Race or Satan (who didn't let the fact that he was a cop stop him from shooting

[1]The nameless detective is not, as this shows, something pulp historian Bill Pronzini brought to the genre with his Nameless Detective novels. It also shows that almost every trick a writer can think of has probably already been thought of.

first and asking questions later) to whip out a pistol and blow somebody away.

Hammett took the vitality that Daly created and fashioned it into a sort of pseudorealism. No, private detectives don't exist except as guys who do divorce work or repossess cars—but if they did, they would be just like the Op or Marlowe or Archer. The best hard-boiled detectives engage in little gun play, because real detectives engage in little gun play. It can never be emphasized enough that Hammett wrote about violence, but that he wasn't a violent writer. Look at any of the Op stories, even *Red Harvest,* and this is obvious. The Op worries in *Red Harvest* that he is going "blood-simple" from all of the mayhem, and in "The Gutting of Couffignal," he solves the case because the crooks had been too violent. Professionals, the Op points out, wouldn't have made the mistake of blowing up so many buildings. And it can't be emphasized enough that every murder in *The Maltese Falcon* takes place offstage, that Spade doesn't carry a gun, and that Spade and Gutman actually talk intellectually about the efficacy of violence. What kind of impression must this have made on the readers of *Black Mask,* where *The Maltese Falcon* appeared in serial form before its book publication?

Marlowe did not appear until 1939, when he walked past the carving of the knight trying to rescue a damsel in distress at the front door of the Sternwood home in *The Big Sleep.* Chandler,

Humphrey Bogart found his niche playing hard-boiled detectives—both Spade, in The Maltese Falcon, *and Marlowe, in* The Big Sleep *with Lauren Bacall.*

though, had been working on his detective since 1933, when he was a forty-five-year-old unemployed oil company executive who had taken up writing detective fiction. Mallory, the hard-boiled hero of the first Chandler story, "Blackmailers Don't Shoot," is Marlowe in every significant detail except his name. If Hammett was the savior of the hard-boiled detective, Chandler was the greatest apostle. He took the framework Hammett created with Spade and the Op and fleshed it out. He codified the rules of the genre in "The Simple Art of Murder" in 1944 with so much skill that few hard-boiled detectives who have appeared since have not in some way been written according to those rules: A man going down mean streets who is not himself mean.

EXAMINING THE CLUES

Carroll John Daly is most famous for Race Williams and his brothers, but Race is far from the most unique of Daly's characters. That honor goes to Vee Brown, always described as a Tin Pan Alley tunesmith by day (who signs his work Vivian) and an avenging angel by night. Vee works for the district attorney's office, and his orders are simple—bring back either a man or a body. He hunts only the meanest, most vicious killers, and did so in two novels and stories for *Dime Detective,* mostly during the Depression. This contradiction is something the psychohistorians could really sink their teeth into.

Marlowe also has something that almost none of his predecessors had: a sense of humor. Marlowe is, if not the first, the best of the wise-cracking detectives. There had been humor in Hammett's work, certainly, and there are those who argue that *The Thin Man* is a sixty thousand-word joke. And some of Hammett's humor was so subtle that his readers needed a postgraduate degree in linguistics to figure it out. Take, for instance, this scene from the 1924 Prohibition-era Op story, "The Golden Horseshoe," when the Op is in a saloon in Tijuana: "I was reading a sign high on a wall behind the bar—'Only genuine pre-war American and British whiskeys served here.' I was trying to count how many lies could be found in those nine words, and had reached four, with promise of more, when the Greek cleared his throat. . . ."

Chandler wasn't as indirect, and the subgenre has been living with his legacy—including countless half-boiled halfwits—ever since. Each of the Marlowe books has so many chuckles that it often seems Marlowe works his way through Los Angeles as if he were a Catskills comic working an audience. No hood, no matter how tough, is safe from Marlowe's wit. No cop, no matter how crooked, can get out of the way of Marlowe's tongue. Most important, the humor is as integral to the story as it is to Marlowe's character. Anyone who doubts Chandler knew what he was doing has overlooked this. On the other hand, this technique makes it nearly impossible to quote chapter and verse to get a laugh here, since so much of the humor depends on the situation. In *The Big Sleep,* Marlowe tells a cheap hood with a bad ear to leave him alone, or he will shoot his other ear off. In this context, it seems juvenile. In the book, it just seems like Marlowe.

The funniest Marlowe book is *Farewell, My Lovely,* a 1940 novel about an ex-con named Moose Malloy, "a big man but not more than six feet five inches tall and not wider than a beer truck," who is looking for his girlfriend. Marlowe is dragged into the case—literally. "A hand I could have sat in came out of the dimness and took hold of my shoulder and squashed it to a pulp." Along the

Philip Marlowe's "business card," as depicted on a hardback edition of Farewell, My Lovely.
(Courtesy Bob Lakin Books)

way, he exchanges witty double entendres with a femme fatale, rides an honest cop unmercifully, and spars with a couple of crooked policemen, one of whom he keeps calling Hemingway. "Who is this Hemingway person at all?" the cop asks. Marlowe, who has just been sapped, hog-tied and is being taken for a ride, doesn't miss a beat. "A guy that keeps saying the same thing over and over until you begin to believe it must be good," he says.

Marlowe was also more introspective than Spade and the Op. This is the continuation of a trend that would peak with Lew Archer: the hard-boiled detective as gumshoe-psychotherapist. Seen at a distance and through the years, this is a discernible pattern. Spade and the Op were manhunters. They rarely wonder why someone commits a crime; to them, motive is only important in how it helps them catch the criminal. Spade does not pause midway through *The Maltese Falcon* to ponder what the black bird symbolizes to Gutman. It doesn't matter why Gutman wants the statue—it only matters that Spade must stop Gutman before he kills again in his attempt to get it.

Marlowe is more philosophical than this, even in his least philosophical moments. In *The Big Sleep*, certainly not his most polished effort, Chandler puts Marlowe through paces no hard-boiled detective had ever been through. The final scene, when Marlowe recites what can only be termed a Shakespearean soliloquy ("What did it matter where you lay once you were dead? . . . Once you were dead, you were sleeping the big sleep. . . ."), was of a style never done before. And it was only the beginning of Chandler's attempt to add this sort of introspection typical of mainstream novels to the hard-boiled subgenre, and ultimately to the entire genre. *The Long Goodbye* (1953) is not the best Marlowe, but it is certainly the most ambitious. Marlowe is concerned not only with discovering whether Terry Lennox committed the murder he is charged with, but also with trying to understand what sort

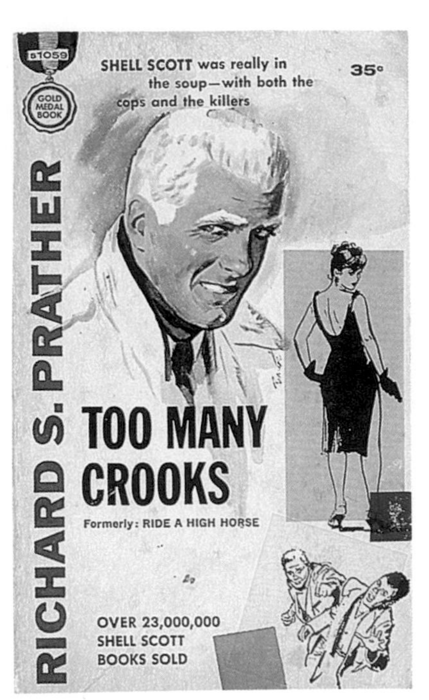

(Courtesy Bob Lakin Books)

of conditions would cause Lennox to commit the murder—as well as with the lives and relationships of almost a half-dozen other people, including a drunken writer who sounds a lot like Chandler.

It was almost inevitable, then, that Archer built on this base. Between Marlowe and Archer, many of the postwar hard-boiled sleuths like Mike Shayne and Shell Scott imitated the surface aspects of Marlowe's charm—his wit, his relationships with women, his long, colorful (and in lesser hands, windy) narrative descriptions—without getting under the surface to the substance. There is nothing wrong with Scott, the crew-cut, white-haired Los Angeles detective created by Richard S. Prather who appeared in ten novels between 1950 and 1975, if the only thing a reader needs to do is to kill an hour in an airport. He was created for a series of paperback originals by a new publisher who thought there was a market for just that sort of adventure.

Ross Macdonald, on the other hand, was burrowing into the substance, and even hollowing out new territory. "The inner shape of a man's life, if he is a man of action," he wrote in 1969, "plots the curve of his movements. If he is a writer, it is what he writes from and about. But it remains as personal and hidden as his skeleton, just as intricate, almost as unchangeable." This is pretty heady stuff for a detective novel, but Macdonald wanted to take the detective novel where not even Chandler had taken it. He wanted to write mainstream novels where the hard-boiled detective was a member of the cast, and not the reason for the play.

This attempt to continue to bring the hard-boiled subgenre into the mainstream was something he was eminently qualified to do, given the direction American literature has taken since the end of World War II. Macdonald was an academic. He earned his doctorate degree from the University of Michigan in 1951, writing his dissertation on the early nineteenth-century English poet Samuel Taylor Coleridge. This gave Macdonald a perspective that no one had ever had before. His training was in *Jane Eyre* and *Moby Dick,* not *Black Mask* and *Dime Detective.* He understood all sorts of things about writing and literature that his predecessors could only guess at. Hammett, for instance, had dropped out of high school and spent the rest of his life trying to catch up. But Macdonald spent most of the first thirty years of his life in a school of some sort, and he was aware of his place in the subgenre. That is one reason why Archer was called Archer—as homage to Spade's partner, Miles Archer. This education also gave Macdonald the background that enabled him, later in his career, to write almost as much about Archer as a critic as he did as a novelist, in an attempt to explain what he was trying to do with the character.

Of course, being an academic is no guarantee of success, despite what everyone thinks today. Macdonald was an academic who could write, and that made the difference. He had to be talented to overcome the almost complete lack of action in Archer's adventures after *The Galton Case* (1958). Macdonald was working in a subgenre where slam and bang had been key ingredients for more than thirty years, and he replaced them with introspection and contemplation. In the typical Archer book of that time, Archer shoots no one, sleeps with no one, chases no one and fights with no one. He does a lot of talking and he does a lot of traveling, often cross-country. The only reason these pseudo-adventures are not as dull as an accounting textbook is that Macdonald knew what to do with a typewriter. He may not have been as good as his critics said (it's hard to see him as the Walker Percy of the hard-boiled crowd), but he was good enough. Archer is insightful, but rarely sanctimonious. In *Sleeping Beauty*, his concern for a daughter who disappears is not that of the professional do-gooder, but that of someone who knows that but for the grace of God, goes himself.

Archer became Harper in Hollywood, and Paul Newman portrayed him in two films, here in The Drowning Pool *(1975).*

(Courtesy Bob Lakin Books)

Archer, in fact, was so successful that he not only influenced a generation of followers (including television's Harry Orwell and Lawrence Block's Matt Scudder), but he also made it possible for Mike Hammer to be even more successful than he probably deserved to be. Hammer is as violent and vicious as Archer is subtle and subdued. If Archer works to heal the tears in society's fabric, Hammer yearns to buzz-saw the entire garment. He is an anarchist in the finest tradition of the political revolutionaries who kept blowing themselves up one hundred years ago in their attempt to perfect the world in their image. Hammer not only believes that eggs must be broken to make omelettes, he also believes the chicken must have its neck wrung and the farmer should be shot for good measure.

"All right, you conniving little punks, I'll play ball, but I'm going to make up a lot of rules you never heard of," Hammer wails in 1951's *One Lonely Night* (far from the most strident of his epics). "You think I'm cornered and it'll be a soft touch. Well, you won't be playing with a guy who's a hero. You'll be up against a guy with a mind gone rotten and a lust for killing! That's the way I was and that's the way I like it!"

This was hard for critics to stomach forty years ago; imagine how much harder it must be in these days. Regardless of his literary merits—and his writing is not nearly as bad as he is given credit for—Hammer has been as influential as he has been critically scorned. Every excess in the hard-boiled line since Mickey Spillane created Hammer in 1947's *I, the Jury* can be traced to Spillane, from those committed by respectable detectives like Robicheaux and Parker's Spenser to the even more fantastic characters who have since passed out of the subgenre—the Exterminators and the Executioners who can't speak a sentence that isn't punctuated with a machine gun clip. The violence that is common in hard-boiled novels and films today is nothing more than a reaction to the near psychotherapeutic plots of the Archer books—something that Spillane must have realized, if only instinctively.

These excesses mean it is almost impossible to find anyone anywhere who has anything nice to say about Hammer; there's even a reference to Spillane's father calling his son's work "crud."

The critic Anthony Boucher, the Howard Haycraft of his era, went so far as to say that *I, the Jury* should be required reading at a Gestapo training class. Yet Spillane's books sold tens of millions, and are ranked among the best-selling U.S. titles ever. One study reported that seven Hammer books were among the twenty-nine best-sellers between 1865 and 1967. Even allowing that there was a bigger audience for books in 1965 than during the previous century, this is an impressive statistic.

Spillane, who professes to be as much of a character as his detective, says he could not care less about any of this. The only important fact to him is the line on his royalty statement that says how much his publisher owes him. This is, after all, the same man who not only made beer commercials, but plugged the beer on the cover photos of the paperback editions of his books in the early 1980s. Spillane claims he doesn't like to be called an author, but a writer, and he refers to his readers as customers. In fact, Hammer's 1989 comeback, *The Killing Man,* was written not because the muse came to Spillane and called forth another Hammer novel after nineteen years, but because Spillane needed the money.

Stacy Keach appeared as Mike Hammer on the mid-eighties television series. Don Stroud played Pat Chambers.

The past two decades have been spent trying to sort out the future of the hard-boiled detective. Would it be Archer or would it be Hammer? Spenser shows just how clearly the battle for the detective's soul has been waged. When he first appeared in *The Godwulf Manuscript* in 1974, he seemed to be, as his cover blurbs pointed out, the heir to the Hammett/Chandler/Macdonald tradition. Spenser was quick-witted, honorable and tough—everything Chandler said the hard-boiled detective should be. "Parker has revitalized and enriched the genre," critic David Geherin wrote in 1985, claiming that Spenser's exploits were not only entertaining, but literary.

But something happened to Spenser a couple of novels later: He turned mean and violent. He had always been quick with his fists, but the violence that started showing up in his adventures was more than a fistfight to advance the plot. Not only did Spenser start shooting people—a lot of people—but his intellectual rationalization of the violence became a common part of the books, especially in the countless conversations he

Parker's Spenser became a television series with Robert Urich starring. Avery Brooks co-starred on "Spenser: For Hire."

Richard Roundtree played Shaft on film and television. Ed Barth (Lt. Al Rossi) was his television costar.

had about manhood with his girlfriend, Susan Silverman. The first appearance of this new attitude came in *The Judas Goat* (1978). Spenser packs enough hardware to take on Mack Bolan (the scene where he loads his suitcase with guns is chilling) for a trip to London to look for a covey of terrorists who maimed a wealthy industrialist after they killed his wife and family. The industrialist tells Spenser he needs a "hungry Captain Midnight" to track the terrorists, and this reference cannot be overlooked. In one sentence, Parker is jettisoning the tradition he was supposed to be the heir to.[2] Marlowe has his faults, but he is not a comic-book character.

This must have been a conscious decision on Parker's part. He is no fool. Parker was an academic who chucked teaching because he found the lifestyle to be a pain in the neck, and he wrote his doctoral dissertation on a relationship between Hammett, Chandler, and Macdonald. He certainly knows where the bodies are buried. If he made this decision, which seems to be an acknowledgment that the Hammett/Chandler/Macdonald tradition is bankrupt, then it seems certain that others, less talented, can only come to the same conclusion. This is one reason why it is so difficult to get excited about the changes in the hard-boiled subgenre over the past decade, which includes the advent of the female hard-boiled sleuth.

Will Sharon McCone, Kinsey Millhone, V. I. Warshawski and their sisters find a way around this entanglement of violence? Or will they turn out to be nothing more than another trend, in much the same way the black private eye was twenty years ago? John Shaft's only legacies, save for the flurry of "Superfly" movies in the 1970s, were Issac Hayes's theme song and the typecasting of actor Richard Roundtree. This cannot be what Ernest Tidyman (who, oddly enough, was white) had in mind when he wrote the seven Shaft novels and two of the three Shaft movies in the 1970s. Shaft was (at first, anyway) an attempt to update the Chandlerian private eye so that he could function in the modern urban environment. When Chandler wrote, white people went slumming in Harlem. When Tidyman wrote *Shaft* in 1970, the only people left in

[2]One critic went so far as to call the Spenser novels pastiche, claiming that it was an example of how "the genre that had begun as the most realistic, the closest to life, became the most artificial, the furthest removed from life."

Harlem were black. Today, all of the books are out of print, and Tidyman is probably better known as the man who won an Oscar for *The French Connection* screenplay. So much for relevance.

Sue Grafton.

(*Photograph by Nick Vaccarro, courtesy Henry Holt*)

Relevance may be the only thing the women have going for them. Although this is a powerful advantage, it may not be enough if one of them cannot find some way to do for modern hard-boiled fiction what Hammett, Chandler, Macdonald—and even Spillane—did for the subgenre during their eras. So far, there has been little evidence of this, Grafton has pointed out. "I write from the inside out," she said, "and I work very hard to operate on a gut level as opposed to an academic or an intellectual one." Is this reaction any different from Parker's? Hillary Waugh points out that the women are different from the men because their tales are replete with mundane, daily tasks like doing laundry. When is the last time, he asks, Lew Archer did his laundry? That may be true, but it's hardly enough to enable the women to stake out a permanent niche.[3]

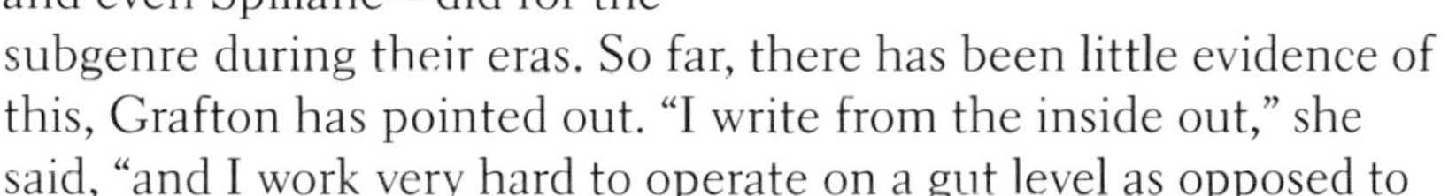

Kathleen Turner, with a big gun, played V. I. Warshawski to almost no success.

(*Photograph by Jane O'Neal, © Hollywood Pictures Company*)

McCone, created by Marcia Muller in 1977 in *Edwin of the Iron Shoes* and generally considered the first of the new hard-boiled women, takes one tack with her politically correct plots and her "Big Chill" atmosphere. It's a technique that Paretsky, whose V. I. Warshawski works out of Chicago, understands and has used, especially in the 1987 novel *Bitter Medicine*. In it, she watches a for-profit hospital butcher the delivery of her Hispanic friend's baby, killing the

[3]It's hard not to be cynical and wonder if the popularity of the women detectives with publishers and critics has as much to do with the new readers they have brought to the subgenre as it has to do with their talent. Millhone, especially, has sold books to millions of people who never would have thought about buying a Mickey Spillane book.

EXAMINING THE CLUES

Hammett and Chandler met just once, at a dinner on January 11, 1936 for a number of *Black Mask* authors who lived in California. Most accounts of the dinner report that Hammett and Chandler barely spoke to each other, save for exchanging pleasantries. A photo was taken at the dinner, and sent to Joseph Shaw, *Black Mask*'s editor. Among the others who attended was Horace McCoy (*They Shoot Horses, Don't They?*), Norbert Davis and W. T. Ballard. Everyone else is smiling at the camera; Hammett and Chandler look bored.

baby and the mother. But this may not be enough. In "Final Resting Place (1990)," McCone is just as concerned with vengeance as Hammer ever was. The only difference is that she is less bloody, which may or may not be an improvement.[4] An old '60s friend of McCone's has asked her to find out who left flowers at the friend's mother's grave. McCone does, and eventually discovers that the mother was murdered by her husband, and the flowers were left by the mother's lover. Does McCone go to the cops? Does she face the murderer herself? Does Hammer belong to the ACLU? Hardly. "Already I sensed a bond between [the daughter and the lover], knew that they had forged a front between a probable killer. Old Carl would get his, one way or the other."

What a terrific '90s, win-win sort of solution. McCone maintains a clear conscience, although she sanctions a revenge no different from that of the most high-handed, hard-fisted, male pig. After all, she emphasizes that she feels certain the two will act "sanely and rationally." Yet she has just helped her two friends play *I, the Jury*. Contrast that with Marlowe's actions at the end of *The Big Sleep*. He is not adverse to saving the Sternwoods from scandal to spare the sickly General Sternwood, but he also accepts responsibility for making sure that there is no scandal. "I'll give you three days," he tells Vivian Reagan. "If you're gone by then—okey. If you're not, out it comes. And don't think I don't mean it." Marlowe does not shrug off what needs to be done because he has every faith and confidence in Vivian; he knows all too well that life is not that simple, and that people very rarely act in their own best interests unless prodded to do so. He has spent much of the novel learning just that.

If the traditional hard-boiled detective has a future, he must acknowledge what Marlowe has learned. Otherwise, he will go the way of Philo Vance. It may seem strange to trust in involved reasoning, since the subgenre's weak point with critics has always been its simplicity and its lack of sophistication. Most of these characters, its detractors have always claimed, are just overgrown children running around playing cops and robbers. They are not subjects that deserve to be taken seriously. But if the genre is to carry on the tradition of Hammett, Chandler and Macdonald, it will have to build on the complexity that Hammett revealed and that Chandler and Macdonald improved upon. The fault with Spillane and his heirs, and this includes the women, is not that they are violent and vengeance prone. The fault is that violence and vengeance is always a simple solution to a complex problem.

---

[4]At least McCone's m.o. is better than Charley Davenport's, the woman hero of the story, "Death of a Fatcat" (1990). Says Charley: "One thing I've learned over the years: The instant someone threatens you, cold-cock him."

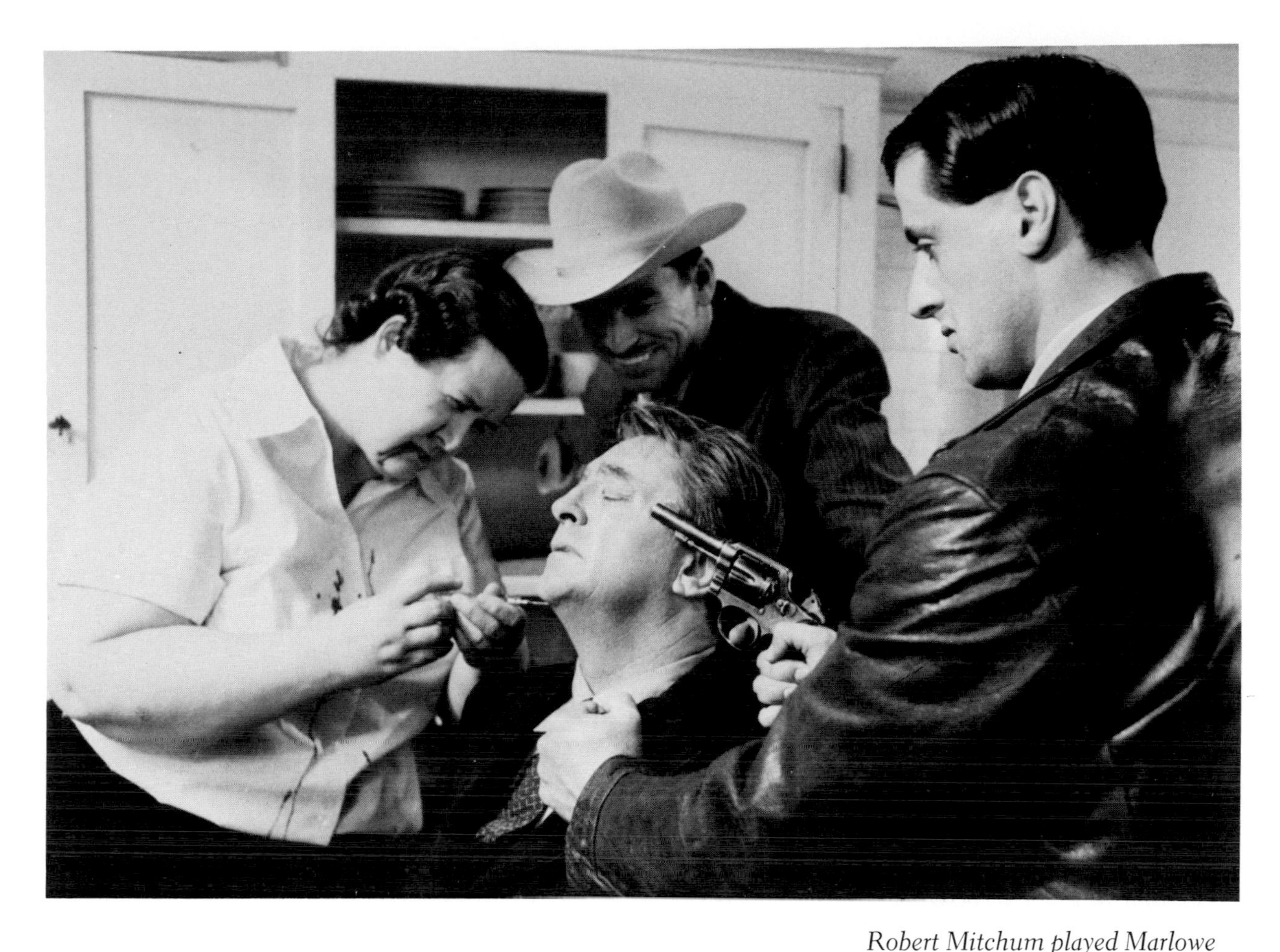

Robert Mitchum played Marlowe twice: in a bad Big Sleep *and a much better* Farewell, My Lovely *here. Even Sylvester Stallone (right, with Burton Gilliam and Kate Murtagh) gets into the act.*

The hard-boiled detective has been stereotyped for so long that too many people have forgotten that a man can be honorable without being simple, and that he can be compassionate without being a fool. Chandler wrote that in "everything that can be called art there is a quality of redemption." The trick for whoever succeeds in moving the traditional hard-boiled detective to the next level will be to combine this philosophy with the energy the genre is famous for. This energy is not radiated by the twists and turns of the plot, but by the narrative itself and how the story is told.

That is what makes Marlowe work. By the time Chandler wrote his novels, he was tired of the formulas he had learned in the pulps, and there is a noticeable lack of gun play and car chases in the Marlowe stories. The energy comes from Marlowe himself, by the language he uses and by the perspective he brings. This is a difficult concept for some people to grasp. One reason why hard-boiled detectives have fared so poorly on television is that the medium's writers and producers don't realize a story can have energy without those elements. One of the reasons "Harry O" last-

Clint Eastwood's Dirty Harry is nothing new—there have been hard-boiled cops since the subgenre started. Harry Guardino plays his boss, here in Dirty Harry *(1971), the first film of that successful series.*

EXAMINING THE CLUES

Ross Macdonald wrote his first four books, all World War II thrillers, under his real name, Kenneth Millar. He switched to John Macdonald for the first Lew Archer novel in 1949 so as not to be confused with his wife, the suspense writer Margaret Millar. This did not sit well with John D. MacDonald, who was churning out paperback originals at the time and had not yet become famous for the Travis McGee series. So Ross Macdonald switched to John Ross Macdonald for the next book, which still didn't please John D. MacDonald. Finally, he became Ross Macdonald, and John D. didn't object.

ed just two seasons was the constant fighting between the network and the show's creative staff. Series creator Howard Rodman wanted a quiet loner who didn't even own a car and who limped from a bullet lodged permanently in his back. He even went so far as to compare Harry Orwell with Marlowe. This boggled the network, which didn't understand how a series could have any action if there wasn't any action. It wanted a detective who was surrounded by pretty girls, drove a fast car, and shot it out with the bad guys every week (not unlike "Spenser: For Hire").

The irony is that better writers are working in the hard-boiled subgenre today than ever before. Parker is more talented than a dozen of the pulp hacks combined, and he isn't appreciably better than many of his contemporaries—Grafton, Paretsky, Valin, Hansen, Estleman, Michael Z. Lewin, Lawrence Block, John Lutz and Jack Livingston among them. That's why it's so hard to believe that if there was a way to salvage the traditional hard-boiled detective, someone would have found it by now. Writers rarely get a chance to quote W. Somerset Maugham in a study of genre literature, but what he said shortly before Chandler died applies here: "I do not see," he wrote in his book *The Decline and Fall of the Detective Story,* "who can succeed Raymond Chandler." He was right. Macdonald finished the job Chandler had started, and when he was done, so was the subgenre. It is getting ready to sleep its big sleep.

MASS MEDIA: A Hard-boiled Sampler

- **Peter Gunn.** If anyone wonders why television can't do hard-boiled, they need look no further than "Peter Gunn." The program had everything going for it: style, ratings (number sixteen in the Nielsens in the 1958–59 season), a great theme song by Henry Mancini, and critical success. Yet it lasted just three seasons, and had to move to a second network for its final season. Television executives don't understand the hard-boiled genre, don't want to understand the genre, and will probably never understand the genre. That's too bad, because "Peter Gunn" showed what could be done if someone—in this case, creator Blake Edwards—cared. Yes, it was often slick, and it inspired all sorts of second-rate imitators like "77 Sunset Strip," but it is one of only a handful of television shows that ever came close to the hard-boiled ideal.

- **J. J. Gittes.** *Chinatown* does not need any more praise as a brilliant piece of filmmaking. What it's here for is to take its rightful place as the movie that wrote the end to Hollywood's hard-boiled tradition. Think about it—how many great detective movies has Hollywood made since *Chinatown?* Director Roman Polanski succeeded where Robert Altman's *The Long Goodbye* failed because he knew what Altman didn't: Damning with faint praise is a lot more effective than bombast. That's why Jack Nicholson's Gittes is so much more effective than Elliot Gould's Philip Marlowe. Gittes is a loser, and he doesn't have to go to any extremes to show it. Gittes is everything the real private detective too often is, and what Hammett ignored and Chandler feared: a sleazy man with few scruples who will do almost anything for a buck.

Jack Nicholson and Faye Dunaway in Roman Polanski's Chinatown *(1974).*

Peter Gunn had a second television incarnation in the late eighties, with Peter Strauss as the cool detective.

• **Paul Auster's New York Trilogy.** These three short works by the poet and essayist are not for everyone. It's probably fair to call *City of Glass, Ghosts,* and *The Locked Room* a series of existential hard-boiled novels, but that's putting labels on something that wasn't meant for labels. Instead, try to imagine a collaboration of Richard Brautigan, Franz Kafka and Ross Macdonald. Some critics thought Auster was on the verge of redefining the hard-boiled genre (granted, only a few elite East Coast critics) when these books appeared in the late 1980s. But it's hard for something to influence something else when no one is sure what's going on in the thing that's supposed to be doing the influencing.

• **Travis McGee.** McGee, created by pulp graduate John D. MacDonald, is an acquired taste. There are those who insist his couple of dozen adventures, identifiable by the colors in their titles, are the next best thing to actually living out a life as a hard-boiled hero. The University of South Florida, for instance, is the site of a McGee newsletter discussing such crucial topics as Plymouth gin (which is all McGee drinks), the condition of his boat, *The Busted Flush,* sidekick Meyer's various economic theories, and other assorted Travisiana. Then there is the rest of the world, which wonders what all of the fuss is about. Travis is well versed in pop philosophy, gets to bed a lot of women, and doesn't pay taxes. Other than that, they say, it's hard to figure out his appeal. McGee is, in the end, a pulp character who outlived the pulps. The others changed, like Perry Mason, or died, like Ed Jenkins, the Phantom Crook. McGee merely moved to paperback originals under a variety of names, until MacDonald wrote *The Deep Blue Good-By* in 1964—Travis's first official appearance. MacDonald found a formula, honed it to perfection, and repeated it for approximately seventy million readers who couldn't get enough of it.

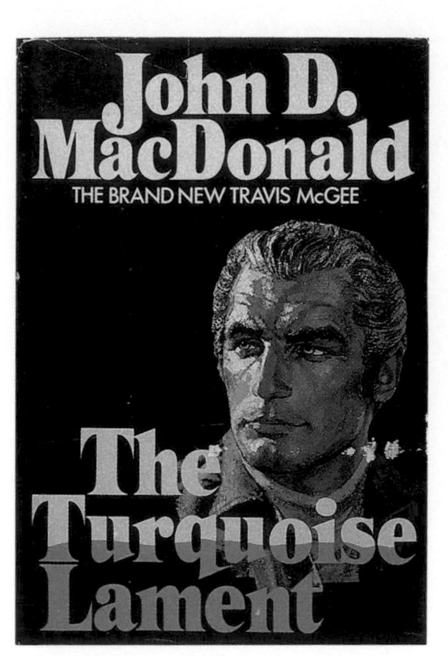

(Courtesy Bob Lakin Books)

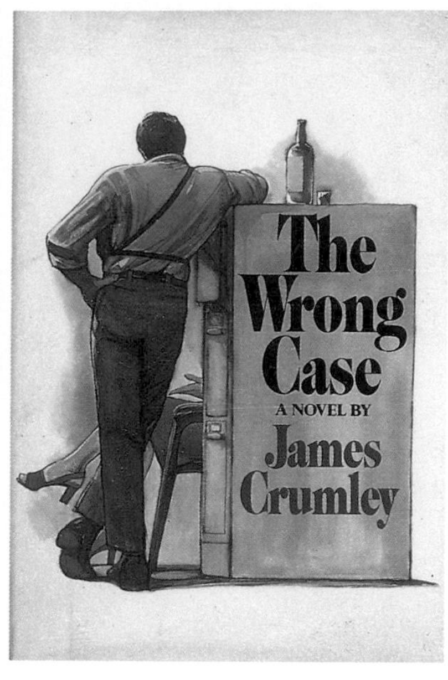

(Courtesy Bob Lakin Books)

• **C. W. Sughrue.** Sughrue is the hero of *The Last Good Kiss* (1978) and *The Mexican Tree Duck* (1993), two of only four hard-boiled novels poet and critic James Crumley has written in the past seventeen years. Sughrue could revive the entire hard-boiled subgenre all by himself if Crumley could just get his creative juices flowing a touch more. Sughrue combines the action which seems so crucial to the hard-boiled novel today with the quality of redemption the rest don't have. Plus, Crumley is as good a writer as anyone, anywhere, as the opening of the book shows: "When I finally caught up with Abraham Trahearne, he was drinking beer with an alcoholic bulldog named Fireball Roberts in a ramshackle joint just outside of Sonoma, California, drinking the heart out of a fine spring afternoon."

THE THIRD DEGREE: Rehabilitating Raymond Chandler

The time has come to restore Raymond Chandler to his rightful place in the world he played such a large role in creating.

In the past two decades, Chandler's memory has endured more sniping than Philip Marlowe took shots from his office bottle. The psycho-historians have looked at Chandler's submissive relationship with his mother, his marriage to a woman eighteen years his senior and his alcoholism, and have wagged their fingers in displeasure. The critics have taken apart his novels and his stories and have found them wanting, denigrating them as over-written, sentimental and childish. One went so far as to call Chandler a poseur, while another has called Marlowe passé, saying that he couldn't get the girl today, and that he probably didn't get the girl in his day.

Chandler deserves none of this. The only thing Raymond Chandler was ever guilty of was trying to make the detective story something better than what it was, and he has been paying for his efforts ever since. He was not a great writer, as Philip Durham pointed out in his landmark critical biography of Chandler, but he was a good one. And he was a good enough writer to be spared the second-guessing and the backhanded compliments that have been his lot since his death in 1959.

Raymond Chandler in February 1958.

(Department of Special Collections, University Research Library, UCLA)

What they have overlooked is what Chandler accomplished. His only peer in the seventy-year history of the hard-boiled detective was Hammett, and this assessment includes Ross

Elliot Gould played Marlowe in Robert Altman's take on The Long Goodbye *(1973).*

Macdonald. Chandler, through Marlowe, struggled valiantly to make the hard-boiled detective respectable company in literary discussions. And if Chandler didn't succeed, it was the battles that he almost always lost that made it possible for a Ross Macdonald novel to appear on the front page of *The New York Times Book Review.* If Hammett's successor had been less talented, had been one of the second-stringers who wrote for *Black Mask* and *Dime Detective* and had not been Chandler, no one would have bothered to take the hard-boiled detective seriously. The character would have been relegated to the literary netherworld populated by science fiction, westerns and romances.

That is almost certainly a perspective that not even Hammett had. This is not a reflection on Hammett's intellect, but on his priorities. Being the first and best hard-boiled writer (which he was) was less important to Hammett than his politics, which he equated with ridding the world of pain and suffering. It's rare to come across evidence of Hammett musing about his place in the literary world, unless the place was a bar, and he was musing with a drink in his hand. This is not to say Hammett didn't have an ego, and that he didn't want to be admired for his work. It's nearly impossible to find a writer who doesn't have an ego and who doesn't crave admiration. What it says is that Hammett didn't worry what people fifty years later would think of his work.

Chandler, on the other hand, did worry. It possessed him. In the 1940s and '50s, for instance, when a host of inferior detectives had radio and television shows, Chandler lobbied for a Marlowe show. He had little respect for either medium (and less for television than radio), but he was not going to rest until Marlowe had what was coming to him. The money was important, for Chandler was always saying he was short of money. But the flap over the television and radio shows had more to do with his reputation than anything else. "I guess there are maybe two kinds of writers," he wrote to his agent around this time, "writers who write stories and writers who write writing." There is no doubt that Chandler considered himself part of the second group.

All he had ever wanted to be was a writer, starting with his days at an English public school. One of Chandler's first jobs was as a writer, as a free-lancer selling sketches, shorts and poetry to a number of English newspapers at the turn of the century. When he couldn't make a living doing this, he was forced to turn to other things, including a stint in the trenches with a Canadian regiment during World War I and his years with a Los Angeles oil company. He only returned to writing during the Depression when he lost his job with the oil company. The key to Chandler, who was born in the United States but raised in Britain, may be found in those earliest years. The man was a failed poet, and every bit of writing he did after his free-lance days was a search for the success he couldn't find as a poet.

Chandler not only knew what Hammett had done with the Op and Sam Spade, but knew what he had to do to improve on Hammett. It's almost irrelevant whether he made good on this challenge, because what is unique about the challenge is that Chandler was the only one who realized it. This is a crucial point that his critics have always failed to acknowledge, which baffled Chandler. Maybe this is why so much of Chandler's critical work,

Klute *(1971), starring Donald Sutherland, was one of the last attempts to portray the traditional Chandlerian private eye on film.*

EXAMINING THE CLUES

William Campbell Gault, whose Brock "The Rock" Callahan is one of the most successful and well-liked of the 1950s hard-boiled detectives, made no bones about who influenced him. Callahan, a former pro football player, is always comparing himself with Marlowe, and coming up on the short end. Nowhere is this more obvious than in *Day of the Ram* (1956), which deals with the murder of a quarterback for the Los Angeles NFL team. The Rock has just been beaten up and arrested in a bookie joint in Santa Monica. "Evidently, you don't know our little town," the Santa Monica police chief tells The Rock. "I read about it," says Callahan, "but the writer called it Bay City." This reference is to Chandler, who modeled his corrupt, fictional Bay City after Santa Monica.

as well as his correspondence (as fascinating as it is numerous) was directed toward explaining himself and what he was trying to do. "The Simple Art of Murder," which appeared in *Atlantic Monthly* in 1944, was a landmark in this direction. Not only was the upscale *Atlantic* an unlikely place for an essay evaluating the mystery story, but the essay itself was as revolutionary as *Red Harvest* had been twenty years before. No one had ever written anything quite like it before (or since, for that matter).

This, more than anything else, may be what has always aggravated the critics about Chandler. He not only broke ground as a writer, but as a critic. There's no obvious excuse for things like the esteemed Anthony Boucher's vicious review of *The Little Sister* (he attacked it for what he called its "scathing hatred of the human race"), or the boring, repetitious discussions about whether Marlowe was a homosexual or not. These are side issues, smokescreens that obscure what is really important. There is no reason for the small-mindedness of work like the essays in *The World of Raymond Chandler,* which once was described as a look at Chandler by his friends. If those were his friends, it's easy to see why he drank. Any critic who dissected the tales of the other Marlow in this fashion would be thrown out of the "critics union."[5]

There has to be another reason for their fury, and the reason is this: Chandler was right. The puzzle doesn't matter in the hard-boiled story; character matters, and modern literature is about character. This premise would be sure to infuriate not only a mystery traditionalist like Boucher, but also mainstream critics, who refuse to believe that if long, dull novels describing the affairs of married college professors and their young, nubile students can be literature, so can the hard-boiled detective story. Sure, Chandler tried too hard, and he wore his ego on his shoulder just so it could be knocked off, but neither of these conditions alters what Chandler accomplished. It may be going too far to compare Chandler with Dickens, as his biographer Frank MacShane, does. But it isn't going too far to realize that what the hard-to-please William Ruehlmann wrote is true. After Chandler, he said, "there were few noteworthy changes. These were, with few exceptions, degenerative rather than developmental."

[5]Oddly, Chandler had never read Joseph Conrad, and had no idea that Conrad's narrator was named Marlow. Chandler's Marlowe was going to be called Mallory, after the chronicler of *Morte d'Arthur* (in keeping with Chandler's chivalric motif), but Chandler's wife said she liked Marlowe better. Marlowe it was.

THE SOLUTION:
Of Glims and Gloms and Whatchacallems. . . .

A sense of humor has never been a necessary piece of equipment for the American hard-boiled detective. Save for Philip Marlowe and his wise-cracking heirs, most hard-boiled detectives have provided as many giggles as Mike Hammer's .45 automatic. It's hard to laugh when you are snarling.

There have been even fewer attempts to bring comedy to other parts of the detective story field. Donald Westlake's Dortmunder is one of the few successful exceptions; Ross H. Spencer's Chance Perdue is less successful (although he can be a lot more juvenile). Most attempts at humor have come from places like Stuart Kaminsky's overrated Toby Peters series, which uses real people from Hollywood's Golden Age in plots featuring Kaminsky's fictional detective.

But one man wrote hard-boiled humor as well as anyone will ever write it. His name was Robert Leslie Bellem (1902–1968), and between the mid-1920s and the mid-1950s, he wrote, as near as anyone can figure, three thousand pulp stories—two stories a week and as many as one million words a year—for every conceivable pulp magazine. Bellem's stories appeared in hard-boiled pulps, adventure pulps, aviation pulps, western pulps and soft-core pulps. But Bellem is best known for creating the hero of the self-titled pulp (for which he wrote all of the stories under a number of pseudonyms): Dan Turner, Hollywood Detective.

The first Dan Turner pulp—a "bookfull" of stuttering roscoes.
(Photograph by Michael Keller Photography, courtesy John Wooley)

Do not labor under the impression that the Dan Turner stories are great literature. They are not even mediocre literature. But that's okay, because Dan wasn't much of a detective, even for a hard-boiled dick who appeared in second-rate pulps. He never solved a case using anything other than luck, lucky guesses and lucky coincidences—as well as a shootout on the final page. The pieces are formulaic, poorly plotted, and involve a lot of groping. The characters are all Hollywood moguls, stars or starlets, and the crime is always committed by an insider who is trying to seize control of some studio or another. Dan spends most of his time getting cracked on the

noggin, kicking the stems out from under frail wrens, and dodging cannons that yammer "kachow, kachow."

But no one read Dan Turner stories then or reads them now for the plot. The charm of the Dan Turner stories, as the preceding indicates, is the language and the character. Dan is proof of Chandler's theory that character is all—but in Dan's case, only after it has been cooked in a microwave. Bellem was a genius at sticking three or four unrelated words together with some slang and a verb or two, and coming up with sentences like this: "I pelted down to the basement, climbed into my bucket and souped the kidneys out of it; bored a hole through the night with my radiator ornament" ("Death's Passport," 1940). Not once do the words car or drive appear, but who notices that they are missing? This use of language is so impressive that the humorist S. J. Perelman, who knew his way around literary circles, said Turner was "the apotheosis of all private detectives" in an essay praising Dan called "Somewhere a Roscoe. . . ."[6]

Bellem was at his finest in describing women's breasts. No one anywhere in the history of literature could possibly have come up with as many terms as he did. And he wasn't especially vulgar about it, either, since he had to satisfy pulp-era moral standards (although his women seemed to wear nightgowns more often than any other form of clothing). That ruled out terms like boobs and

[6]Perelman always seemed to show up on the fringes of the hard-boiled crowd. He was a drinking buddy of Hammett and Lillian Hellman's, and his "Farewell, My Lovely Appetizer" is the classic hard-boiled parody.

tits. Instead, breasts were called whatcha-callems, thingumabobs, thems and thoses, mounded yumphs, perky pretty pretties, creamy bon bons, and tiddlywinks—among others.

Turner first appeared in *Spicy Detective* in June 1934, and the private skulk was in every issue of the magazine until it folded in 1947. He was the star of his own pulp from 1942 to 1950, often appearing in two or three stories. Bellem's output was so spectacular that to say it was prodigious doesn't seem to do him justice. It also accounts for the failure of his stories to contain much plot, even for a pulp story. What it doesn't account for is whether Bellem knew what he was doing, or was just writing to make his deadlines.

Bill Pronzini, whose Turner chapter in *Gun in Cheek* is the delishful morsel of Turner scholarship and will bring a glimmer to anyone's gloms, tends to think that the deadline was Bellem's most important concern, and discounts any idea that he was any sort of alchemist of language. There is more than a passing relationship to the style popularized by James Thurber, who was practicing his skill at the *New Yorker* at about this time. On the other hand, there's a consistency to Bellem's writing that lends credence to the theory that Dan was more than a chucklehead who swilled scotch. If he stole from Thurber, he at least stole from the best, and that says something for Bellem's intelligence, if not his talent. But what matters more is that for all of the triteness and formula in Bellem's stories—roscoes do a lot of sneezing—there are few recurring bad examples of Bellem's style.[7] As silly as all of it sounds at times, it gets the author's point across, and no writer can hope for more than that.

But the incident that really shows that Bellem was not just another million-word-a-year man came in the late 1950s, when he had to find a job after the collapse of the pulps. Robert Leslie Bellem went to work writing television shows (among them: "Perry Mason," "77 Sunset Strip" and "Superman"). If writing for television doesn't require a sense of humor, what does?

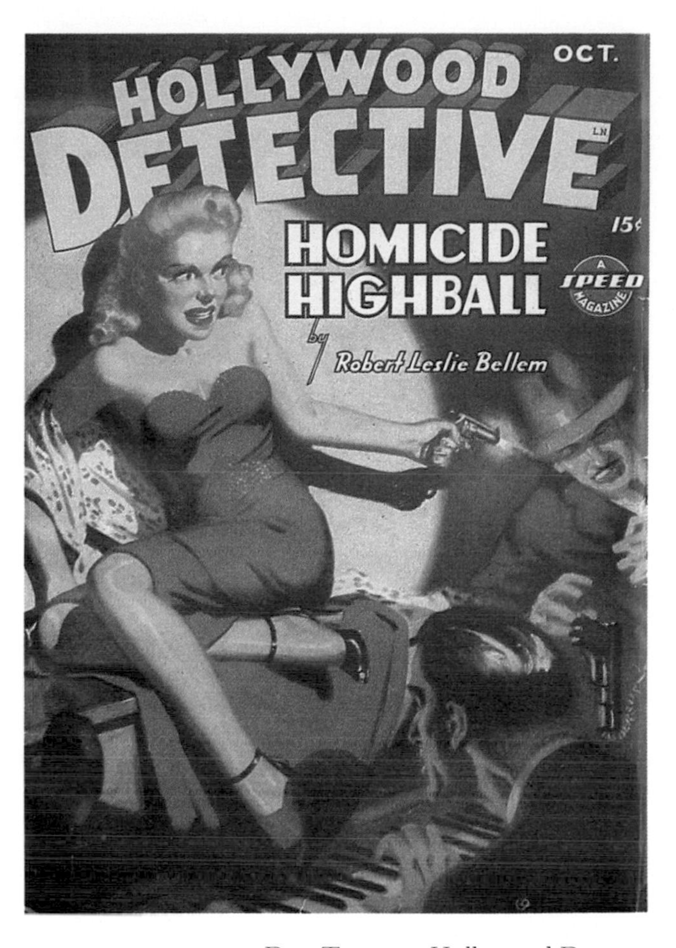

Dan Turner—Hollywood Detective *became simply* Hollywood Detective *after three issues.*

(*Photograph by Michael Keller Photography, courtesy John Wooley*)

[7]Bellem's most annoying habit is his repeated use of the word "she-male" when all of his readers know "frail," "wren," "jane" or "cupcake" would have been more appropriate.

THE RAP SHEET: The Traditional Detective

M.O.: The traditional fictional detective in the United States has been out of favor for the past six decades, a poor stepson to the hard-boiled detective. The traditional detective in this country, since its heyday in the years following World War I, has usually been a woman, usually of the upper classes, and usually of an occupation that normally has little to do with solving crimes. One thing that has not changed is that the traditional detective is almost always an amateur. The hero of these stories has been forced to become a detective because a friend is involved, or because she feels like snooping around. Most important, the traditional detective does not solve the crime through the use of muscle or brawn, like the hard-boiled detective, or through science or procedure, like the policeman. Instead, the traditional detective solves crimes by pulling together, in her mind, the disparate threads of the case. Then she weaves a solution that has remained hidden from everyone, including the professionals. This last criteria means certain policemen, especially those (like Columbo) created for television, are included in this group. These policemen do not use police-like tools, but follow the routine ascribed to the traditional detective.

Perpetrators: Edgar Allan Poe's C. Auguste Dupin, Rex Stout's Nero Wolfe, Ellery Queen's Ellery Queen, S. S. Van Dine's Philo Vance, Harry Kemelman's Rabbi Small, Amanda Cross's Kate Fansler, and television's Jessica Fletcher.

Aliases: Busybody, snoop, meddler, blabbermouth, gossip.

The Snoops

3

"Philo Vance/Needs a kick in the pance."
—OGDEN NASH

Even someone who doesn't like S. S. Van Dine's Philo Vance can't help but feel sorry for Van Dine, a pseudonym for the scholar Willard Huntington Wright. In a decade, Vance and Van Dine went from the pinnacle of success in their subgenre to near obscurity. Their descent was as swift and mysterious as that of a baseball player who wakes up one day as a .180 hitter after batting .330 during the first part of his career. In 1930, Van Dine (1888–1939) was at the height of his popularity. He had published five Vance books in five years, each had been a best-seller, and each had won critical raves. Said critic Howard Haycraft: Van

William Powell was the first screen Philo Vance. He shares a scholarly moment here with Florence Eldridge (left, Sibela Greene) and Jean Arthur (Ada Greene) in The Greene Murder Case *(1929)*
(Photofest)

Dine had "magnificently smashed the old tabus into smithereens for all time." Hollywood, meanwhile, had released four Vance movies in 1929 and 1930—and A movies, too, starring William Powell (three times) and Basil Rathbone (once) as Vance.

There had never been a more popular American fictional detective than Vance, and his popularity at times in the late 1920s and early 1930s rivaled that of Sherlock Holmes. Vance appeared regularly on newspaper best-seller lists during his heyday, something that had been unheard of before then. Vance was certainly as well known as his most famous contemporary, Lord Peter Wimsey (and even more insufferable, if that's possible). Vance, for all of his egocentric, superior and aristocratic behavior, seemed to have assured the success of the traditional, English-style detective on this side of the Atlantic.

Yet by 1939, Van Dine was dead (as well as broke, leaving an estate that was hardly worth enough to be called an estate). His later Vance books—seven in the next decade—were not as successful financially or critically as the first five, and by the end he had stooped to trying to drop names to make the books relevant. How else to explain 1938's *The Gracie Allen Murder Case?* Although Hollywood made ten more Vance films through 1947, most were forgettable "B" efforts, starring actors like Warren William (who also played Perry Mason in several films of that series) and directed by people like Basil Wrangell. Vance, in fact, has fallen on such hard times that not only are his books out of print, but he is not listed anywhere in H. R. F. Keating's listing of the 100 best crime and mystery novels of all time. So much for immortality.

(Courtesy Bob Lakin Books)

Van Dine was always a little confused by what happened, but someone as erudite as he was should have stumbled on the answer. Even Haycraft, one of Vance's biggest fans, finally did.

"For all of his wide and undeniable influence and achievements," Haycraft wrote in *Murder for Pleasure* as he placed Vance among the detective immortals, "S. S. Van Dine was essentially a developer, an adapter and polisher of other men's techniques, rather than a true innovator."

The times had changed, but Vance had not. By 1939, the techniques Van Dine had polished and improved upon were no longer important. They had been replaced by the work of a true innovator—Dashiell Hammett, who gave the world the hard-boiled detective.

Vance's failure to become anything more than a souvenir of the Roaring Twenties—as outdated as Calvin Coolidge—is, in its own way, as significant a development as the birth of the hard-boiled hero. When Vance began to fade from the scene during the Depression, the death of the traditional, English-style Great Detective in this country was assured. No longer would American sleuths drop their "g's" like British nobles. No longer would readers be forced to sift through monologues on subjects like Sanskrit, always inserted in the plot to show the detective's brilliance—even though the monologues were uniformly boring. The traditional detective would almost surely remain on the American scene, but he would be forever changed. And he has been better for the change.

This is not to say that the hard-boiled detective is the culmination of years of development of the American fictional detective. Far from it—repeated bashings to the skull can be just as dull to read about or to watch as discourses on Egyptology. But what is important is the sensibility that the hard-boiled detective brought to the traditional genre. The traditional detectives who survived and prospered—like Ellery Queen and Nero Wolfe, and extending today to television heroes like Columbo and Jessica Fletcher—did so because they seemed more plausible than Vance. This is the naturalism, to use the literary term, that Hammett brought to the genre.

Consider these contrasts as examples:

- The names of the characters themselves. Wright picked S. S. Van Dine as a pseudonym, which sounds more like a ship than a writer. Then there is the detective, Philo Vance. Has anyone ever actually been named Philo? If Van Dine was trying to create an atmosphere of aloofness and superiority with these names, he succeeded. If he was trying to create any sort of permanency, he failed miserably. In many ways, Wolfe is just as inaccessible as Vance—but a fat, slovenly detective named Nero Wolfe doesn't seem as ridiculous as a skinny little runt named Philo Vance.
- Vance lives in the top two floors of a mansion on East 38th Street in Manhattan, and he lives on the money he inherited from his wealthy aunt. He has no children, no family, and no responsibilities, other than to meddle in "interestin'" murder cases. He collects antiques, goes fox hunting, and his bookshelves include first

Basil Rathbone's fame today rests with his Sherlock Holmes portrayals, but he took a turn as the dapper American Philo Vance (right) in The Bishop Murder Case *(1930).*

editions(!) by Leonardo da Vinci. On the other hand, Charlie Chan seems as if he barely has enough time to solve cases because he is too busy overseeing his ever increasing brood of children. When the Chan book series started in 1925, he had nine children; when it ended seven years later, he had eleven. Much of the accessibility of the Chan series (as well as the humor) comes from this contradiction: How many Great Detectives have to deal with family problems?

- Vance's arrogance is an accepted part of the quintessential amateur detective, as outlined by Poe, perfected by Doyle, polished by Sayers, and practiced by Christie. The cops don't know anything, the suspects don't know anything, and the bumbling assistant doesn't know anything. The only person who knows anything is Philo Vance, and he is fond of reminding everyone of that. The law, Vance claims, is for imbeciles. Police procedure is a "masterpiece of absurdity," and Vance goes out of his way to point this out. He once said he wouldn't be surprised to see a judge tell a criminal: "I know, and the jury knows, that you committed the crime, but in view of the legally admissible evidence, I declare you innocent. Go and sing again." The only way to solve a crime and to punish the criminal is to call in Vance—whose official standing in a case consists almost solely of this arrogance. No one hires him to investigate; he more or less materializes whenever something piques his interest. This is a markedly different attitude from even the most arrogant of his successors in the traditional field, who often intervene on the flimsiest of excuses. Queen, especially the early Queen, is no wallflower, but eventually learns humility. After the first decade or so, there is always an instant when Queen is baffled by the case, and admits he has no idea of what is going on. Queen's creators were smart enough to realize it was kind of silly to have some half-baked writer stumbling around in murder cases without any reason to do so. That's why they invented Ellery's father, New York City police inspector Richard Queen, who can bring his work home with him.

This difference is nowhere more apparent than in Rex Stout's Nero Wolfe. Stout (1886–1975) created a detective with few redeeming features—he is fat, he is lazy, and he is arrogant. Wolfe thinks nothing of launching into those long, turgid monologues that detectives like Vance favor, and he once got so angry with two changes in the third edition of a Webster's dictionary that he burned it. Yet Wolfe has lasted, starring in forty-eight books between 1934's *Fer-de-lance* and a posthumous 1975 outing, *A Family Affair.* His books are still in print, and take up almost as much room on bookstore shelves as Christie's do. The only reason Hollywood didn't do for Wolfe what it did for Sherlock Holmes—only two Wolfe movies were ever made—was that Stout didn't

EXAMINING THE CLUES

Dashiell Hammett was not the only American detective writer who made a reputation from his politics. Rex Stout was active in left-wing causes, especially during the Depression and World War II. But most important (for writers, anyway), Stout was a champion of copyright law reform. He played a crucial role in one mid-twentieth-century change in the law, and was an advocate of increased rights for authors until he died. Stout met Mark Twain in 1909, and they did not discuss Huck Finn or Twain's place in literature. Stout's biographer says they discussed copyright law, a subject of especial interest to Twain. He was always convinced that his publishers were out to cheat him in any way possible.

approve of the films, and wouldn't sell the rights to any other books.[1] Wolfe, for all his blustering, has a human side, and it is his human side that is responsible for his success.

Stout was an educated man—often described as a child prodigy—who had written a number of literary novels before *Fer-de-lance* was serialized in *The Saturday Evening Post.* He had made his fortune at age forty-one (one source says four hundred thousand dollars) from inventing a savings program for school children. He banked the proceeds, and retired to write books. When the first four, of a literary bent that accorded him a place in New York literary circles, had failed to elicit much interest beyond that circle, he switched to Wolfe. Although Wolfe has his eccentricities, they don't overwhelm his character—or get in the way of earning a buck. In fact, Stout always used part of the beginning of each Wolfe story to describe the financial straits Wolfe is in, why work is the only remedy, and how much money the work will bring in. Wolfe needs, by one estimate, ten thousand dollars a month in World War II–era prices to survive.

(Courtesy Bob Lakin Books)

This sort of detail balances the personality of a character whose ego can best be described as about as big as his bulk—always referred to as one-seventh of a ton. A team of earnest graduate students could earn dozens of advanced degrees delving into Wolfe's whims. Detailing each and every one, from his anxiety about leaving his home to his paranoia toward women, would not leave room for much else in this book. Wolfe's daily schedule—which is not supposed to vary unless the Apocalypse is at hand—will prove the point. Wolfe gets up each morning around 8:00 A.M., breakfasting in bed. After breakfast, he dresses (always a three-piece suit, tie and yellow shirt) and retires to his rooftop greenhouse, where he fiddles with his ten thousand orchids until 11:00 A.M. From 11 until 1:15 P.M., he detects, discussing cases with his assistant, Archie Goodwin. Then it's lunch until 2:00 P.M. or so, then two more

[1]An interesting note: A Nero Wolfe television series lasted just one-half a season on NBC in 1981. It starred William Conrad as Wolfe, which seems like a perfect choice. Perhaps the flaw came in casting Lee Horsley ("Matt Houston," "Paradise") as Archie. The show also suffered because of its time slot—it was opposite the "Dukes of Hazzard"—and its timing—it was scheduled to debut during the 1981–82 writers' strike, which delayed the start of the 1981 season. Stout hated television, and refused to let it have any of his books while he was alive. He once said he wouldn't let television near his work, even if all he had created was "Jack and the Beanstalk."

hours of work before two final hours spent in the greenhouse. Dinner is served at 7:15 P.M. (after forty-five minutes more to clear up the day's business). Entertainment after dinner—a repast so immense that it deserves to be called Wolfeian[2]—usually consists of Wolfe holding forth on whichever subject amuses him in a fashion so tedious that Archie always includes it in his list of things to nag Wolfe about. This schedule, which also features five quarts of beer daily, is Wolfe's ideal, and he will go to almost any extreme to make sure nothing disturbs it.

Nero Wolfe—orchid in hand—as portrayed on his paperback editions.

Yet as goofy as this routine is (Wolfe treats the orchids better than he treats people), there is a certain charm to it. It makes Wolfe vulnerable in a way that very few other Great Detectives are. Wolfe may be a genius, but he can be a big baby, and that's reassuring to the reader. This balancing act between vulnerability and genius is a testament to Stout's skill as a writer. It would have been easier to create a detective like Vance, whom Stout read and liked, than it was to create Wolfe. After all, every traditional detective before Wolfe was like Vance. Yet for all of the similarities with previous traditional detectives, Wolfe differs in a couple of key ways.

One is Wolfe's emphasis on work and the work ethic. This is unique among most traditional private detectives, whose motivation is usually boredom or conceit. It is also a peculiarly American habit, whether the detective is hard-boiled or traditional. Holmes ignores payments for the challenge of a good puzzle, and Miss Marple certainly never talks about pride of work or professionalism in her tales. But every American hard-boiled private eye has an obligatory passage or two not only detailing his busted bank account, but also the efforts to give the client value for money received. Vance doesn't work because he needs the money, but because he needs amusement. That is part of the reason why detectives like Vance and Wolfe (each having five letters, by the way), conceived in such similar ways, could be so strikingly different. Van Dine and Stout were both brilliant, well-educated men. Van Dine was a genuine man of letters, who was an expert on Nietzche. He began writing mysteries in the mid-1920s after a two-

[2]There is a group of Wolfe fans who meet yearly to re-create meals from the books, as well as a Wolfe cookbook, *The Nero Wolfe Cookbook*. A typical Wolfe repast is beef braised in red wine, lamb-stuffed eggplant, carrottes flamandes, and lemon-sherry pudding with brown sugar sauce.

year stint recuperating from exhaustion and overwork that had damaged his heart. During that period, Van Dine's doctors told him he couldn't do any serious reading, so he read mysteries. The mysteries he read, he said, were so poorly written that he decided he could write a better one. He dashed three outlines off to Maxwell Perkins at Scribner's, and Vance was born. This does not seem all that different from Wolfe's birth. Stout gave up writing novels few people were reading to write detective stories that, he emphasized shortly after the series started, would one day rate among the two or three best in the world.

Edward Arnold played Wolfe in Meet Nero Wolfe (1936), *here in the orchid greenhouse with Lionel Stander as Archie (left).*

Yet they are different, and the vehicle for displaying this difference—Archie Goodwin—is Stout's greatest contribution to the subgenre. He realized that the world would little note nor long remember one more eccentric detective, and so took pains to make his different. Who remembers, after all, an obese New York detective named Jim Hanvey, who was popular in the 1920s? That's why Stout came up with Archie—for the first time pairing a traditional Great Detective with a hard-boiled sidekick. Archie is not a remarkable hard-boiled detective, and he certainly isn't any smarter or any tougher than his compatriots in the pulps. But he is a brilliant idea. Critics can expostulate on the psychological ramifications of such divergent personalities—Wolfe is slothful, Archie is active; Wolfe is arrogant, Archie is humble; Archie is yin, Wolfe is yang; etcetera—but the practical results are not nearly as complex. Wolfe, who was born in the Balkans, is a European. Archie, who was born in Indiana, is so American that his birthplace just happens to be the small town where Stout's mother grew up. In 1934, in the aftermath of World War I when the first Wolfe book was published, Americans had two uses for Europeans—little and none. The interplay between Wolfe and Archie starts there.[3]

Stout was a pioneer, and Archie was the tool he used to blaze a trail. Like Queen, Stout helped to change the direction of the

[3]Stout was never very expansive on the creative process he used to devise Wolfe and Archie. His biographer, John McAleer, makes a special point of Stout's refusal to discuss the issue.

EXAMINING THE CLUES

The term "red herring," used in traditional mysteries to describe false clues, may date from seventeenth-century England. Apparently, anti-hunting advocates would buy herring, smoke them (which turned them red), and use the smoked herrings to disrupt fox hunts. The scent of the fish would throw the hounds off the track.

traditional detective anyway. He adapted many of the techniques that were successful in the hard-boiled subgenre; Archie is only one example of this. Those critics, like Haycraft, who thought of the hard-boiled writers and detectives as heretics, were blinded by their faith and weren't able to see what Stout had done. A modern critic, T. J. Binyon, puts Wolfe into perspective as well as anyone, calling him a magnificent creation. Binyon writes that he "has a solidity and a reality that transcends the boundaries of fiction."

Archie moves the plot along in a way it had never been moved along before. One of the problems with most Great Detectives is that their sidekicks are so dull as to be almost unmemorable. Watson, of course, is an exception, but who can remember the names of the sidekicks in the Poirot, Vance, and Dupin stories?[4] And even when they are memorable, they are fools, knaves and blunderers. Watson, as immortalized by Nigel Bruce in the Basil Rathbone/Holmes movies, is barely bright enough to tie his shoes by himself. Even a more restrained Watson, like Edward Hardwicke in the Jeremy Brett television films, is stuck with the character. No matter how hard he tries to play Watson straight, he is stuck on the short end of Holmes's "Elementary, my dear Watson"—and gee, you certainly are a boob.

Archie is nothing like that. He is traditional only in the sense that he is a sidekick, and even then his character is strong enough to have stood on its own if Stout had wanted to write a hard-boiled series. Archie is not present in the Wolfe stories to reinforce, by his ignorance, the genius of the Great Detective. He is there to shake things up—to interrupt Wolfe's monologues, to prod Wolfe to action, to remind him the bank account balance is low enough to kiss a curb without stooping. That is why he is not a bumbler, why he likes girls (and why they like him, much to Wolfe's consternation), why he carries a gun, and why he cracks wise. Every time Wolfe does something silly, Archie is on hand to deflate him. "You are simply too conceited, too eccentric and too fat to work for," he once tells Wolfe, which just about covers every situation. Another memorable exchange in the Wolfe series comes when Wolfe contemplates leaving—or, as he occasionally does, leaves—his brownstone. In *The League of Frightened Men* (1935), Archie asks him to step outside to catch a glimpse of a witness who is sitting in a car: "I don't know, Archie. I don't know why you persist in trying to badger me into frantic sorties."

[4]Captain Hastings, S. S. Van Dine and unnamed. Christie was as sharp a marketer as she was a writer. Although there is no mention of it in her autobiography, the stolidly English Hastings must have been invented as a counterweight to the foreigner Poirot. Someone with some authority (hence the military title) had to be on hand to keep track of the Belgian lest Christie's English readers get alarmed.

At no time do Archie and Wolfe play ring-around-the-rosey with such skill and as often as when it comes to the subject of money. Wolfe loves it, but hates to do the work necessary to accumulate it. "He would be here reading books, drinking beer and having Fritz tell anyone who called he was engaged," Archie explains to the reader in the novelette *Bullet for One* (1950). "It wasn't the first time he had decided a case wasn't worth the effort. On such occasions, my mission was to keep after him until I had jarred him loose. . . ." This is the ultimate marriage of the traditional, English armchair detective who solves cases using only his brain, and the hard-boiled American detective who believes that nothing will happen unless someone kicks in a few doors. Wolfe doesn't even like to get out of his specially designed seven-thousand-dollar armchair to detect, while Archie spends most of his time running around New York City knocking on doors and reporting the interviews to Wolfe—verbatim, by the way, complete with any body language, signs of discomfort and the like.

The shortlived television "Nero Wolfe" featured William Conrad (left) as Wolfe and Lee Horsley as Archie. Former First Daughter Patti Davis guest-starred in an episode.

Authors after Stout have managed to retain this sensibility without resorting to an Archie-like sidekick to play off of. Archie, by his very success, may well be the last of the great sidekicks who accompany the traditional American detective. Most of the traditional detectives who have succeeded Queen and Wolfe have done so as solo acts (save for the baffled policeman who requests their help). This process is nothing more than the continuing Americanization of the traditional detective. Stout showed that a Watson could be more than a chalkboard for the Great Detective to write on. Once this was done, it made the sidekick irrelevant. This is part of the Chandlerian belief that character—one character—is all. It's hard to believe that Stout would have used Archie exclusively as a foil if he had written the first story ten years later. Then, what influenced him would have been more hard-boiled, and it would have been easier to see what was possible by focusing on Archie and dumping Wolfe, or by writing two series. After Archie, the sidekick evolved into the buddy, for better or worse.

Of all of the solo acts who succeeded Wolfe and Queen, few are more completely American than Harry Kemelman's Rabbi David Small. The rabbi, who first appeared in 1964's *Friday, the Rabbi Slept Late,* fits all of the criteria for the traditional enthusiast—the books are ingeniously plotted, Kemelman is careful to include the correct number and proper display of clues, and he has a good gimmick. The rabbi solves his cases using pilpul, a form of reasoning outlined in the Jewish Talmud, a holy book. But the real success of the books—which have run through the seven days of the week—comes from their ability to make Rabbi Small more than some Jew who fronts a congregation in Barnard's Crossing, Massachusetts. He may be Jewish, but he is an American Jew. There is an authentic quality to the books that is missing from the rabbi's most notable predecessor, G. K. Chesterton's Father Brown. Father Brown is a sleuth whose day job happens to be hearing confessions; David Small is a rabbi who happens to wander into murders. Chesterton (or his publisher) almost certainly toned down the Catholicism in the Father Brown stories so as not to upset the book-buying public in turn-of-the-century Anglican Britain, where religion was still a reason to fight wars. On the other hand, anyone who has picked up one of the Rabbi Small books learns almost as much about the

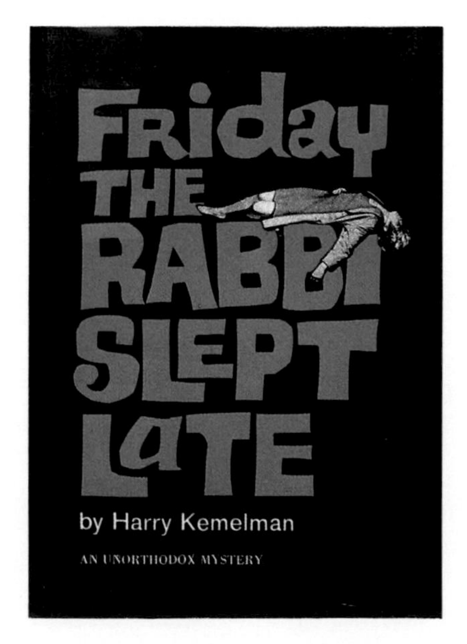

(Courtesy Bob Lakin Books)

politics of running a congregation as Herman Melville's audience learned about whaling. This is a similarity that is not made lightly. Kemelman is no Melville, and does not pretend to be (although he isn't nearly as dull as often as Melville is). But there is a sense of permanence to the Small books, in much the same way there is a sense of salt water to *Moby Dick*. The most vivid parts of any of the Small tales are not the murders and the detection, but the rabbi's constant battles to retain his pulpit in the face of congregants who want to oust him. They are more concerned with the bottom line than the eternal soul, and Rabbi Small is a lousy fund raiser who writes unexciting sermons and who too often serves as the conscience of the community. This is a phenomenon that is not unique to Judaism; this sort of infighting goes on regularly whether the house of worship is Catholic, Protestant, Muslim, or Druid.

In this, Kemelman not only accomplished one of his goals (he has said he wanted the books to give a sense, through fiction, of what Judaism was like), but also succeeded where someone like Dorothy L. Sayers ultimately failed. The reader learns as much about bell ringing in her *The Nine Tailors* as Rabbi Small teaches about religion, but there is a sense in this Sayers book (as there is in *Murder Must Advertise*, set in an ad agency) that the bells are just a backdrop for Lord Peter to go through his paces. When he is done, he will return to London, free and clear and with the money and prestige that go with being the second son of the fifteenth Duke of Denver. Rabbi Small, on the other hand, doesn't have anywhere else to go. In this sense, the rabbi is as plausible as Wimsey is not.

Wolfe's heirs have been especially popular with television audiences. Two of the most enduring American fictional detectives are television characters: Peter Falk's Lieutenant Columbo and Angela Lansbury's Jessica Fletcher of "Murder, She Wrote." Television, in fact, has a much more successful relationship with traditional detectives than it has with their hard-boiled counterparts (a contradiction which will be explained in chapter 5). But this doesn't mean there have been any ratings guarantees. Past network schedules are chock full of shows like "The Eddie Capra Mysteries" (one season in 1978) and "Partners in Crime" (one-half a season in 1984). Even Ellery Queen has had his troubles. The Jim Hutton version was one of the biggest bombs of the mid-1970s, barely lasting two seasons. Yet Columbo and Jessica Fletcher have managed to combine television longevity with some sort of distinction.

Trying to apply non-television rules of analysis to television is a sticky business, since television operates on a different principle than publishing or filmmaking. Television is a marketing medium, first and foremost. Television programs exist only to sell soap, as vehicles to place around advertising. Publishers make their money from selling books; filmmakers make their money by selling film tickets. The networks don't get rich from selling shows; they get rich from selling ad time on shows. This may be good or bad, but it is undeniably true (although the increasing popularity of cable may alter it). This concept also influences how network executives think about shows. When Christie came up with *Murder on the Orient Express,* she didn't worry how it would chart with eighteen- to twenty-two-year-old women. On the other hand, that's the sort of thing any competent television executive worries about regularly. It's one reason why formulas are so important in developing

Angela Lansbury as Jessica Fletcher in "Murder, She Wrote."

shows. Producers think they can look at the numbers to see what kind of shows to make. If they want to appeal to thirty- to forty-five-year-old men, they check the surveys and the focus groups, drop in a star, a situation and a supporting cast, and generate an instant hit.

It doesn't always work that way, of course, but that's never stopped anyone from using the system. What makes "Columbo" and "Murder, She Wrote" so interesting in this context is that neither of them fits into the television system. Their stars are not beautiful, their formats are not action/adventure-oriented, and they are not geared toward the younger side of the market that every producer pursues with a drive similar to that which powers teenage boys in heat. Falk was far from a typical television leading man. He had spent his career playing best friends and heavies in Hollywood (an Oscar nomination as the gangster in *A Pocketful of Miracles* in 1961), as well as appearing in art house films in the late 1960s. His only experience with a television drama series had come in 1965, when he played the lead in a lawyer show called "The Trials of O'Brien" on CBS that didn't return for the 1966 season. Lansbury was an even more unusual star. She, too, had never done a series, but she had two other handicaps. First, she was a respected stage and screen actor (three Oscar nominations) who didn't need television—and she was going to work in a medium that had little use for respected stage and screen actors. Jaclyn Smith is television's idea of a respected actor. Second, Lansbury was fifty-nine when "Murder, She Wrote" debuted in 1984. This was unheard of. Television executives casting a fifty-nine year old woman to front an expensive, hour-long series is about as unthinkable as Wolfe giving up his time with his orchids for anything less than a nuclear war (and even then, as Archie has pointed out, Wolfe would have to think about it).

"Just one more thing . . ."

Yet each detective succeeded. One reason was that each program was created by the same people, the team of veteran television writer/producers William Link and the late Richard Levinson. They had devised the Columbo character for a one-time appearance on 1960–61 series called "The Chevy Mystery Show," refined him in a play called *Prescription: Murder* in the early 1960s, and then perfected him for a made-for-television movie in 1968 that served as the pilot for the first "Columbo" series (1971–77). Levinson and Link created Fletcher with Peter Fischer in the

MASS MEDIA: A Traditional Sampler

• **Kate Fansler.** It's no surprise this detective was an immediate hit with critics—she is a literature professor at a New York City university. This just happens to be what her creator, Amanda Cross (pen name for Carolyn Heilbroner) is at New York's Columbia University. But she must have other attributes, or she wouldn't have appeared on Keating's 100 best list (*Death in a Tenured Position,* 1981). Kate is a traditional detective for people who don't like to read stories featuring traditional detectives. In this, she is the opposite of her English colleagues, those British profs who solve murders while being so damn clever that anyone who doesn't have an old school tie will be completely baffled by what's happening. Kate may not always be believable when she uses literary criticism to solve crimes, but she does it in admirable style. Her sense of humor is so dry that it's hard to tell if she is kidding or not. In *In the Last Analysis* (1964), the first in the series, Kate must clear a psychiatrist friend who is accused of murdering one of his young women patients who was one of Kate's students. She skewers therapy with such a sure hand that it's a pleasure to read—but there's an off chance her criticism is legitimate.

• The women hard-boiled detectives detailed in the previous chapter were not the first American women detectives, although they have certainly proved to be the most popular. When the traditional detective in this country was in disrepute during the heyday of the *Black Mask* style following World War II, women carried the flame. There may not have been many of them—one study says that during the first one hundred years of crime fiction, there were only one hundred or so recurring women detectives, most of them British—but they were good enough to buck the trend. Among the most prominent was Hildegarde Withers, a former New York City school teacher, current spinster and hero of novels and short stories created by Hollywood scenarist Stuart Palmer ("The Falcon," "Bulldog Drummond"). Withers was featured in print almost until Palmer died in 1968, and even had her own movie series in the 1930s and a made-for-television movie in 1971. Her relationship with her ex-beau, New York cop Oscar Piper, moves the books, which are exactly what they seem to be. Palmer said he based Hildegarde on his high school English teacher.

• **John Putnam Thatcher.** This is how fascinating Thatcher is—he is an investment banker who comes across as a human being. This is due to the skill of Emma Lathen (pen name for Mary J. Latsis and Martha Hennissart), who has created a character who can wear a pin-striped suit and not be a pill. Thatcher is senior vice-president for the Sloan Guaranty Trust, New York's biggest investment banking house, and his cases revolve around the Sloan's clients. In *Banking for Death* (1961), the first Thatcher, he decides the Sloan's resources must be used to solve a murder

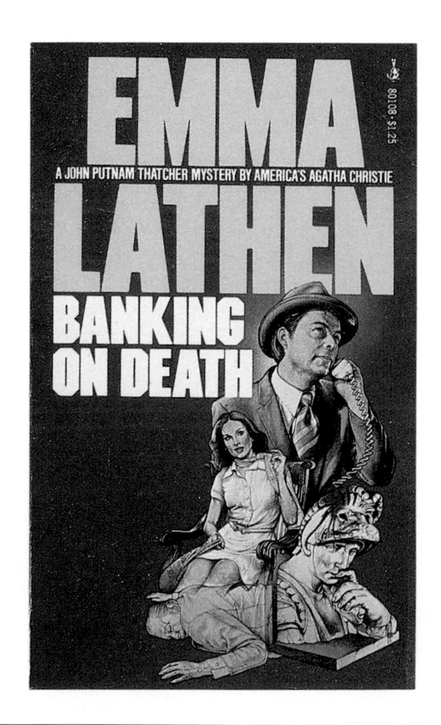

because it administers a trust for two small boys whose mother is the chief suspect. How many heroes in detective fiction are motivated by fiduciary duty?

• **Peter Cutler Sargeant II.** Gore Vidal never took much pride in writing his three Peter Sargeant mysteries (under the pen name Edgar Box), but he should have. They are the Dan Turner of the traditional field. Plot is even more irrelevant in these books than usual, but plot is not what Vidal was interested in. He wanted to make money while writing about his favorite topics: sex and politics. Peter is a public relations man with a healthy sexual appetite who always seems to get involved with beautiful women and right-wing Neanderthals. Typical is *Death before Bedtime* (1953), where Peter is working for a U.S. senator whose daughter is as liberal with her charms as her father is conservative in his politics.

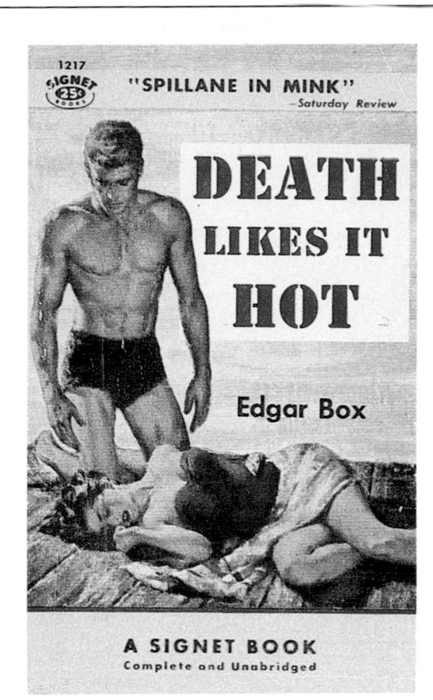

(Courtesy Bob Lakin Books)

early 1980s in an attempt to do a television detective show that wasn't like every other television detective show.

Levinson and Link were self-admitted mystery buffs, which helped them devise their characters. It also helps to explain why the characters fit into the mainstream of fictional American detectives in a way that few other television characters ever have. Columbo, they explained, was an Americanized version of the policeman Petrovich in Dostoyevsky's *Crime and Punishment* who hounded Raskolnikov until he confessed. Jessica, they emphasized, is a typical English detective strained of her Englishness and injected with a healthy dose of Americanness— to not only drive the show, but to please the networks, which think British English is a foreign language.

But the most important reason for each program's success is that each is firmly rooted in the philosophy popularized by Stout. Columbo and Jessica may be Great Detectives, but they are Great Detectives with a heart. Their character is all. The plots in these programs are often silly, especially in Jessica's case. How many murders can there be in a small town in Maine? But the plots don't matter, which would be heresy to the English writers who gathered for meetings of the famed Detection Club. In this country, even for traditional detectives, plot will always be secondary to character.

THE THIRD DEGREE:
In Praise of Charlie Chan

An unlikely thing happened in Hollywood between 1931 and 1949—an Asian was portrayed sympathetically on the screen. Of course, it was hard to play Charlie Chan any other way.

There are any number of nits to pick with the Chan series, which covered forty-four films for two studios and featured four actors as Chan. None of the leads, for instance, was Chinese, Asian or Hawaiian. The plots often stereotyped the rest of the characters, while Chan is often saddled with dialogue that would break the heart of someone who cared about those things. And there is a black chauffeur in some of the series's entries to provide comic relief.

But there is no denying that Chan is the hero of a series of films at a time when most Asians (and other nonwhites, for that matter) were discriminated against culturally, economically and politically. This is remarkable. It is a testament to the flexibility of the American system—where anything is possible if there is a buck to be made—and a testament to the imagination of Earl Der Biggers (1884–1933), who created Chan in six novels that appeared between 1925 and 1932. "Sinister and wicked Chinese are old stuff," he once said, "but an amiable Chinese on the side of law and order had never been used."

Below right: Warner Oland (right, with Keye Luke) started the long-running Chan movie series in 1931.

In fact, almost every Chinese or Asian character appearing before Chan's debut was an insidious devil, part of the Yellow Peril that hounded the West between the two world wars. The most famous was Dr. Fu Manchu, a creation of Sax Rohmer, who was bent on world domination and the destruction of the Western way of life—which, it was always emphasized, was weak and decadent. This view was so prevalent that it not only spawned Fu Manchu books, movies, radio and television shows, but also showed up in any number of other places. Several adventure pulps specialized in the Yellow Peril, with stories so thick in "atmosphere" that readers could smell the opium. Their covers were so lurid that the only thing missing from the face of the villain was a couple of fangs and some drool. This attitude lasted well into the 1960s, when an enlightened West should have known better. Ian Fleming, whose James Bond is in so many ways modern, suave and sophisticated, had a weak spot for the old-fashioned, simple Oriental villain such as Dr. No or Goldfinger's evil henchman Oddjob.

(Courtesy Bob Lakin Books)

Yet Sgt. (later Inspector) Charlie Chan of the Honolulu Police Department—meek, simple, humble, overweight, and family-loving Charlie, with his eleven kids—was a colossal hit.

Much of the success came from the Hollywood system, which strived to give filmgoers the sorts of characters they wanted to see. Certainly no one wanted Fu Manchu and his ilk to exist; why not reinforce the image of the friendly, helpful Chinese made popular by writers such as Pearl Buck? In this, the films stereotype Chan as much as they do the supporting cast. But at least his character isn't plotting to ravage a nubile young girl as part of a white slavery ring, one of the favorite schemes of the various Yellow Peril villains. And what overshadows this stereotyping is that Chan is a respected and powerful figure at a time when all respected and powerful figures in American culture were white. No one in the movies ever questions Charlie's authority, or refuses to allow him to investigate a case because of his race. This alone places the Chan movies decades ahead of their time, both cinematically and culturally.

Sidney Toler as Chan.

Roland Winters was the final movie Chan, here in Docks of New Orleans *(1948).*

The movies could have been even further ahead of their time if they had not toned down certain aspects of the novelistic Chan's personality. Der Biggers wanted to create a sympathetic character, but he did not create a saint. The Chan of the books has a temper that is more than the annoyance he shows when his Number 1 or Number 2 son aggravates him. He does not suffer fools as gladly as the inscrutable Chan of the movies does. More amazing, to Occidentals anyway, is that Chan does not like the Japanese. This may come as a shock to Westerners who tend to lump all Asians together into one neat minority group, but the Chinese have little use for the Japanese, who don't like the Koreans, who would just as soon have nothing to do with the Chinese. This circle is endless. In this respect, it's no surprise that Chan would not like the Japanese—any Japanese. It may not be a morally correct attitude, but it is accurate of its time and place. Consider this scene from *Charlie Chan Carries On* (1930), when Chan's assistant Kashimo, a Japanese American, loses the evidence needed to convict three gamblers. "I would much prefer to make oration on efficiency of Japanese race," he tells the court after Kashimo's mistake makes him a laughingstock. Later, he tells Kashimo—who does not appear in the movies—that "you began work as a supreme bumbler, but I think you improve as you go forward. What laughter there must have been among the gods when you made detective."

Chan is also aware of his place in a United States where Jim Crow laws are as common as his aphorisms. Later in *Charlie Chan Carries On,* a murder suspect tells him that the Chinese are her favorite race in the world. Chan will have little of this. "We are not highly valued in the United States," he says, "where we are appraised as laundrymen. . . . You have great country, rich and proud, and sure of itself. About the rest of the world—pardon me—it knows little and cares extremely less."

This sort of anger and bitterness is missing from the jovial Chan of the movies, who has a saying for every occasion and almost as many sons as sayings. At times, the films resemble a "My Three Sons" reunion more than murder mysteries. Nevertheless, they are an impressive achievement. As Chan would say: "He who runs with light conscience makes the most speed."

THE SOLUTION: The Mysterious Case of Nick and Nora Charles

This chapter is an unlikely place to find a mention of Dashiell Hammett, whose characters revolutionized the American fictional detective and who was about as traditional as Philo Vance was innovative. Nevertheless, this is where Nick and Nora Charles belong.

Maybe.

Hammett was a brilliant writer, whose work deserves to be studied for generations to come. His efforts, starting with the Continental Op short stories, proceeding through the Op novels and *The Maltese Falcon,* and ending with *The Glass Key,* showed the range, versatility and literary merit of the hard-boiled character. And then, at the peak of his success in 1934, desperate for money, he wrote *The Thin Man.*

The husband-and-wife Charleses have nothing in common with any of Hammett's previous heroes, and the novel is equally as alien from the rest. Hammett's heroes have a code; the Charleses have a bottle. Hammett's other novels provide gritty realism; the Charleses provide plenty of parties where they get to use their bottle. The first four books are hard-boiled in plot and outcome; the Charleses' book is as traditional as any English mystery, right down to the scene in the drawing room where the detective explains the case to an assembled crowd of sycophants and hangers-on (especially in the movie version).

(Library of Congress)

And yet Nick and Nora were for thirty years the most popular of Hammett's creations. The six movies in the "The Thin Man" series were among the best made and most acclaimed in the history of Hollywood sequels and series, there was a decade-long "Thin Man" radio show in the 1940s, a television series in the late 1950s, and a made-for-television movie in the 1970s. Who is kidding whom here?

The best guess is that Hammett was kidding everyone—himself, his hard-boiled fans, and anyone who thought he was taking the traditional form seriously. By 1934, he was drinking even more heavily than the Charleses. He had written nothing more substantial than movie scripts, plot treatments and the like since 1931. He had had it, and it doesn't require a very close

Nick Charles (William Powell) takes target practice with Nora (Myrna Loy) looking on disapprovingly in The Thin Man *(1934). Hammett's couple premiered on the silver screen successfully, prompting a Thin Man movie series.*
(Photofest)

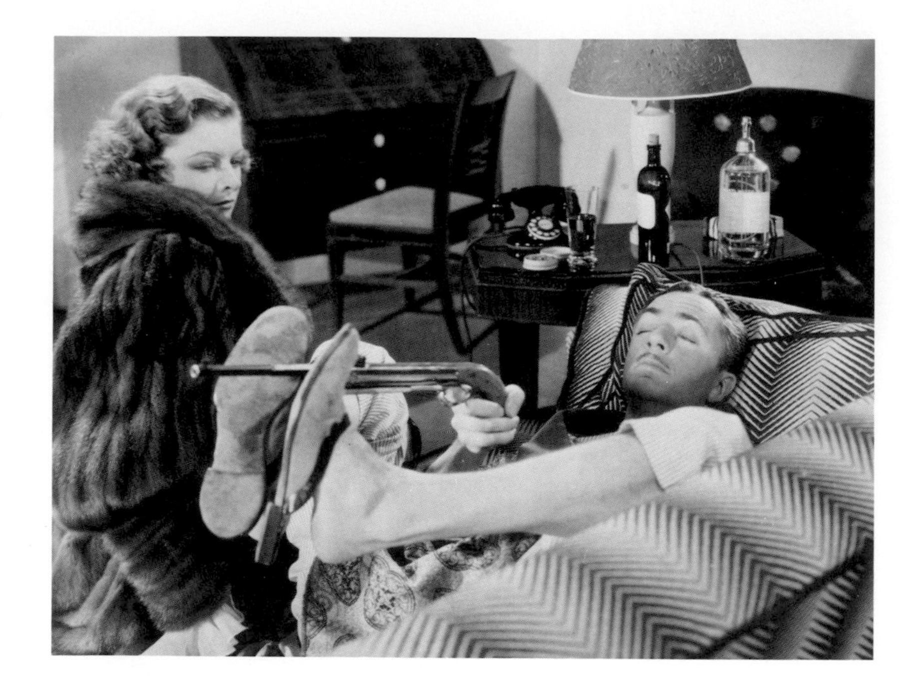

reading of *The Thin Man* to see he knew it. Nick Charles is a former detective, like Hammett; who drinks heavily, like Hammett; and who no longer does any productive work, like Hammett. Nora is Lillian Hellman, Hammett's longtime companion, and the resemblance is even more obvious. In the introduction to one of Hammett's short story collections, Hellman wrote: "It was a happy day when I was given half the manuscript to read and was told that I was Nora."

What better way for Hammett to get even with himself for failing to live up to his code than by writing a book that mocked that code? Hammett's lifestyle during this period was especially notorious among his Hollywood and New York friends. Any of the three Hammett biographies, including the official one by Diane Johnson, outline his excesses more than adequately. He drank, gambled and fornicated with little regard for anything or anyone except his drinking, gambling and fornicating. Then, he would write Hellman, telling her how miserable his conduct had been, and ask her forgiveness. No one needs a psychiatrist to figure out this sort of behavior.

Best yet, he got paid a lot of money for *The Thin Man*. The film rights alone sold for $21,000, a fortune during the Depression—and no one saw that the entire episode was really a joke. Hammett had a sense of humor, but it was, as previously mentioned, often black and very subtle. The best way to look at Nick and Nora Charles is with Hammett's sense of humor. His publisher, Alfred Knopf, and his fans wanted another book; fine, they could have this one, which features Sam Spade drinking all of the time. Spade isn't as crooked as he is supposed to be because he is too busy getting drunk. They didn't get the joke. How else to explain the movie series, or the letters from Knopf begging for another, similar book? Critics such as Howard Haycraft, who had wrung their hands at the havoc Hammett's breakthrough had wrought on their beloved garden parties, would be happy, too. After all, isn't this book just like one of their beloved garden parties? No one kicks down any doors, the gun play is kept to a minimum, and the puzzle is paramount. Even Haycraft praised the book in *Murder for Pleasure,* noting its humor. He didn't get the joke, either. This is not to detract from *The Thin Man.* It's a funny book, and Nick and Nora are a pleasure to spend a weekend with. But they are such a betrayal of everything Hammett had written about that it's difficult to believe that more people didn't notice. Hillary Waugh, the normally astute critic and author, once wrote that *The Thin Man* "is a real, bonafide mystery tale." If Waugh can be fooled, anyone can be.

The passing of time has, however, made the joke obvious. Johnson writes that "the problem is think well of yourself; Nick Charles doesn't seem to. The Op, Spade, Ned Beaumont, struggling in worlds they don't like or approve of, devise for themselves their own codes of behavior, but Nick, an alcoholic ex-detective, leads a social life he seems to despise, drinks, . . . has changed his name, . . . and is in some sense a visitor or an imposter."

EXAMINING THE CLUES

One of the firmest rules about writing is that if it's hard to do by yourself, it's infinitely harder to do with a coauthor. Yet Frederic Danny and Manfred Lee wrote their hundreds of Ellery Queen scripts, novels and the like together without a hint of any discord. This speaks not only of their patience, but of their method. The two men worked independently on each project, and then met at an office on Fifth Avenue in New York City to hash out their differences. They also regarded the Queen series as a business, which eliminated much of the potential for disagreement. Few writers will make changes in their work when they consider their work to be art; if they take a more realistic view, it's a lot easier to edit.

Frederic Dannay (left) and Manfred B. Lee contemplate their Edgar and Raven awards from the Mystery Writers of America in 1967.

(Ellery Queen's Mystery Magazine)

HE RAP SHEET: Policemen

M.O.: The fictional policeman, since World War II, has usually been a reasonable facsimile of his real-life counterpart. He works out of a squad room, usually with a partner, and his story is the story of the procedure that policemen go through to solve a crime. The hero in these stories is less the single character than it is the process itself, and the people who are part of the process. Not all fictional policemen fit into this category. Some, like Chester Himes's Coffin Ed Johnson and Grave Digger Jones or Caroll John Daly's Satan Hall, are hard-boiled detectives. Others, like television's Columbo or Earl Der Biggers's Charlie Chan, are traditional detectives. These characters are policemen in name only. Their çases involve little accepted police work. The hard-boiled group eschews police methods in favor of violence; the traditional group acts more like a classical Great Detective than it does policemen.

Perpetrators: Ed McBain's 87th Precinct, Lawrence Treat's Mitch Taylor, John Ball's Virgil Tibbs, K. C. Constantine's Mario Balzic, Tony Hillerman's Joe Leaphorn and Jim Chee, and Jack Webb's Joe Friday.

Aliases: Fuzz, pig, flatfoot, John Law, The Man, gendarme, bluecoat, bobby, constable.

The Sheriffs

4

"This is the city. Los Angeles, California. I work here. I carry a badge."

—SGT. JOE FRIDAY

On January 3, 1952, Jack Webb changed not only television, but the history of the police brotherhood of the fictional detective. Before Webb, fictional cops were either hard-boiled mavericks like Carroll John Daly's Satan Hall, buffoons like the English cops who played second banana to Sherlock Holmes, or aristocrats hiding behind a badge, like Ngaio Marsh's Roderick Alleyn. After Webb, fictional cops would be more like actual policemen than anyone had ever thought possible.

The first fictional policeman was probably Inspector Bucket in Charles Dickens's *Bleak House* (1852–53), based on the real-life Inspector Charles Field of the Metropolitan Police. Bucket is, at any rate, the first policeman who shows up in fiction with his very own case to solve—even though, in the finest Dickensian tradition, Bucket's case is just one part of a long and complicated narrative. He doesn't even show up until chapter 22. One reason why there were so few fictional policemen before this time is that there were few police forces in existence. It took London almost two decades after the Sûreté was formed to put together the Metropolitan Police in 1829. Before that, law and order had been the responsibility of the military. In countries such as Britain, where there was a small standing army, the cities often went unpoliced save for a handful of magistrates or constables—usually described in the literature as inept, corrupt, or both. This was not always a problem, though, since the cities were small and most people still lived widely scattered in rural areas.

The first detective who is credited with actually featuring in the give and take of the plot is usually said to be Sergeant Cuff (again based on a real person) in Wilkie Collins's *Moonstone* (1868). Sergeant Cuff must solve a jewel robbery, which may or may not be a jewel robbery. Along the way, the massive book—three vol-

cop shows what Ed Asner would do for television newsrooms two decades later. Flint, played by Paul Burke, was about as good looking as, but no more good looking than, a real cop would be. Plots on "Naked City" were often long—an hour-long version of "Dragnet." Sgt. Frank Arcaro got to go from door to door interviewing neighbors, suspects and witnesses, while Parker and Flint figured out what to do with the information Arcaro discovered. On one episode late in the series's run, the main characters spent most of their time complaining about how tired and overworked they were. Several conventions were in New York, and each cop was working double shifts. Flint even finagled a day in court so he could avoid working on a particularly troublesome murder. The day in court would give him the chance to doze while waiting to testify. Otherwise, he would be out pounding the pavements in the search for the murderer.

That's hardly the sort of Superman-like behavior of most fictional detectives. But Joe Friday, his partners and successors are not supermen. They are as ordinary and as average as television characters can be—the kind of people who might even go bowling. They just happen to be cops in the way that other people happen to be auto mechanics or plumbers. This was a revolutionary concept when Webb devised it for the "Dragnet" radio series in 1949, and it was even more revolutionary when he was able to devise a look to go with it. Imagine Los Angeles as a real city—not the fantasyland of the movie studios or the glossy brochures of the tourist bureaus but a Los Angeles of corner taverns and blue-collar hotels and cramped bungalows. Maybe it was the cheap sets or the primitive black-and-white camera work, but Webb made Los Angeles look dingy, and at the same time dignified. For perhaps the only time in its history as a fictional backdrop, Los Angeles looked like the working-class town it really was.

In the Los Angeles of "Dragnet," real people committed real crimes for real reasons—muggings and robberies and car thefts, not murder mystery weekends at moguls' mansions. In one 1953 episode, Friday and Officer Frank Smith (played by Ben Alexander) must catch a group of young toughs who are cruising the streets, causing trouble. There is nothing glamorous about the crimes (purse snatchings and the like), nothing glamorous about the victims (two of whom are Mexicans who speak no English), and nothing glamorous about the cops' methods (which are so dull that Friday's narration seems exciting by contrast). In one scene, Friday and Smith stake out a hotel by standing in a linen closet. This is hardly the sort of thing that most fictional detectives, including the hard-boiled realists, do. But it is exactly the sort of thing real policemen do.

"Dragnet" was not Webb's first effort in the detective genre, and that experience helped him to firm up his ideas. He had produced and starred in three postwar private eye radio series typical of the Mike Shayne school that was popular at the time. He had also played the heavy in a couple of crime movies. He knew the genre, and he knew what would be fresh and different because the things he had been doing weren't fresh and different.

No police writer had ever attempted to describe a crime and its solution the way Webb described it. This deadpan technique is a common thread academics find running through American literature, from James Fenimore Cooper through the dime novels to today. Hemingway explained the technique when he said his goal was to "write truly." Webb probably didn't consider the problem in quite those terms, but the result was the same. "We built the series on pure authenticity," he told an interviewer. "As such we made every effort to hire good but unrecognizable actors, meaning no recognizable stars, who might detract our audience from the almost documentary realism we were trying to achieve." His watchword was routine—the daily, boring, grinding routine of the policeman. The cops go to the office, they have coffee, they interview suspects, they complain about their caseload. In fact, character—and now not just one individual, but a precinct house full of people—has now moved the puzzle even further away from the center of the action in these stories. To a policeman, crime is crime. It's no more difficult to solve a murder than it is a robbery (and often easier, since murders aren't planned as thoroughly as robberies).

Today, this sort of action is a cliché, but in 1952, it was almost too real to have ever been used in detective fiction. *The Glass Key*, perhaps Hammett's most naturalistic novel, still concerns itself with the machinations of politicians and gangsters, people who are larger than life. The police procedural focuses on people who are not larger than life, but resolutely part of it. The cops are anonymous because their methods are interchangeable. Anyone with a reasonable amount of intelligence can be trained to ask the right questions. It does not require a hard-boiled superman or a traditional genius. Meanwhile, the victims are people whose anonymity is broken only by the circumstances of the crime that involves them, and who, when their involvement ends, will return to anonymity. The first reviews of the "Dragnet" radio show pointed this out, and not favorably. "It may have been factually accurate," reported *Variety*, "but dramatically it was artificial."

So much for the critics. By the time "Dragnet" had concluded its second season in 1954, Webb was one of the most powerful men in Hollywood, his program had won two Emmys and his ratings were second only to Lucille Ball's. Webb had established a format

EXAMINING THE CLUES

• Sue Grafton's Kinsey Millhone, whose adventures started with *"A" Is for Alibi* in 1982 and have worked their way through J, does not have a monopoly on alphabet book titles. Lawrence Treat is best known for *V As in Victim*, but over the past five decades has written books called *B As in Banshee* (1940), *D As in Dead* (1941), *Q As in Quicksand* (1947), and a short story, "H As in Homocide" (1964), and a collection of short stories, *P As in Police* (1970).

that was to be copied for the next four decades—not always successfully, especially when the copies appeared on television and on film, but copied nonetheless. Since Webb, television has not been able to duplicate the show's success, and the police procedural has flourished in the novel, thanks to Waugh, Lawrence Treat and Ed McBain.[2] Their work firmed up the rules and established more precedents for what was to follow.

Waugh based *Last Seen Wearing . . .* (1952) on the actual disappearance and murder of a college-age girl, and then detailed the painstaking efforts two state cops went through to solve the killing. His story actually began when he picked up a true-crime book, and noticed the deadpan style—no frills, no adornments, only the facts. He then wrote *Last Seen Wearing . . .*, trying to capture that true crime atmosphere. Waugh succeeded (his book is among the Keating 100), and he almost did it too well. It took two years to sell the novel, for it was too different for any publisher to take a chance on. The cops in *Last Seen Wearing . . .* do not appear again, however. Waugh followed up its success with a series of procedurals about a small town chief named Fred Fellows who works in the fictitious Connecticut city of Stockford. Typical of Fellows, always identifiable by his paunch, is *The Missing Man* (1964), where Fellows must piece together the murder of a young woman.

Treat's *V As in Victim* (1945) is generally acknowledged to be the first precinct-style police procedural. Stories in the series have appeared for four decades, chronicling the day-to-day activities of Det. Mitch Taylor and his colleagues, including Lt. Bill Decker and Det. Jub Freeman. What distinguishes the Treat stories is not the writing—Treat's style is often wooden, even for a police procedural—or the author's intention to be a pioneer. Treat's modesty is becoming. He has gone on record many times as disclaiming any intention of inventing anything. "I didn't know I was writing procedurals until somebody invented the term and said that that was the kind of thing I was writing," he once told Waugh. What distinguishes the Treat stories is Mitch Taylor, as ordinary a cop as anyone can imagine. Mitch is not above considering taking a bribe. He isn't very bright. He fights with his wife. In short, he is just like a thousand guys people pass driving to work each morning, and about as

---

[2]In one of those twists that keep critics up nights scratching their heads, the British—who never could master the hard-boiled detective, and whose traditional detectives still seem to be stuck in the nineteenth century—have embraced the police procedural with equal parts skill and enthusiasm. The BBC version of "Dragnet," set in Liverpool and called "Z Cars," ran from 1960 to 1978. The literary equivalents are best represented in the Gideon of Scotland Yard series by the prolific John Creasey, who has as many pseudonyms as Gideon has crimes to solve.

different as possible from the tens of thousands of fictional detectives who had preceded him in the genre. "Mitch had two worlds. One, the police world, was a perpetual and losing battle against lieutenants, work and bad breaks" (*Big Shot,* 1951). There is something comforting about this lament. Perhaps, to be literary for a moment, it reinforces for the reader that the law in a democracy is nothing more than the people who enforce it—ordinary, average people like Mitch Taylor, whose concerns aren't that different from the reader's.

McBain's 87th Precinct novels and short stories (which must total somewhere around one hundred) take Treat's concept and do it one better. His detectives are more interesting than Mitch Taylor and his colleagues, and occasionally come perilously close to glamour. His shootouts play like the missing reel from a *Lethal Weapon* movie. This, no doubt, has much to do with McBain's film back-

Cop Hater *was the first 87th Precinct novel.*
(Courtesy Bob Lakin Books)

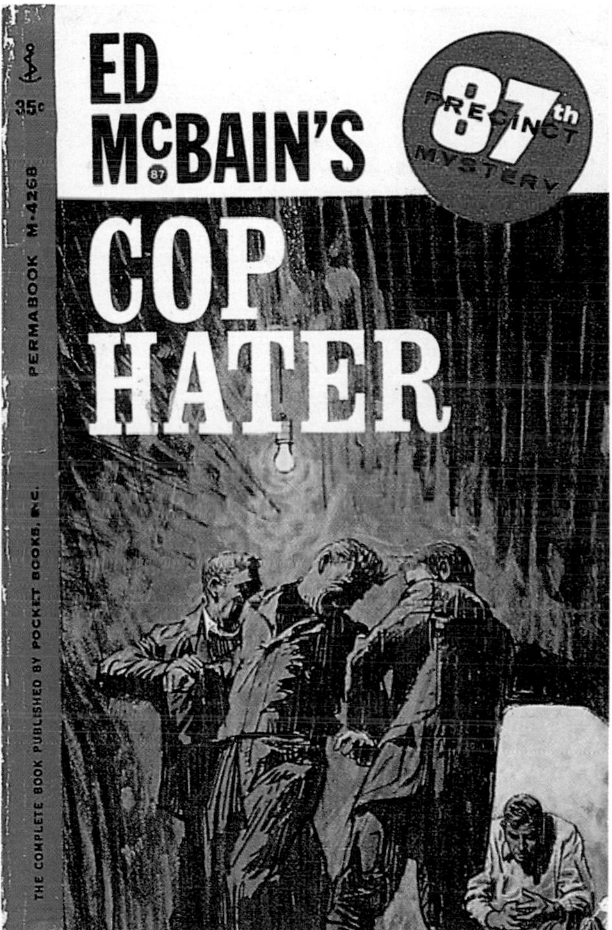

ground. He got his start in Hollywood when his first novel, *The Blackboard Jungle* (written under what may be his real name, Evan Hunter), was turned into the Glenn Ford–Sidney Poitier film. Still, despite these bursts of slickness, McBain understands the grit and realism that make up police routine. McBain has written that "it occurred to me that if I came home late one night and found my wife slaughtered in her bed, I would not call the little old lady next door, and I would not call an insurance investigator, or a reporter, or a private eye, or even a jockey. I might call my lawyer, but only to find out what I should do next. He would undoubtedly advise me to call the cops."

And McBain has the cops down to their nightsticks. The focal point of most of the 87th Precinct stories, which started in 1956 with *Cop Hater,* is Det. Steve Carella, who is a little smarter and a little more handsome than the average detective. But he is not so much smarter and so much more handsome as to be offensive. Carella is the married son of Italian immigrants, which gives McBain the opportunity to work family in. The rest of the 87th Precinct crew gives McBain the opportunity to work in the rest of the tensions of modern urban life—race, politics, religion and sex. There is Meyer Meyer, whose Jewish father had an especially ironic sense of humor; Bert Kling, the perpetual Andy Hardy type; Monaghan and Monroe, whose unintentional Abbott and Costello act provides the comic relief; Cotton Hawes, the son of a minister; and Eileen Burke, a later addition to the series. The city they work, says McBain, is a fictional place called Isola, but it is New York in everything but name—weather, geography and urban blight.

(Courtesy Bob Lakin Books)

Everyone has their favorite part of an 87th Precinct story, but it's hard to beat the times the cops work themselves into a corner. Carella and his partner, a black detective named Arthur Brown, are looking for the person who killed the mistress of a wealthy New York lawyer in *Widows* (1991), a late entry in the series that shows McBain hasn't slowed down at all. Not only can't Carella and Brown solve the crime, but they aren't even doing a very good job of pretending to solve the crime. That gives McBain an opportunity for the 87th Precinct boss, Lt. Peter Byrnes, to chew his men out: "He was telling his assembled detectives what he hoped they should have known by now. 'When you're stuck,' he said, 'you go back to the beginning. You start where it started.'" And then McBain spends six pages describing the squad's attempt to sort out why Carella and Brown have accomplished nothing. Six pages in a 332-page novel is the equivalent of watching Starsky and Hutch's boss spend almost a minute telling them how stupid they were being. This was about as unlikely to happen as it might have been welcome.

McBain has been so skilled at his work, in fact, that he has almost single-handedly kept others from entering the field. In an informal survey of several dozen detective authors, writers and critics undertaken for this book, hardly anyone mentioned a police procedural author after McBain. The one they did mention, Joseph Wambaugh, is almost more significant for what he hasn't done than for what he has. Wambaugh, a former Los Angeles policeman, has not only written a number of well-received police procedural novels (*The New Centurions, The Glitter Dome,* and *The Blue Knight,* among others), but was one of the men responsible for the 1970s surge in realistic television cop shows sparked by "Police Story," which he helped to create. Wambaugh, however, has never made a sustained effort to create a series character or to devise the sort of precinct house which would be a symbol for what he feels is real and genuine about police work. This is too bad. The police subgenre has not aged gracefully, and is in need of updating. McBain decided long ago not to update it when he chose not to let his characters age. That's why crankiness is the only thing missing from the 87th Precinct novels. There is no one who represents the crabbiness that lives in every station house (and in every work place, for that matter) in the twenty-year men who have calendars on their desks where they mark off the days to retirement. Wambaugh's decision not to create a consistent character may be as telling as if he had created one. By not coming up with someone like Carella or Friday, Wambaugh is saying that no one symbol can stand for the infinite diversity among policemen.

And nothing can be more realistic than that.

Joseph Wambaugh (right) and William Holden on the set of TV mini-series, "The Blue Knight." Holden played Bumper Morgan.

MASS MEDIA: A Police Sampler

• **Virgil Tibbs.** There are actually two Virgil Tibbses (not including the Tibbs who plays a supporting role in the television show "In the Heat of the Night"). One is John Ball's black police detective. This Tibbs is the top homicide investigator for the Pasadena Police Department, and he first appeared in the novel *In the Heat of the Night* (1965). He bears more than a passing resemblance to Jackie Robinson, the baseball player. Both were children of the Deep South at a time when Jim Crow was the norm, both worked their way through a California college (Robinson at UCLA, where he was a three-sport star, and Tibbs at the University of California at Berkeley), and both were pioneers in their profession. Robinson broke baseball's color barrier, while Tibbs was one of the first black fictional policemen. The second Tibbs looks just like Sidney Poitier, who played him in the Oscar-winning *Heat* and in its sequels, *They Call Me MISTER Tibbs!* and *The Organization.* One interesting sidelight: In the books, Tibbs works for the Pasadena police. In the first Tibbs movie, he works for the Philadelphia police. The *Heat* movie is worth seeing if only for the scene where Rod Steiger, playing the Southern police chief, calls Philly to check on Tibbs. Steiger's character just can't believe a Negro can be a police detective. In the second and third Tibbs movies, he works for the San Francisco police. This is one reason why Hollywood will always hold a place in the heart of filmgoers.

In the Heat of the Night, *starring Sidney Poitier and Rod Steiger, won an Edgar Award for best motion picture in 1967. The novel also won the Edgar for best first novel in 1965 for John Ball.*

• **Gabriel Wager.** This Denver-based cop, created by Rex Burns (pen name for Raoul Stephen Schler), is unique for a couple of reasons. First, he's Hispanic, and there haven't been a lot of Hispanics in this subgenre (just as there haven't been in any of the other subgenres under discussion). Second, Burns loves acronyms, and Wager often seems to be fighting crime with initials (the novels even come with glossaries, so the reader won't get too confused). The Wager stories also offer authentic atmosphere, as well as an unlikely locale. Denver (which has a sizable Hispanic population) isn't the scene of many detective books. However, like books from a number of other authors, Wager seems to have gotten lost in the glare of Waugh, Treat, McBain and Wambaugh. Wager is mentioned just once in Bill Pronizini and Marica Muller's critical guide *1001 Midnights*, for example, even though lesser police characters—Dell Shannon's Luis Mendoza, with two mentions—are included more often.

• **Mike Stone and Steve Keller.** These days, when Michael Douglas is best known for his steamy leading-man roles, it's hard to believe that he got his start playing Karl Malden's cool, younger partner in television's "The Streets of San Francisco" (1972–77). It's hard to forget his wide ties, plaid jackets and 1970s-style hair-spray hairdo. Although cop buddy shows are a staple of television and the movies, something about "Streets" elevated it above the usual level of mediocrity (see "Hunter" or "Red Heat" for examples). It was also a notch better than the usual fare offered by producer Quinn Martin ("The FBI," "Barnaby Jones," "Twelve O'Clock High"). The credit for its success goes to the actors. No one watched "Streets" to get a firsthand look at police procedure (although it was closer to the truth than many of its contemporaries). The plots usually involved Stone and Keller driving around for forty-five minutes, stopping for coffee, brainstorming the solution, and then arresting the bad guy. Instead, viewers watched to see Malden and Douglas trade barbs. It was obvious that Douglas was going places. Malden is one of the great underrated actors of American show business. He's so interesting that he could read from the telephone book and almost certainly attract an audience.

Karl Malden as Detective Mike Stone on "The Streets of San Francisco."

THE THIRD DEGREE:
When Is a Policeman a Policeman?

One of the worst habits critics have is categorizing everything. None of them are happy unless the entire world has been relegated to its proper cubbyhole: Which brings the discussion to the adventures of Navajo tribal cops Jim Chee and Joe Leaphorn, and the tales of Pennsylvania police chief Mario Balzic. Where do they go?

Their stories aren't police procedurals in the classic, "Dragnet" sense. They aren't hard-boiled enough to fit, along with their police comrades like Coffin Ed Johnson and Grave Digger Jones or Dirty Harry Callahan, among the hard-boiled detectives. They certainly aren't lawyers and spies, and they are just as apparently not traditional, drawing room detectives. The two Navajos spend too much time driving around the Four Corners area of the Southwest to spend any time in a drawing room, while Balzic wouldn't know a drawing room if it came up and poured him a cold one. Yet the men are traditional policemen.

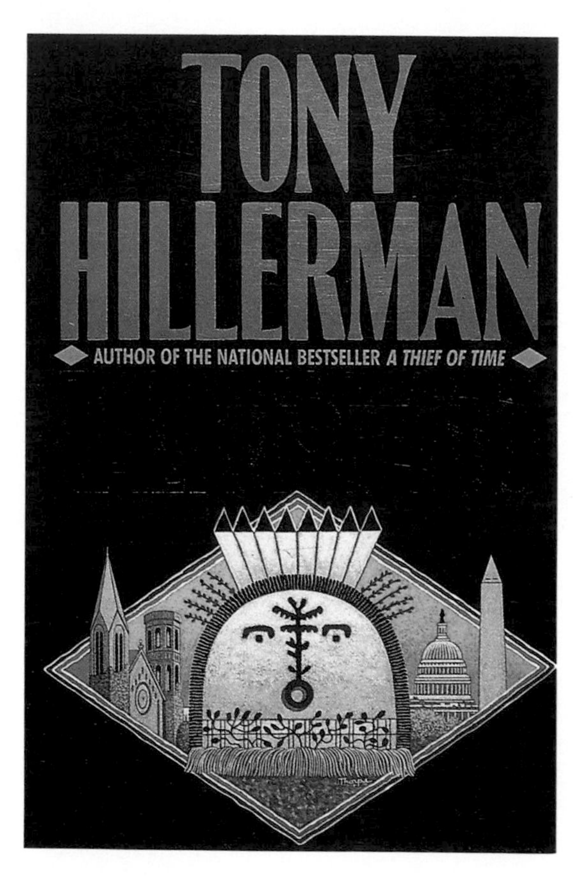

What does this mean? Where do they fit in the hierarchy? It means, and they fit, into the police category. The Constantine/ Hillerman detectives are legitimate characters even though they don't fit the Jack Webb archetype—really the first instance in the police subgenre. In this, the three men are the zenith of a long and not very illustrious line of American fictional policemen, both before and after Jack Webb injected a healthy dose of realism into the profession.

American fictional cops were, before Webb, caricatures. At first, they were second-stringers who couldn't compare to the men from Scotland Yard. These English policemen were witty and talented, and if they weren't peers like Roderick Alleyn, they often wound up as lords at the end of their careers, like John Appleby. Not only did these kinds of cops solve crimes, but they looked good doing it. Later, they were created only to offer comic relief. How many times has the cop with the Irish brogue provided a few laughs in a slow moment in some hard-boiled detective movie? How many cops have been like John Guild, Nick Charles's foil in *The Thin Man?* Guild is supposed to be one of New York's best detectives, but he spends most of the time telling Nick how pretty Nora is. Ed McBain, in explaining why he wrote about hard-boiled private eyes before he devised the 87th Precinct, put it best: "The bad guys were the cops. The good guys were anybody else trying to solve murders. . . . If only the cops would let the private eyes and the lawyers and the little old ladies with knitting needles get on with their work everybody would be a lot happier."

The few American fictional cops who were heroes before 1925, when Charlie Chan made his first appearance, were secondary characters from writers like Mary Roberts Rinehart and Anna Katherine Green. And Chan was not a policeman in the critical sense. He was a traditional, English-style detective whose job coincidentally called for him to show up at the Honolulu police headquarters. In manner and form, the Chan stories (both on the screen and on the page), resemble a Lord Peter Wimsey story more than a "Dragnet" story. Chan works alone (save for a goofball assistant in the books), does not fill out reports, does not use even the most basic police methods (fingerprints and the like), features a drawing room denouement, and solves his cases only after going into what H. R. F. Keating calls the Great Detective trance, where he is visited by the muse of detection. After Chan, police heroes are a motley assortment: the elderly, plodding French–Canadian created by Rufus King, New York's Lieutenant Valcour (1929); another New York cop, Inspector McKee, nicknamed "The Scotsman" by author Helen Reilly (1930); and George Bagby's Inspector Schmidt (1935), the flatfoot who is always complaining about his aching feet. The Schmidt stories are entertaining (Bagby is a pen name for Aaron Marc Stein, a well-known critic and author), but none of them—like their colleagues before "Dragnet"—have shown much staying power.

This is where the Hillerman stories and the six Balzic novels are different. They are not resplendent examples of the police procedural. The plots in the Hillerman books are usually an excuse to explain some anthropological point about the native peoples who inhabited the Southwest before the Europeans arrived; the Balzic stories are equally as sociological. The various ethnic groups who live in western Pennsylvania are as worthy of study as the Navajos, although they are not nearly as trendy. The ethnic and racial composition of Hillerman's and Balzic's books, in fact, tend to obscure what's important about them. Too many discussions of these three characters point out their ethnic origins, but leave it at that. This does a disservice to the characters. Chee and Leaphorn are more than characters to place on a list with other detectives who come from aboriginal stock (which is why they are usually lumped with an Australian half-caste named Inspector Napoleon Bonaparte). Chee and Leaphorn have more in common with Inspector Maigret than they do with Tonto, even though Tonto is an Indian. Anyone who does that sort of categorizing misses Hillerman's point: that the Navajo culture is worthy of respect, and from this respect will come understanding of common problems and solutions to those problems.

The Chee/Leaphorn series, which started in 1970 with the Leaphorn novel *The Blessing Way* and in 1983 with a Chee book, *The Dark Wind*, has probably done more to explain the native Southwestern way of life to those of European ancestry than a library of textbooks. Hillerman, who attended an Indian boarding school for eight years, knows what he writes about. Leaphorn is a lieutenant for the law and order division of the Navajo nation, while Chee is a sergeant in the tribal police. This gives Hillerman plenty of opportunities to paint a portrait of the way of life of the Navajos and Zunis who live in Arizona and New Mexico and who eke out a living on the reservations. The United States has always had a fascinating, if not always reputable, relationship with its native peoples. In one sense, all of those treaties the United States signed (and later broke) made each tribe a sovereign nation like Canada, independent not only of the states but of the federal government. In another sense, this independence is as unrealistic as it sounds—which is why all of the treaties were broken in the first place. The only reason some poor slob living on the Navajo reservation in Arizona doesn't pay federal income tax is not because his tribe is independent of the United States but because he is unemployed. This is the dichotomy that Hillerman exploits, in much the same way Chester Himes did with Grave Digger Jones and Coffin Ed Johnson. Chee and Leaphorn must enforce the rules of a system that they aren't part of, if only because it will prevent greater suffering than if they don't enforce the rules. Chee, for example, is faced not only with a crime in *The Ghostway*, but with a dilemma. Should he leave the reservation to join the FBI, forsaking his family and tradition (a theme throughout Hillerman's books) for a new life? Compounding the problem

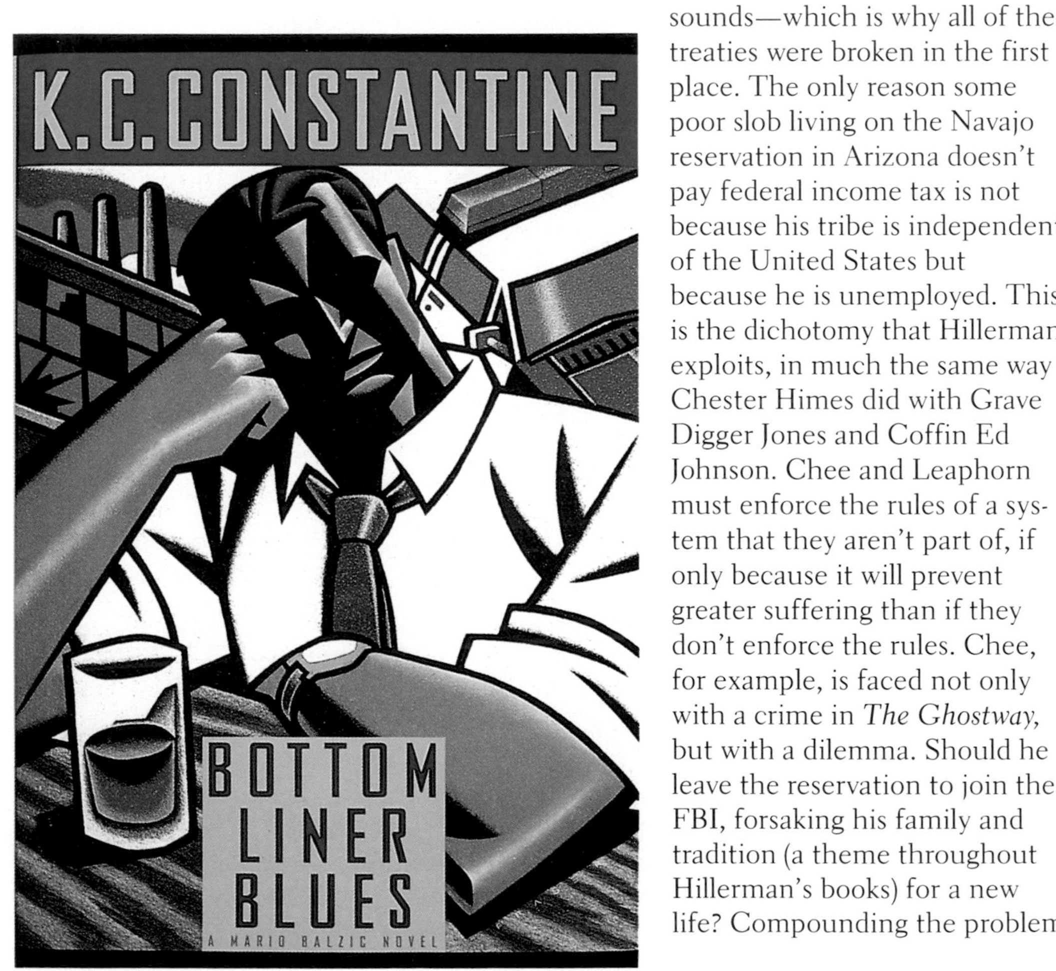

(Courtesy Mysterious Press)

is his desire to be with his Anglo girlfriend, who won't stay on the reservation with him.

Balzic, created by the mysterious K. C. Constantine, has never been as popular as Chee or Leaphorn, and it's easy to see why. The Navajos have gotten more publicity, for one. Hillerman has had a major U.S. publisher for years, and has become a minor celebrity in his own right. He has even written nonfiction books about the Southwest. Constantine is one of the most leakproof pseudonyms in literature, as much a secret as Deep Throat is to American history. The man (or woman) refuses to be identified, which cuts down on the opportunities for publicity.

This is too bad, for the Balzic books may very well be literature—and this is not damning with faint praise. The Serbo-Italian Balzic, who first appeared in *The Rocksburg Railroad Murders* (1972), is as authentic as Huck Finn. Anyone who has ever spent time in a small town in the Midwest or Pennsylvania knows someone like Balzic. He works in a town that is thoroughly blue collar as well as extremely diverse culturally,[3] and is dying so slowly that hardly anyone notices. Rocksburg is populated with guys named Janeski and Bielski and Muscotti, men who call themselves bohunks and don't think anything of calling others worse. There are dozens of small gems in each Balzic book, and they have little to do with the plot or the puzzle the chief has to solve. Truth be told, the mysteries are straight forward, and it's rarely difficult to figure out who committed the crime. This, as would be expected, has lowered Constantine's reputation with mainstream reviewers (who already object to his language). They always seem to compliment Constantine's books by wondering why, if he is so talented, the puzzles aren't more complicated. This is as foolish as asking why Mark Twain wrote in dialect. In *The Man Who Liked to Look at Himself* (1973), Balzic shines as few others before him have. He is describing a bar fight between a black man and a Pole to one of his sergeants: "He felt that he had probably talked too much. He'd noticed a certain distance in Stramsky's eyes when he was telling that one about Woznichak. Had he told it before? He couldn't remember, but he probably had. He loved that story too much not to have told it before." That passage is as natural as anything in American literature, let alone the detective genre.

EXAMINING THE CLUES

- Ed McBain always begins his 87th Precinct books by choosing a title, and then writing the book to fit the title. That explains such colorful appellations as *So Long as You Both Shall Live, Hail, Hail the Gang's All Here,* and *Sadie When She Died* (it makes sense after reading the book). The last, incidentally, is McBain's favorite 87th Precinct book, according to a 1984 interview. He was so fond of the title that he not only used it for a 1972 novel, but for a 1972 short story. His least favorite is *So Long as They Both Shall Live,* which apparently didn't live up to the title.

---

[3]Language, in fact, is another of the reasons Balzic hasn't gotten the attention he deserves. There are quite a few four-letter words, as well as enough racial slurs to infuriate an entire brigade of do-gooders. But none of it is out of place. It's obvious that Constantine knows how his characters live, and that this language is as much a part of them as the coal mines and steel mills that used to dot the area.

THE SOLUTION: The Ten Silliest Cop Shows in Television History

Television does not hold a monopoly on silly fictional policemen. There have been silly cops in books, the movies and radio, but television seems to do it better than any other medium. After all, many television shows are silly regardless of genre, as efforts like "My Mother the Car" and "Supertrain" show.

Here, then, are the ten silliest cop shows in the history of television. The list does not include those shows intended to be silly, such as "Carter Country" or "Car 54, Where Are You?," or programs that were silly but didn't have anything to do with policemen, like "Charlie's Angels." Also excluded are programs which were so silly that they didn't last long enough for anyone to notice, such as "Street Hawk" or "Max Monroe: Loose Cannon." Also missing from the list is the incredibly silly second version of "Dragnet," out of respect for Jack Webb's accomplishments with the first "Dragnet."

A final warning: Some of the programs on this list may have been entertaining, but they were still pretty silly.

Below left: "Adam-12," starring Martin Milner (left) and Kent McCord, was produced by Jack Webb. Obviously, Webb's taste in cop shows had slipped.

Below right: David Soul and Paul Michael Glaser in "Starsky and Hutch."

1. "Starsky and Hutch" (1975–79). Paul Michael Glaser and David Soul are accomplished actors, and Glaser has even made a name for himself as a director. So how did they manage to wind up in the middle of this mess? "Starsky and Hutch" described the exploits of a pair of hip, streetwise cops who had no respect for authority, the Constitution, or anything else that might prevent them from squealing around town in their bright red 1974 Ford Torino. This was the kind of program that people who hate television always point to, and with good rea-

son. It was sexist, racist and violent, and those were its redeeming features. The plots had even less to recommend them. What's worse about "Starsky and Hutch" is that it was immensely popular, spawning the usual array of merchandise (lunch boxes, action figures) and making teenybopper stars of Glaser and Soul during its four-season run.

2. "SWAT" (1975–76). How silly was this, which featured the weekly adventures of a Special Weapons and Tactics team? It was so silly that Robert Urich, who would go on to play Dan Tanna in "Vegas" two years later, was probably the best actor among the bunch. The plots were sadly predictable, even for a bad television show. Each week, some nut would start something that the city's regular cops couldn't handle. Then Lt. Hondo Harrelson (Steve Forrest) and his men would be called in. They would arrive with more firepower than the armies of some small countries, dressed in fatigues and riding in an armored van. After a suitable wait, the SWAT team would blast the hell out of the nut. Thankfully, this program lasted just one season. ABC, which aired it, actually listened when viewers complained it was too violent, and canceled it despite adequate ratings.

3. "T. J. Hooker" (1982–87). This is the program that proved that William Shatner was not the sole reason for the success of "Star Trek." Shatner, as the title character, was as bad in this as the rest of the cast, and that's saying a lot. His colleagues on a big city police force were played by Adrian Zmed, who left this show to host "Dance Fever," and Heather Locklear, best known for her fitness club commercials and the "Dynasty" evening soap. Hooker was a former detective who thought it would be more interesting to be a patrolman, and the show chronicled his duties on the street. However, these duties never seemed to include writing traffic tickets, breaking up domestic disturbances or any of the other things real street cops do. Instead, Hooker spent a lot of time in car chases with murderers. This program was so silly that it made "Adam-12" look like cinema vérité.

The "Hooker" team, ready for action.

4. “The Mod Squad” (1968–73). This program was based on the experiences of Bud Ruskin, who formed a group of young-looking undercover officers for the Los Angeles County Sheriff’s Department. Of course, Ruskin did this in the 1950s, but what’s a decade or two to a television network? “The Mod Squad” was ABC’s attempt to cash in on the youth culture of the late 1960s and early 1970s, but it was only moderately successful. Although the show made the Nielsen top twenty-five ratings three times in its five-season run, it never cracked the top ten. Could it have been because the people it was aimed at knew it was too silly to watch? Only a television executive would believe that viewers would believe that the cops would recruit a car thief from Beverly Hills (Pete), the daughter of a prostitute (Julie), and a huge black kid from Watts with an

The Mod Squad.

equally huge Afro (Linc) to fight crime. It's interesting that the Mod Squadders never arrested any kids. All of the crimes, oddly enough, were committed by adults. Peggy Lipton, who played Julie, can still be seen in some of Jane Fonda's workout videos.

5. "Burke's Law" (1963–66). This show was entertaining, thanks to star Gene Barry, one of those actors who knows how to make television work for him. Its scripts, often written by Richard Levinson and partner William Link, were usually engaging. But its ratings never excited ABC (which went so far as to change the format and the title to "Amos Burke—Secret Agent" for its final season) and it was never a top-twenty-five show. But it was definitely silly. What other explanation is there for a program about a Los Angeles chief of detectives who just happened to be a multimillionaire, lived in a mansion, and was driven to work each day in a chauffeured limousine? Burke also never seemed to investigate any murders involving people beneath him on the socioeconomic scale. Nice work if you can get it. An even sillier note: "Burke's Law" spun off "Honey West," the sex-and-danger private eye series starring Anne Francis, which might make this list if it included silly private eye series.

6. "The Rookies" (1972–76). Kate Jackson may be a great actress, but the world will never know. Her material is always so abysmal. "The Rookies," her first big break, detailed the day-to-day experiences of three first-year cops in a large Southern California city. It wasn't as silly as Jackson's other two action series—"Charlie's Angels" and "Scarecrow and Mrs. King"—but that doesn't mean it wasn't silly in its own right. Georg Sanford Brown, who played one of the three cops (Jackson was married to the third of the trio), may have been so embarrassed by his part in the program that he stopped acting. He has since become a well-known and respected television director, and won an Emmy in the 1985–86 season for directing an episode of "Cagney & Lacey."

The stars of "The Rookies": Gerald S. O'Loughlin (Lt. Eddie Ryker), Georg Stanford Brown (Officer Terry Webster), and Michael Ontkean (Officer Willie Gillis)—all of whom went on to better projects.

7. “The Protectors” (1969–70). Relevance comes to the television cop show. “The Protectors” was one section of the three-part “Bold Ones”—NBC’s tales of doctors, cops and lawyers who may have been older than thirty, but were still in touch with the world around them. The program starred Leslie Nielsen as a big-city police chief who grappled with all of those momentous changes (“You mean we can’t beat the hell out of suspects anymore?”), while Hari Rhodes was the hip black district attorney who was his guide into the new reality. Nielsen got the last laugh, though, as anyone who has seen him slapstick his way through the “Naked Gun” movies and television show will testify. Why be silly unintentionally when it’s possible to be paid to be silly?

8. “Sidekicks” (1986–87). It’s hard to believe someone got paid for dreaming this one up. How it lasted an entire season is too silly to even think about. “Sidekicks” told the story of Jake Rizzo, a bachelor cop who one day discovered a ten-year-old kid on his doorstep. But this was no ordinary preteen—the kid was a karate expert endowed with mystical powers who could kick his way through legions of bad guys. Needless to say, Jake couldn’t solve any cases without the kid’s help. As remarkable as it seems, this was played as a drama.

9. “Treasury Men in Action” (1950–55). One of the reasons there are so few programs from the early days of television on this list is that there were few cop shows in the early days of television. This one, however, more than made up for the lack of such programming with its silly, Junior G-man approach. The shows were based on actual cases, and detailed the various law enforcement agencies of the Treasury Department in their never-ending struggle to bring evil-doers to justice. There was no regular cast, but a journeyman character actor named Walter Greaza appeared every week as the chief of whichever law enforcement unit was being featured. The plots were formulaic to a fault (the T-men chased a lot of tax evaders, counterfeiters and moonshiners), and each show ended with a moral, emphasizing that the government always gets the bad guys. In fact, government officials sometimes appeared on the show during its four seasons, three on ABC and one, the second, on NBC. Greaza was a busy man in 1951. Not only did he star in “Treasury Men,” but he played one of Martin Kane’s police contacts in “Martin Kane, Private Eye,” television’s first private eye show. “Kane” was also shown live on Thursday night, which meant that Greaza had to run from show to show. Fortunately, he had time. The two were an hour apart on the

NBC schedule that season, separated by the "Ford Festival," a musical variety show.

10. "Baretta" (1975–78). Let's get something out of the way. Yes, Robert Blake was terrific, winning an Emmy as the streetwise cop who lived in a flop house with a cockatoo as a pet and had all of these luscious women cousins. And yes, the theme song, sung by Sammy Davis, Jr., was about as good as television theme songs get. And yes, it was popular, earning two Nielsen top-twenty-five spots in its three and a half seasons on the air. But this show was patently silly, the sort of program real policemen use as an example to show how television misses the point. "Baretta" was about as authentic a portrayal of police work as a pinball machine is to baseball. The Blake character did pretty much as he pleased, regardless of what the consequences would be. He didn't file reports, didn't have a partner, didn't listen to his boss, and didn't dress in anything other than jeans, t-shirts and a cloth cap.

Others deserving mention (but in no particular order): "McMillan and Wife" (1971–77)—Susan St. James was surprisingly sexy, and her banter with Rock Hudson was charming, but this had about as much to do with police work as "Baretta" did. "CHiPS" (1978–83)—This program did not get worse when Erik Estrada sat out part of the 1981 season in a contract dispute. "21 Jump Street" (1987–91)—TV is often criticized for having thirty-year-old actors play teenagers. In this show, that was the entire idea, making it a "Mod Squad" for the '80s.

THE RAP SHEET: Lawyers

M.O.: The lawyer is not usually classified in a separate category. Most deliberations tend to include the lawyer in the group which most resembles him. Ed McBain's Matthew Hope or Stephen Greenleaf's John Marshall Tanner, for instance, fit into the hard-boiled category. There are lawyers who are traditional detectives, like William Faulkner's Gavin Stevens (no kidding), and police procedural lawyers, such as Erle Stanley Gardner's Doug Selby, a district attorney. Yet the failure to include a separate category for lawyers means that the most famous lawyers of all time don't have any room at the inn. These lawyers, such as Perry Mason, work to clear clients wrongly accused of murder, and every action in their adventure leads to a climactic final scene. This final scene comes in the courtroom, where the lawyer proves his client's innocence using the combination of genius, good luck and persistence that Mason made famous.

Perpetrators: Erle Stanley Gardner's Perry Mason, Arthur Train's Ephraim Tutt, Craig Rice's John J. Malone, Carolyn Wheat's Cassandra Jameson, and Melville Davisson Post's Randolph Mason.

Aliases: Barrister, counselor, shyster, attorney, solicitor, mouthpiece, jurist, pettifogger.

The Shysters

5

"Perry Mason is a household word. . . . There won't be another."

—Jon Tuska

In the early 1920s, a failed businessman and overworked lawyer was looking for a way to supplement his income to better support his wife and young daughter. He thought that writing fiction would be a quick and easy way to pick up a couple of bucks. After all, the newsstands were full of pulp magazines, each containing dozens of stories. How hard would it be to peddle to that market? He was sure it wasn't very particular in its needs or its taste, what with its gaudy covers and hastily written and edited efforts. In the next couple of years, the lawyer sold a number of pieces to the pulps, with titles like "Nellie's Naughty Nightie" and "The Shrieking Skeleton."

But the stories weren't very good, and the lawyer wasn't very happy with his efforts. "My stories were terrible," he once said. "I didn't know how to plot [and] I had no natural aptitude as a writer."

But he persevered, in much the same way he had clung to his law practice. In 1926, for example, he sold one million words to the pulps (and he was still taking cases). By the beginning of the next decade, he had become one of the most respected writers in the pulps, and his work appeared regularly in the leading pulp titles. His characters were famous throughout the cheap magazines. The best known were Ed Jenkins, the Phantom Crook (an annual favorite in *Black Mask* reader polls); Pete Wennick, a wrongfully disbarred lawyer who worked as a law clerk and who was hell with women; and two-fisted district attorney Ken Corning.

But all of this success was not enough. It was lucrative—he earned $20,000 from the pulps in 1932, a fabulous sum at the beginning of the Depression—but it wasn't where the lawyer wanted to stop. "I've never been mediocre in anything," he told his agent, pointing out that for ten years he got by on three hours of

Gardner started out in crime pulps like the famous Black Mask.

(Photo by Michael Keller Photography, courtesy John Wooley)

sleep a night—working as an attorney during the day and writing pulp fiction in the evening. It was time to take the next step, and to reach a larger audience that promised an even more lucrative payoff. But the problems the lawyer faced now seemed just as insurmountable as those he had faced when he had started. Joseph "Cap" Shaw, the legendary editor at *Black Mask* and the man who had encouraged Dashiell Hammett and given Raymond Chandler his start, took one look at the lawyer's breakthrough project, a novel about a Los Angeles defense attorney, and turned it down. The lawyer, still persevering, wrote a second novel about the L.A. attorney, who worked closely with his secretary and a private detective.

Then one of those things happened that only seem to happen in fiction. Thayer Hobson, the president of William Morrow & Company, a major New York publisher, saw the two novels about the L.A. attorney and liked them. He liked them so much that he agreed to publish them, on the condition that the lawyer change the name of the fictional attorney. The character had been called Stark, and then Keene, but Hobson didn't like either name. His suggestion was Mason, and in 1933, Morrow published Erle Stanley Gardner's *The Case of the Velvet Claws*, the first Perry Mason mystery.

(Courtesy Bob Lakin Books)

It would be a cliché to say that the rest is history, but it would also be undeniably true. Since that time, Mason has become more than a character in a book. He has become an industry, with production figures to rival anything that any other set of characters (or some industries, for that matter) could have accumulated. The statistics are so staggering as to be almost impossible to believe. The eighty-two Mason novels have sold more than 200 million copies; at his height, Mason was selling twenty thousand copies a day. That's almost three times as many in one day as the average book sells during its lifetime. The Mason radio show ran on CBS for twelve seasons (and also spawned "The Edge of Night," a television soap opera). There were six Mason movies in the 1930s, and there would have been more except that Gardner disapproved of what Hollywood did to his character, and refused to sell the rights to additional books. Finally, there is the Mason television show. The original ran from 1957 to 1966, and is one of only four mystery dramas to last nine or more seasons (the others are "Dragnet," "Hawaii 5-0," and "The FBI").[1] Its 271 episodes are still shown today, often on more than one station in the same market, and were as much an influence on future lawyer shows as "Dragnet" was on cop shows.The Mason revival movies, with Raymond Burr re-creating the title role, have been a staple of the NBC schedule since 1985.

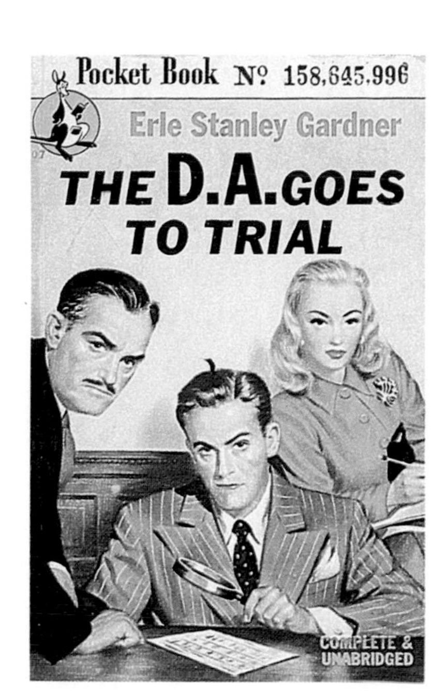

Another Gardner lawyer-detective was District Attorney Doug Selby, who had his own series.

This success, though, is just the beginning of Mason's legacy. Mason is an icon. Not only is he the synthesis of every fictional lawyer ever created, but he is also the ideal for every real lawyer who has ever walked in front of a jury. This is no joke: it's almost impossible to serve on a jury in the United States without having one of the attorneys in the case apologize for not being like Mason. He was more than good; he was perfect—and he was so perfect that it has been useless for anyone else to compete with him.

The American fictional detective's law division didn't begin with Mason, but it almost surely ends there. No one has ever been able to duplicate Mason's success, including Gardner. His Doug Selby series, written from the district attorney's point of view, is okay, but its nine books don't even come close to matching Mason's popularity. Almost every other attorney/detective who followed Mason chose, in the words of one of their creators, to imitate Mason. Carolyn Wheat, whose Cassandra Jameson does for lawyers what Kinsey Millhone and V. I. Warshawski did for the hard-boiled detective, points out that "fellow mystery authors chose defenders over prosecutors as heroes" because of Mason's success. He spoiled forever the idea of the lawyer/detective as anything other than a champion of the underdog.

This can be traced to Mason's roots in the hard-boiled subgenre, where the detective who doesn't take a case for the underdog is the exception that proves the rule. The early Mason books

EXAMINING THE CLUES

When Ed McBain started his Matthew Hope series in 1978, about a Florida lawyer who always gets tangled up in murder, he realized he was getting into an area he didn't want to get into. "I know in my heart of hearts," wrote McBain, "that Matthew Hope does not have any legitimate reason for becoming involved in a murder investigation. He should be at a real estate closing instead of in a morgue. He should be writing a brief instead of chasing down clues." Still, he hasn't let that get in the way of the series. There are a half dozen books, and Hope has managed to find a way to look for clues when he should be drawing up merger papers.

---

[1]The only blemish on Mason's record is the 1973–74 series, starring Monte Markham. It lasted barely one-half season, and missed the point entirely. In fact, it seemed as if it was conceived by network officials eager to prove they didn't need Gardner's advice. He had died in 1970 after exercising near dictatorial control over the Raymond Burr series (much to CBS's chagrin).

and stories, published between 1933 and the mid-1940s or so, are firmly a part of the hard-boiled tradition. Mason uses a gun, gets in fistfights, is regularly threatened with disbarment, and doesn't always engage in all of the courtroom pyrotechnics that are the highlight of the later books and the television series. Gardner, in an interview given soon after the Mason series became popular, said that he was worried that Mason might be too heavily influenced by the Hammett style as practiced in *Black Mask*. In another instance, he even went so far as to describe an early Mason case as "smash-bang action which is really the basis of Perry Mason's exploits." This will no doubt be news to Raymond Burr, whose Mason did little more than get in and out of cars and walk to and fro in a courtroom.[2]

The change in Mason came after Gardner abandoned the pulps for the higher paying slicks, such as *Collier's* and *The Saturday Evening Post*. The slick audiences were, at least demographically, more sophisticated than pulp audiences. That called for a slicker hero, and Gardner was nothing if not talented enough to give the public want it wanted. The Mason of the early books punches out someone who chokes his secretary, Della Street. In another early case, he and his private-eye cohort, Paul Drake, are sued for defamation of character. The pulp Mason tampers with

---

[2]Gardner fought a losing battle with Cap Shaw at *Black Mask* over what Gardner called the "Hammetization" of the magazine. Shaw liked Hammett's style so much, Gardner complained, that he tried to force every writer to write like Hammett.

Gardner later moved to the slicks. Rico Tomaso illustrated "The Case of the Lame Canary" in a 1937 Saturday Evening Post.

witnesses, often hiding them out in cheap motels under assumed names. He does these things, he says, because the truth is "the only weapon powerful enough; a lawyer doing the things I have done and relying on anything less powerful would be disbarred in a month."

The slick Mason (and especially the Mason of the television show) was continually paying for the excesses of the pulp Mason. Although Mason's character had mellowed, the attitudes of his adversaries toward him hadn't. This is why district attorney Hamilton Burger is constantly carping about all of Mason's legal shenanigans on the television show when the most outrageous thing Mason ever does is to badger a witness. It's also why, in a short story written for *Collier's* in 1953, a judge asks Mason what sort of pressure he put on a recalcitrant witness (who also happens to be guilty of murder) after the witness has skipped town. "'Just a moment, Judge,' Mason said. 'The only pressure I brought to bear on him was to cross-examine him.'" The judge must have known the early Mason, who was not above tampering with a witness to get a client off the hook.

(Courtesy Bob Lakin Books)

In this, Mason was no different than his most illustrious predecessor, the slimy Gilded Age barrister Randolph Mason (who apparently is the source for Perry Mason's name). Randolph Mason was created by Melville Davisson Post, the same man who gave the world the kindly and God-fearing Uncle Abner. But the two were as different as Sherlock Holmes and Mike Hammer. Uncle Abner quoted the Scriptures in his cases; Randolph Mason flaunted them. Mason proved that the second half of the twentieth century has no monopoly on ambulance chasers. One client, facing a certain guilty verdict, asked Mason what he should do. Mason told him to murder the only witness against him.

In this, Mason is part of a long and glorious tradition in the English-speaking world. In the past thousand years, there have been many dramatic changes in social, cultural and political life. A fourteenth-century banker, for instance, and his twentieth-century counterpart would have almost nothing in common despite their professional backgrounds—save for a hatred for lawyers. Dickens wrote about corrupt lawyers in *Bleak House*; Shakespeare wrote about corrupt lawyers regularly; Chaucer wrote about corrupt lawyers in *The Canterbury Tales*. Even nonfiction accounts of life

over the past millennium emphasize this distaste for men of law. The letters, diaries and personal papers of the Pastons, an influential fifteenth-century English family, have survived. The Pastons seem to have spent a great deal of their time in lawsuits and counter-lawsuits against their neighbors and business partners in an attempt to increase their already substantial family holdings. "I suppose that in all Christendom are not so many pleaders, attorneys and men of law as be in England only," wrote the fifteenth-century printer William Caxton.

Truth be told, there are very few sympathetic accounts of lawyers in English or American literature in mainstream fiction, let alone in the detective genre. For every character like Horace Rumpole, there are dozens like S. S. Van Dine, who was a lawyer before he became Philo Vance's narrator and sycophant. For every character like John Marshall Tanner, there are dozens more like the attorneys who frequent Ross Macdonald's later Lew Archer novels. They are at best incompetent and are at worst murderous, and it is a trend that must be significant, given the psychological bent of these books. Typical of the lawyers Archer comes across is Gordon Sable in *The Galton Case* (1959), who seems to have a successful practice and beautiful young wife. But appearances are deceiving.

All Post did with Randolph Mason was to adapt this stereotype to his own uses. Mason, wrote Post, was created in part in reaction to Sherlock Holmes's omnipotence. He is a lawyer who uses his formidable legal knowledge to find loopholes in the system to cheat justice. The first two volumes of Mason stories were written in 1896 and 1897, and it's no coincidence that they appeared at the same time that the American legal and political systems were undergoing the shock of the Populist and Progressive movements. The two groups (the Populists in the final decade of the nineteenth century and the Progressives in the first two decades of the twentieth) contended that the system was skewed in favor of big business and its political cronies, and that the ordinary citizen didn't have an equal opportunity to compete. Their political agendas, although often differing in procedure, were philosophically similar. Something, they argued, must be done to the system to end the stranglehold that the wealthy and powerful held. Mason was an example of the sort of lawyer who gave the Populists and the Progressives fits. His kind were the tools of the elite, the lawyers who always helped banks foreclose on family farms and robber barons to steal small businesses. The law is supposed to be blind, but Mason always managed to find a way to let it borrow a seeing-eye dog.

In *The Strange Schemes of Randolph Mason,* the lawyer is described as "a mysterious legal misanthrope, having no sense of moral obligation, but learned in the law, who by virtue of the strange tilt in his mind is pleased to strive with the difficulties of his clients as though they were mere problems involving no matter of right or equity or common justice." This description bears more than a passing similarity to the answer most lawyers give whenever anyone asks them why they defend child molesters, rapists, mass murderers, drug dealers and the like. To them, guilt or innocence is irrelevant. What makes the Mason stories readable even today is that a late-twentieth-century lawyer would regard Post's description of Mason as a compliment, not a criticism—save for the part about the strange tilt of mind that allowed a lawyer to overlook his moral obligations. One of the law's great strengths from this point of view is that almost every lawyer, no matter how repugnant the case, considers it an advantage to be morally neutral.

THE STRANGE SCHEMES

OF

RANDOLPH MASON.

INTRODUCTION.

THE teller of strange tales is not the least among benefactors of men. His cup of Lethe is welcome at times even to the strongest, when the *tædium vitæ* of the commonplace is in its meridian. To the aching victim of evil fortune, it is ofttimes the divine anæsthetic.

To-day a bitter critic calls down to the story-teller, bidding him turn out with the hewers of wood and the drawers of water, for the reason that there is no new thing, and the pieces with which he seeks to build are ancient and well worn. " At best," he cries, " the great one among you can

9

Mason would no doubt feel as at home today helping shady land developers fleece the taxpayers as he did a hundred years ago. Mason's cases included almost every controversial political topic of his day. He advised speculators who were trying to corner the market in grain futures. He represented greedy cattlemen. He worked for a political machine in an unnamed western state. This timeliness may have been intentional. Post was a lawyer himself, and had been butting his head against the legal system for several years—practicing both criminal and corporation law—when he wrote the first Mason volume. He earned his law degree in West Virginia in 1892, and there is little doubt that he sympathized with what Populists and Progressives described as the excesses of the legal and political systems that helped to impoverish people in rural states like West Virginia. Mason always insisted that he experienced firsthand the abuses he wrote about, and he always insisted that the Mason stories were written to show that the system needed to be reformed. In at least one instance, an abuse Post wrote about led to a change in the law. In the short story "The Corpus Delecti," Mason gets a guilty murderer off after some judicial hanky-panky—strictly within the letter of the law, of course. The laws in several states were later amended to close the loophole Mason exploited in the story.

Post's most eloquent defense of the need for reform came in the second Mason volume, *The Man of Last Resort,* after the critics had a field day skewering the first volume for its moral turpitude. In the second book's preface, Post wrote that the legal system was corrupt, and that "a skillful rogue could commit crimes in such a

Erle Stanley Gardner.

(Photography Collection, Humanities Research Center, The University of Texas at Austin)

way as to render the law powerless to punish him." That, he said, is why he wrote what he did, and that perhaps his writing showed what needed to be changed and how it should be changed.[3]

One of Gardner's great skills was in taking this drive and determination—this energy—and adapting it to the conditions of the time in which he wrote. During Prohibition and the beginning of the Depression, the reforming zeal that had pervaded the country when Post wrote was long gone. The Populist candidate for president in 1892 got eleven percent of the vote; by 1928, the Progressives were spent, and didn't even field a national candidate. If anyone was going to stick up for the common man, he was going to have to do it within a system that already existed—no matter how corrupt and venal that system might be. What's most amazing about the Perry Mason stories is not that Mason never loses a case (and that the cases don't even get past the preliminary hearing), but that he does so without relying on the time-honored and battle-tested tools of his trade. He doesn't bribe a witness or intimidate a jury or pay off a judge. All he does is present the evidence, and it is always enough. The only time it looks like Mason loses comes when his client holds out on him, and doesn't want to be acquitted (*The Case of the Terrified Typist,* 1956). Even then, he finds the evidence on his own, and is able to reverse the jury verdict. Mason's rule for solving a case is simple (and owes a lot to Holmes): If his client is innocent, then someone else is guilty. His job is to find the facts that prove this.

What may be even more amazing is that the American public believed all of it; more than believed it, they rejoiced in it. Mason was the lawyer they always hoped for, even though reality told them most lawyers were to be avoided at all costs. "He always has to remember he's part of the machinery by which justice is dispensed," Mason says. "When it comes to a matter of justice or injustice, there isn't such a thing as big or little. Injustice is a social malignancy." In this way, Mason is the legal version of Chandler's knight. Although he was created at a time when, as Chandler wrote, mobsters ruled cities, Mason was able to win in a corrupt system without becoming corrupt himself. He always let blind justice decide, and blind justice always saw correctly. Perry Mason's legacy is that the system can never be corrupted completely, no matter how corrupt it seems to be.

---

[3]However, by the time the third Mason series of stories appeared in 1909 (*The Corrector of Destinies*) the shyster had turned into a do-gooder. It's hard to get a handle on why Mason changed. Did Post figure that the political reforms of the past twenty years had made the sinister Mason obsolete, or was he just spoiled by success? By then, Post was one of the highest paid magazine writers in the country.

MASS MEDIA: A Lawyer Sampler

• **Ephraim Tutt.** Arthur Train's turn-of-the-century lawyer is always described as part Abraham Lincoln, part Robin Hood and part Uncle Sam. In this, Train, a lawyer himself, was creating a character that fit his conception of the law. "The law offers greater opportunities to be at one and the same time a Christian and a horse-trader than any other profession." In a dozen or so volumes of short stories and a novel, all written between 1920 and 1945, Tutt lived up to that description. His tales have dated about as well as the New York he lived in has, but what may be most important about Tutt is the role he played in establishing a link between Randolph Mason and Perry Mason. This may or may not have something to do with the name of Tutt's opponent in many cases, prosecutor Hezikiah Mason.

• **Cassandra Jameson.** Jameson works for the New York public defender's office, which is in keeping with the political philosophy of someone who was at Kent State in 1970 when the National Guard killed three students. The first James novel, written in 1983, is *Dead Man's Thoughts*, and it established a pattern. Cass is a good lawyer who knows her way around a courtroom and who is on the correct side of every political issue—and Carolyn Wheat knows what to do with characters and plot, as well. Whether Cass breaks out the way Kinsey Millhone and V. I. Warshawski have is another question. Being a woman might help, but she still has Perry Mason's legacy to overcome.

• **John J. Malone.** After Perry Mason, and before television, there was Malone,

Arthur Train's homespun Ephraim Tutt, as depicted by Arthur William Brown in The Saturday Evening Post.

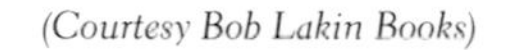
(Courtesy Bob Lakin Books)

- **Paul Biegler.** When Robert Traver wrote *Anatomy of a Murder* in 1954, he wanted to show the day-to-day ups and downs of a murder trial. Forty years later, his technique is still successful. Biegler, a worn-out ex-district attorney, is the right combination of fictional sleuth and real-life lawyer, and the puzzle is impressive. Best yet, this is one of those books that wasn't ruined by Hollywood in 1959's movie version. Jimmy Stewart has rarely been better, and the way he stares at the marvelously trampy Lee Remick, who may or may not have been raped, sends shivers through viewers.

"Chicago's noisiest and most noted criminal lawyer." The books, written by Craig Rice (a pseudonym of Georgianna Rice), were popular in the 1940s, and help to show how Mason's success arrested development in the subgenre. Malone is even more of a character than Mason. He is fat, red-faced, smokes too much, drinks too much, and is preoccupied with his fees. On the other hand, he sounds a lot like a real lawyer. When was the last time Perry Mason ever insisted on being paid?

Above: George Murphy (Jake Justus), Carole Landis (Helene Justus), and Pat O'Brien (John J. Malone) brought Craig Rice's funloving Chicago trio to the big screen in Having Wonderful Crime *(1946).*
Below: James Stewart played Paul Biegler in the film adaptation of Anatomy of a Murder, *here with Ben Gazzara.*

THE THIRD DEGREE: He Who Must Be Obeyed

The theme of this book, as anyone who has managed to get this far has noticed, is that the American fictional detective is a unique sort, whether of the hard-boiled, traditional, police or lawyer variety.

Yet there is one area where the British have a monopoly on being unique, and it isn't Sherlock Holmes and it isn't Peter Wimsey. Holmes, for all his greatness, is Poe's C. Auguste Dupin with an English accent, while Wimsey and his cohorts have their counterpart in Philo Vance. In fact, the British affront to American honor comes in an area that an American invented and that an American perfected. Perry Mason is as much a legend as Holmes, but there are no lawyers in the American canon quite like John Mortimer's Horace Rumpole.

This is a serious matter. Stop for a moment and consider Rumpole, especially as played by Leo McKern in the English television series shown in this country on public television. Rumpole is a professional. Rumpole has a sense of humor. Rumpole's cases rarely revolve around the cryptic and esoteric, as so many of his countrymen's do. Breaking and entering is breaking and entering, which is the sort of crime that doesn't involve slow acting poisons injected with pygmy blow darts. Rumpole defends anyone who can pay him, whether guilty or not—and he has a decided preference for the underdog. Save for his eccentricities, which are as English as a London fog, Rumpole would fit nicely with the other American detectives chronicled here. He is such a marvelous character, whether muttering under his breath at his wife or sipping a glass of Chateau Thames Embankment or playing the ingenue during a trial (a neat trick for the crusty-looking McKern), that he deserves to be an American.

Yet Rumpole is English. This simple statement says a lot about the way other Americans view (and consequently write about) lawyers. It says a lot about the differences in the two legal systems, and how Americans view those differences. It says a lot about how American lawyers view their profession. Mortimer, a lawyer himself, pokes fun at the British legal system in a way that is hard to imagine for an American lawyer who is writing a book about a fictional attorney. It also says a lot that Rumpole is not even considered to be a detective by most critics (either American or British). His name is noticeably absent in many of the most respected references, ostensibly because his pieces have very little traditional detecting in them. The puzzle hardly exists in Rumpole, which should make him even more attractive, especially to

EXAMINING THE CLUES

Erle Stanley Gardner was not only a prolific writer of Perry Mason stories, but also of Doug Selby stories, Donald Lam and Bertha Cool stories (twenty-nine novels), and nonfiction on topics ranging from travel to the environment. But next to the Mason stories, Gardner's most treasured project was The Court of Last Resort, which lasted from 1948 to 1958. Its purpose was to convince the authorities to reopen criminal cases where men and women had been wrongly convicted. Gardner put together a panel of volunteer experts in the various aspects of criminology, who went over the cases looking for flaws in the evidence that would merit reversing a verdict. Gardner wrote seventy-five articles for *Argosy* magazine describing his court, and helped NBC produce a television version of the court in 1957. In the series, which dramatized a season's worth of cases, Gardner was played by actor Paul Birch, apparently the only time Birch appeared in a prime time television series.

Americans. If character is all, there is more than enough of Rumpole to go around.

But Rumpole is more than a funny face. His stories, short novels and television plays are amusing and entertaining, but they are also revealing. They offer a glimpse of the underside of the Anglo-American justice system in ways that few others on either side of the Atlantic do—or seem to want to do. It's much easier to write about super-lawyers who can be played in the movies by stars like Harrison Ford, complete with gratuitous nude scenes, lots of cursing and enough stab-in-the-back power politics to fuel a vendetta for a century. This is the less than desirable side of Mason's legacy, both Randolph and Perry. They were so good and so successful that there was little incentive for those who came later to compete with them on their turf. Although some writers did (and they are noted in the section above), many others opted for an easier path—the glitzy, seductive world depicted on television programs like "L.A. Law" and in books like *The Firm*. There's nothing that could be called wrong with the choice that these writers made, but in many respects their books are as unreal as those of Philo Vance, even if they were written by lawyers. Most attorneys do not sleep with beautiful women in their offices or plot the destinies of huge conglomerates or defend political activists who have been repressed by the decadent capitalist system. Most lawyers draw up wills and contracts while refusing to answer a direct question with a direct answer.

Most lawyers are not glamorous, and neither is their work. This is a point that is almost always overlooked in the fictional world of the lawyer. One reason is that the people who are supposed to know about these things claim that the masses wouldn't be interested if the situation weren't glamorous. This is silly—baseball is popular with tens of millions, and it often has as much glamour as an old tennis shoe. Execution makes something interesting, not situation. It is also not the real reason. Most writers, faced with a choice between creating a character who works out of a nondescript office block and defends shoplifters, and creating one with a suite on the one hundredth floor of a high-rise, a blonde secretary, and a caseload that reads like the "Playboy Advisor" will choose the latter every time. This is the other crucial difference from the Rumpole stories. Americans may hate lawyers, but they also respect and envy them because they are perceived as being wealthy and glamorous. What mother doesn't want her child to grow up to be one?

This is how that system works. One of the television networks made a big deal about a lawyer show in the late 1980s called "Shannon's Deal." This program, it claimed, was going to be real and gritty and authentic. So what did the network come up with?

A disillusioned corporate lawyer (who just happened to have a gambling problem) with a cute, wise-cracking secretary, and a jazz-oriented score. This is hardly breaking new ground.

In his way, Mortimer is as naturalistic as Dashiell Hammett. Rumpole reminds the reader that there is more to the scales of justice than murderers, rapists, and drug dealers standing at the dock, even though they seem to be the only ones on trial in every book, television program and movie. The Rumpole stories are often about second-story men who have never used a gun in their lives, pickpockets whose forte is stealth and not violence, and extended families for whom crime is a way of life, just as other families go into farming or selling shoes. Best yet, Rumpole doesn't always get them off. They are, after all, professional criminals, and professional criminals commit crimes. Even Mason, forced to defend someone who used a gun to make a living, might have suffered a conviction every once in a while.

THE SOLUTION: The Case of the Television Lawyer

In television, nothing succeeds like success. That's why if one network has a hit with a certain kind of show, every network (including the original one) piles on that kind of show. In the late 1950s, Westerns were king. From the three networks combined there were, on average, almost thirty such programs a season between 1958 and 1961, and in 1958, eight of the top ten rated shows were Westerns. In the early 1980s, the networks were obsessed with glitzy soap operas like "Dallas" and "Dynasty." During the 1984–85 season, "Dallas" and "Dynasty" were the two top-rated shows, and three other nighttime soaps were in the Nielsen top twelve. More than a dozen similar programs, most of them expensive, hour-long shows, were on network schedules at the start of that season. Also typical was the trend in the early 1990s, after the success of "Beverly Hills, 90210," when every network raced to offer programs about wealthy and glamorous—yet sensitive—young people.

Raymond Burr as television's Perry Mason faces off with hapless district attorney Hamilton Burger (William Talman).

Yet television has never embraced lawyer shows the way

it has almost every other genre. This is even more contradictory given the tremendous success of "Perry Mason," which is not only the most successful lawyer show in television history but one of the most successful shows of any kind in the medium's almost fifty years of existence. In the entire history of television, there have been fewer than three dozen dramas featuring lawyers going about their work. The old Dumont network had just one in its decade of existence, and the new Fox network has had just one in its six years on the air. Even more amazing is that more than a quarter of these lawyer shows were of the "L.A. Law" variety, hatched in the late 1980s to take advantage of the ground blazed by the sex-and-legal-pad atmosphere of "L.A. Law." Given that another couple were dramatizations of actual court cases, and that several more were police dramas which just happened to feature lawyers, it turns out that in the forty-six years of network television, there have been fewer than two dozen programs starring defense lawyers trying to get their clients acquitted. Of these two dozen or so, only four lasted three seasons or longer: "Perry Mason," "The Defenders" (CBS, 1961–65), "Matlock" (NBC/ABC, 1986–), and "Owen Marshall, Counsellor at Law" (ABC, 1971–74). This is not what could be called a role of honor.

These are astounding figures, even in a medium like television where the life span of a series is often measured in weeks and not seasons. Despite the incredible success of "Perry Mason"—one of only four mystery dramas to last nine seasons or more—the networks have had little enthusiasm for the genre. To get an idea of

"Owen Marshall, Counselor-at-Law" was one of only four lawyer programs on television to last more than three seasons. In it, Arthur Hill, who played Marshall, did his best Marcus Welby impression.

how astonishing this is, imagine "Dallas" and "Dynasty" finishing one and two in the ratings and not generating any spinoffs or imitators—no "Knots Landing," no "Colbys," no "Falcon Crest."

Yet this is what the networks did, and what they have continued to do. There are any number of reasons for their failure to follow up on the success of "Perry Mason"—the cost of doing an hour-long series is one, as is the difficulty of providing material for a weekly, hour-long series and the aforementioned lack of characters from other mediums to transfer to television—but two stand out. First, Mason creator Erle Stanley Gardner demanded (and received) creative control over the television series, something that the networks like about as much as public affairs programming in prime time. Don't be so sure that someone, somewhere, is not still holding a grudge about Gardner's insistence that the television Mason bear more than a passing resemblance to his creation. Gardner was so determined to retain control of his character that he once turned down a reported $1 million offer for the television rights to the character.

Gardner had been burned once, when Hollywood made six Mason movies in the 1930s, and he wasn't going to see his character desecrated again. The Mason movies, starring a journeyman named Warren William, had little to do with the books and more to do with the countless and profitable serials and series ("Boston Blackie," "Crime Doctor") that Hollywood churned out. In the second film, *The Case of the Curious Bride*, Della Street is renamed Claire Dodd for one of those reasons known only to moguls.

Warren William, not the most memorable Perry Mason, in the first Mason movie, The Case of the Howling Dog *(1934).*

Mason and Claire get married in *The Case of the Velvet Claws*. Gardner was convinced the same thing would happen once more—especially after he saw some sample scripts. Gardner wrote to a friend: "It is the god-damndest assortment of crap ever witnessed. Mason becomes a smart-aleck, a wisecracker, a man who looks upon murder only as an opportunity for a new quip."

The second reason is the most important. Mason, despite all of the clichés he invented, does not fit any of television's clichés. The shows are talky, with little action. The characters are not young, glamorous or beautiful, and there are no cute kids waiting in the wings. There is no sex and barely any hint of sex. The climax is not a car chase, but a scene in a courtroom where people shout at each other. Mason and his friends and colleagues do not have any hang-ups, eccentricities or quirks. In other words, they have almost nothing in common with almost every other character to turn up in a television show since 1946.

This was similar to the obstacles the producers of "Murder, She Wrote" faced when they were struggling with CBS executives to get it on the air in 1984. "The show's all talk, there's no action, it's slow," said Richard Levinson, one of its creators. "It features 'mature performers,' and it's a whodunit. The smart money in town didn't give it a prayer." In many respects, "Murder, She Wrote" is the same program as "Perry Mason," with Jessica Fletcher's persistent snooping substituting for Mason's legal wheeling and dealing. Yet the smart money kissed off Jessica. The networks concentrated on the usual assortment—nineteen, as near as it can be figured—of detective shows in 1984, all of which had the requisite car chases, gorgeous women and sexy detectives. These nineteen included such all-time greats as "Riptide," "Hawaiian Heat," and "Cover Up." None of them are still on the air. Whether this made an impression on the smart money is doubtful.

And "Perry Mason" is still around, too. It has bested so many other shows that the smart money bet on that it's hard to figure out why the smart money hasn't changed its mind. It's one thing when the popularity of "Perry Mason" forced the cancellation of something called "The Roaring Twenties," a newspaper detective show that ABC threw up against it in 1960 and 1961. But it's something else entirely when "Perry Mason" not only beat the venerable "Bonanza," which was on NBC at the same time as "Mason" in 1959 and 1960, but forced it to another night. During the height of the Western craze, "Bonanza" never finished higher than seventeen in the Nielsens when it was opposite "Perry Mason"; "Perry Mason" was ten and sixteen. In its first season on Sunday, away from Perry, Paul Drake and Della Street, and where it would become a national institution over the next two decades, "Bonanza" was the second most highly rated show in the country.

So much for the smart money. As mentioned previously, television exists not to sell television programs, but to sell the products advertised in its commercials. One day, perhaps, television executives will realize that a courtroom drama can sell just as much soap as yet another squealing, shoot-'em-up starring a couple of actors who will not be remembered in three seasons. Until then, there will always be reruns of "Perry Mason."

THE RAP SHEET: Spies

M.O.: The spy, despite his shady background, deserves a role in the discussion of the American fictional detective. Too often, like lawyers, spies are not accorded their own category because it is said their stories don't always involve a puzzle. This is nit-picking. For one thing, this opinion overlooks the classical puzzle nature in many spy stories (that is, to be fair, often obscured by the spy atmosphere). For another, more important, reason, it overlooks a basic principle of the American fictional detective. The puzzle isn't the most important thing; character is. And spy stories are often about little more than character, whether they are tales of violence or analysis.

Perpetrators: Bill Granger's Devlin, television's Alexander Scott and Kelly Robinson, William F. Buckley's Blackford Oakes, Bill Ballinger's Joaquin Hawkes, Tom Clancy's Jack Ryan.

Aliases: Spook, clandestine operative, secret agent, mole, counterspy, agent provocateur.

The Spooks

6

"Admirable though he may be in terms of character and probity, the fact remains that, in his professional capacity, the spy is ipso facto a liar and a thief. He may be worse."

—ERIC AMBLER

When it comes to sneakiness, Americans always feel a little uncomfortable. This may be a difficult statement to accept for anyone who has lived through the past two decades, when the United States seemed to have a monopoly on skullduggery and underhandedness, but it is nonetheless true. It is a recurring theme in American national life, where Americans demand a level of honesty unmatched almost anywhere else in the world (even if they don't always live up to that standard). In what other country than the United States is it a felony to bribe a foreign government? Europeans, in particular, are often baffled by this approach. Many of them still have little idea why Richard Nixon was forced to resign, since their governments often commit crimes that make Nixon look like a third-string bench warmer. The French, for instance, once sank a ship operated by an environmental group, killing a couple of people in the process—for no other reason than the ship was used to monitor French nuclear testing.

This attitude is equally as true when it comes to American literature. The Europeans love writers like Thomas Hardy and Marcel Proust, whose style is as sophisticated, complicated and devious as any conspiracy dreamed up by the CIA. Americans, on the other hand, like their literature direct and to the point as created by writers like Twain, Hemingway and Hammett. There is never a doubt as to where they stand, no hidden meanings or messages to decipher. One reason why the famous Flitcraft parable in *The Maltese Falcon*—where Sam Spade describes his search for a man who abandoned his family—is so famous is because it was an unexpectedly circuitous way to make a point in that sort of novel.

It should come as no surprise, then, that the greatest practitioners of the spy subgenre, and the greatest fictional spies, are not Americans. Except for James Fenimore Cooper, who invented the spy in 1821 in a book called *The Spy,* few Americans have distinguished themselves. Joseph Conrad's *Secret Agent,* the first modern spy novel, was the work of a Pole who emigrated to France and then lived in England. John le Carré and his extraordinarily nondescript George Smiley are English, as are Eric Ambler's legion of traveling salesmen who always seem to be in the wrong Balkan country at the wrong time. There is a subtlety and a level of dissembling in these books, as the spy must peel away layer upon layer upon layer in a way that is almost impossible for Americans to understand. Charles Latimer, the detective story author who is the hero of *A Coffin for Dimitrios* (1939) shows a patience and a diligence that few Americans would understand, let alone practice.

By contrast, consider the Continental Op short story, "This King Business (1928)," which tells of the Op's travels to a small, unimportant Balkan country to find a missing American heir. The Op, of course, does not resort to any Ambler-like machinations: he charges straight ahead, and the only thing he sidesteps are bullets. There is an attempted coup, some chases and a number of murders, beatings and scenes of torture. In the usual bloody pulp climax, the Op rescues the heir (who was involved in some sort of hare-brained scheme to make him king) and restores some semblance of democratic government to the country.

"This King Business" is not the best Op tale, although it foreshadows the American-European corruption theme of *The Maltese Falcon.* It is darkly humorous in a number of places (and could even be read as a satire of the spy and intrigue stories popular at the time). Among its comedic features are a sanctimonious U.S. embassy official who runs the embassy in the country. "They'd certainly rob him," he tells the Op about the two villains in the story and their relationship to the missing heir. "I'm positive they're robbing him. But I don't think they would. Perhaps he isn't acquainted with them." There is even some skullduggery involved, but no more than is present in any of the other Op stories about gangsters in San Francisco, such as "The Big Knockover" or "$106,000 Blood Money." The themes in "This King Business" are the themes Hammett wrote about his entire life: power and the lengths people will go to get it, and professionalism. Hammett's gangsters (in this case, the coup plotters) want power, and only the Op's professionalism stands in their way. Ambler's characters, on the other hand, are constantly thrust into situations in which they are powerless. This makes them victims, much like the client the Op rescues in "This King Business." This powerlessness provides many of the thrills in Ambler's books—which, after all, are almost universally referred to as thrillers.

Even James Bond, the world's most famous spy, is much more European than he seems. The surface Bond is little different from any of the *Black Mask* hard-boiled heroes—quick with his fists, quick with his gun, and quick with women. In fact, the Bond of the movies (who is slightly more melodramatic and progressively more comic than the Bond of the books) is a dead ringer for Erle Stanley Gardner's Ed Jenkins, who starred in a number of cliff-hanging, gimmick-laden serials in *Black Mask*. But underneath all of this flash is a darker, more insidious world of half-truths, quarter-truths and lies. They may have become clichés in the forty years since Bond's first appearance, but that doesn't detract from their ultimate meaning. Bond's boss doesn't have a name, but a letter. Bond doesn't have a name, but a number. Bond's intelligence agency doesn't have a name, but initials—when it is referred to at all. The British government acknowledges that Bond is a commander in the Royal Navy, but not an intelligence agent—and then claims that his legitimate job is as a traveling salesman for a British export firm that doesn't export anything. The layers start to pile up on each other.

This sort of deceit is as alien to the American mind as a baseball game played in the snow. The United States didn't even have a national spy agency until after World War II started, when the Office of Strategic Services was formed. After the war ended, the OSS was closed, and the Central Intelligence Agency replaced it.

Robert Culp (Kelly Robinson) and Bill Cosby (Alexander Scott) in the groundbreaking television show, "I Spy."

EXAMINING THE CLUES

William F. Buckley never used a pseudonym for his Blackford Oakes spy novels, which is extremely unusual in his social set. The literati don't like to put their own names on their genre work for fear of embarrassment. For instance, a one-time poet laureate of England, Sir Cecil Day Lewis, wrote about the extremely eccentric Nigel Strangeways

using the name Nicholas Blake. But Buckley, who has never pretended not to be a snob, had a more important reason for using his own name. Buckley, the conservative's conservative, wanted everyone to notice the political content of the Oakes books. They manage to refight every major ideological battle of the Cold War. Not between the Soviet Union and the United States, of course, but between the American left and right. The Soviets don't come off nearly as badly as the American left does. But what else would a reader expect from Buckley?

The CIA is the U.S. equivalent of the British Secret Service—each runs spy organizations in foreign countries. The U.S. Secret Service, despite its name, is a domestic police agency that is part of the Treasury Department. It catches counterfeiters and protects presidents. It does not do any spying. The United States doesn't have any sort of government secrecy act (even Britain, the most open of other Western countries, does), and ex-U.S. spies are as apt to write tell-all books as are retired film stars. A super-secret spy agency has always seemed to be a peculiarity in the United States, where openness is a political trait valued above almost anything else. It's almost impossible to imagine an American spy agency kidnapping a foreign criminal in the way the Israelis went to Argentina to snatch Adolph Eichmann. In fact, the few times U.S. agencies have attempted something like that, they have failed. Does anyone remember the CIA plot to hire the Mafia to kill Fidel Castro by poisoning his cigars?

U.S. fictional spies lack the cunning and finesse of their European counterparts because Americans would much prefer to solve problems by kicking in the door with guns blazing. The Op is in his Balkan country for less than a day when he has to throttle a native soldier trying to kill the heir. This is a reflection of the American psyche that values direct action—the naturalism reflected in the work of Hemingway and Hammett—more than anything else. The Bond movies (despite the comic book nature of many of the plots) are an excellent example of this. In *Dr. No,* the first, Bond is closest to the Bond of the book—a hard, bitter man who trusts no one and who thinks nothing of double-crossing anyone, including a woman. But when Roger Moore replaced Sean Connery as Bond a decade later, in films like *Live and Let Die* and *The Spy Who Loved Me,* the plots had discarded whatever subtlety there had been in favor of blowing things up. By this time, since the Bond movies were major box office hits in the United States, it made sense to give American audiences what they liked—and they liked lots of scenes of lots of things getting blown up.

This is why American spies are, for the most part, an undistinguished lot. The United States is probably the only country in the world where ex-Watergate conspirator E. Howard Hunt could have written and sold a successful series of spy novels, one of them featuring a forgettable CIA agent named Peter Ward. In one respect, Ward is not significant at all. The ten Ward books were hardly noticed at all when they were published as paperback originals in the mid-1960s, and probably wouldn't have attracted any attention later if Hunt, who supposedly worked for the CIA, hadn't been mixed up with Nixon's Watergate cover-up. Yet for all of their mediocrity, the Ward books are important because they are typical of the sort of American fictional spy who keeps popping up. These spies aren't meant to be pastiches of Bond, like Matt Helm, or parodies, like Maxwell Smart. They are meant to stand on their own. Hunt, writing as David St. John, seemed to know this. As long as the action keeps moving, it doesn't matter whether Ward is a plausible character or not, or whether the plot makes any sense at all. Hunt realized that if he threw in a couple of evil villains, some likely-sounding jargon, and just enough sex, he had a winner. His books feature lots of Chinese Communists, always referred to as Chicomms (shades of the Red Peril), glossy details of Ward's affair with a nightclub singer, and dozens of passages like this, from *Return to Vorkuta* (1965): "As far as he knew the addressee was notional, simply a drop box that served as the Headquarters end of his S/W link. The test letter contained no secret writing, but it implicitly informed Jim Hopwood that he was in Madrid, and told the S/W technicians how long his routine communications would be in transit." This may or may not be true, but it sounds like the truth, doesn't it?

(Courtesy Bob Lakin Books)

In fact, Hunt came closer than he probably knew to fashioning a uniquely American fictional spy. The secret was the use of passages like the one above, which had just enough truth in it to sound like the truth. This is the technique that Hammett discovered and that Chandler crusaded for—putting murder back in the hands of people who commit it for a reason. In this case, it was putting spying back in the hands of people who spy for a reason, and not, to paraphrase Chandler again, who spy only as a plot device, like Ambler's salesmen. This is how le Carré improved on Ambler, and it is something an insurance agent named Tom Clancy stumbled on in 1984. Clancy's method was so obscure that when he wrote a book about an intelligence analyst named Jack Ryan, the only publisher who would try it was almost as obscure as Clancy. *The Hunt for Red October* has since become the cornerstone of Clancy's authorial empire, and the advances he receives for his books rival those of Stephen King and Danielle Steele, who make more money with their writing than some small countries make with their entire economies.

The Ryan books, from *Red October* on, are fiction pure and simple, and Clancy is a terrific stylist only if the rest of the writing universe was made up of insurance agents. Yet Clancy has some-

Author Tom Clancy on the set of The Hunt for Red October.

how managed to inject a sense of naturalism and realism in his books that no one else had. Clancy just didn't include realistic-sounding passages, like Hunt did; he made them the basis for the entire novel. Clancy weaved technology and a documentary-style narrative in a way that no one had previously been successful with. This comes closer to what the American intelligence community is really like than any other fictional description ever has. It's not bombs and blondes, but the dull, tedious work of gathering and analyzing intelligence. William Colby, who ran the Central Intelligence Agency for Gerald Ford and was stuck with cleaning up after the spy scandals of the late 1960s and early 1970s, always insisted that episodes like the Castro business were an exception. "Today intelligence is an intellectual process of assembling information from press, radio, books and speeches," he told an interviewer during his tenure. "Which is why we're called the Central Intelligence Agency. All this information is centralized and studied by experts. And then there are electronics, computers, technology."

Clancy, through Ryan, found a way to make this gathering of information by such sterile means sound compelling. In truth, most U.S. spying consists of a guy in a white shirt and striped tie sitting at a desk poring over satellite photos. That's how, for example, the U.S. government knew Iraq was going to invade Kuwait in 1991. That's how, allowing for the technology of the time, the United States broke an important Japanese code in World War II. That's how the Union knew what the Confederacy was going to do at the Battle of Antietam in 1862. There were no clandestine meet-

EXAMINING THE CLUES

American television loves spy series, but only on its own terms. In the decade or so that encompassed the James Bond craze, network television aired almost two dozen spy series. Of that two dozen, almost all of them were spoofs or parodies like "The Man from U.N.C.L.E." or "The Wild, Wild West." The exceptions were shows like "Mission: Impossible," which had an element of unreality of its own. On the other hand, British television has almost always accepted spies for what they were. In that same period, the only BBC production that had its tongue placed anywhere near in its cheek was "The Avengers." The rest were hard, tough dramatic series like "Secret Agent," or the even more bizarre "The Prisoner."

Alec Baldwin as Jack Ryan in the missile bay of the submarine Red October *in* The Hunt for Red October *(1990).*

ings in the night, no showdowns with evil geniuses—just the plodding, sterile routine of intelligence work.[1] Yet Ryan is not sterile, and neither are his adventures. One reason is that Clancy has obeyed one of the cardinal rules of American detective fiction by making his character memorable. Jack Ryan is an Everyman who just happens to be a spy. He has a wife and kids and a dog and a station wagon, and in this respect he has much in common with Ambler's heroes. This was just different enough in this country to make it interesting. It is such an unusual concept for a fictional spy that Hollywood, faced with the dilemma of turning *Red October* into a movie, opted to play it safe and cast a bigger star in a supporting role than the star it chose to play Ryan. The film's producers couldn't believe a character like Ryan—who is not larger than life—could support the movie by himself.

The other reason Ryan is so successful is that there is an authenticity and a genuineness to the books that make up for a multitude of sins. It's why *Red October*, as silly as its plot sounds, is fascinating reading. A top-level Soviet submarine commander, the best of their best, is not going to defect with his sub because he is disillusioned with the system. He *is* the system, and fifty years of Soviet policy had been dedicated to keeping him and his kind happy. When the Soviet Union collapsed, it wasn't because the military was disenchanted, and subsequent developments have shown that they are more unhappy under the new regime than they were under the old. But this apparent contradiction is no

[1]Whether a government believes its intelligence or not is another story—which, as interesting as it may be, isn't part of this discussion.

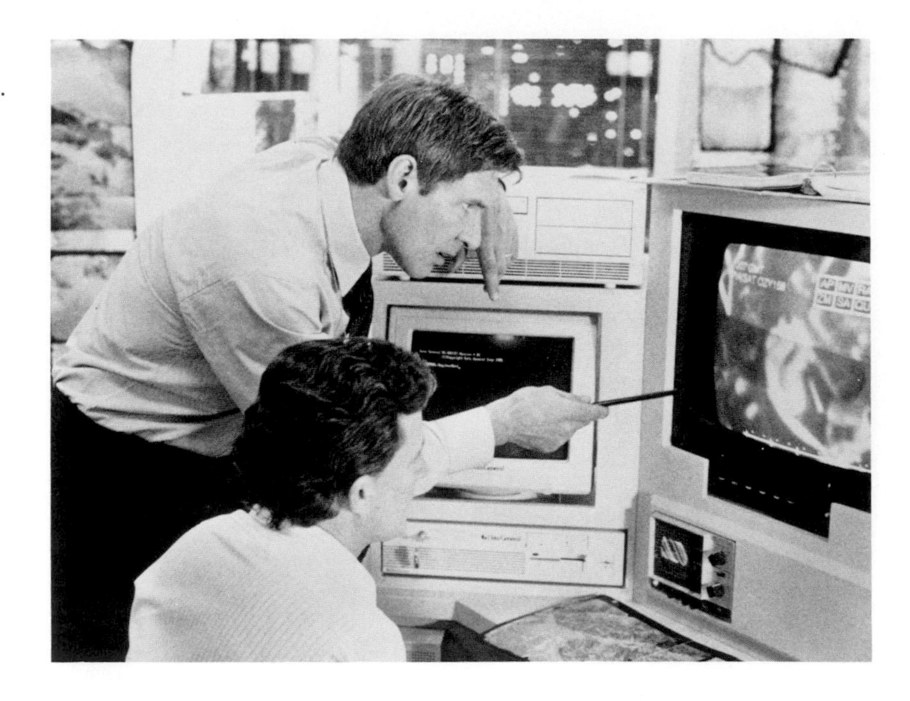

Harrison Ford took over the Ryan character in 1992's Patriot Games.

(Photograph by Merrick Morton, © Paramount Pictures Corporation)

problem for Clancy, who simply ignores it. Instead, he writes about nuclear sub docking procedures and guided missile destroyer radio communications and COMSUBLANT and ESM and LHF MAST lowerings. The plot may not be real, but the workings of the plot certainly seem plausible.

This is also why Ryan did not go away when the Soviet Union did. He is an Everyman who works for a system, and there will always be a threat to the system requiring his services, whether the threat is from drug dealers *(A Clear and Present Danger)* or foreign terrorists *(Patriot Games)*. There will always be a need for a fellow in a white shirt and tie to pore over satellite photos. In one respect, Ryan is as unreal as Peter Ward, as different from a real spook as Philip Marlowe is from a real private eye. But in another, more important respect, he is as real as Marlowe is. Both are, to use Chandler's analogy, honorable men in an unhonorable world, and those streets are plenty mean. Do not be mistaken, though. Clancy is not Chandler or Hammett; in fact, he is barely on par with the best of the second-teamers who followed Hammett and Chandler. Someday, perhaps, a more talented writer than Clancy will turn Clancy's formula—for that is what he has discovered—into something original. When this happens, some author will finally do for the American fictional spy what Hammett and Chandler did for the hard-boiled detective, what Jack Webb did for the police procedural, and what John le Carré has already done for the British fictional spy. It is something worth waiting for.

MASS MEDIA: A Spies Sampler

• **Alexander Scott and Kelly Robinson.** The duo who played in "I Spy" for three seasons on NBC starting in 1965 are already famous for breaking the television color barrier. Bill Cosby, who played Scott, was the first black to star in a dramatic network series. This is all well and good, but it overshadows another important, albeit more subtle, achievement. Scott and Robinson were not only not very good spies, but they were constantly questioning why they were being asked to go around the world on secret missions for a government that didn't seem to know what it was doing. This was a remarkably subversive attitude, often disguised by the low-key banter between the two men. Anyone who remembers "I Spy" as glamorous should go back and watch it again. Creator Sheldon Leonard sent his characters all over the world, but their assignments were far from glamorous. The two men spent most of the their time getting beat up, tied up, or both. They rarely knew what was going on, whether with their bosses or with their assignments. Their degree of dissatisfaction was unusual in spies, who are almost always painted as fierce patriots.

• **Devlin.** This hero, also known as The November Man, stars in a number of books by former Chicago newspaperman Bill Granger. Devlin, though, has never broken out the way his contemporary, Jack Ryan, has. There have been no Devlin movies, and the Devlin books, while respectable sellers, have never approached the Ryan levels. In one respect, this is hard to understand. There is a dark, somber atmosphere in the Devlin books that is missing from the Ryan stories. To add insult to injury, Granger is a much better writer than Clancy. But Granger made a big mistake when he created Devlin, and this almost certainly accounts for his failure to cross out of the subgenre: Devlin is a whiner. It's one thing for a spy to question his job, but it's another to hate it the way Devlin hates his. He sounds like a stenographer trying to find clean pantyhose on Monday morning. It's very difficult to care about whether he solves his puzzle (for his assignments are often almost traditional in their structure) when he spends as much time as he does bellyaching about the raw deal he gets from his agency.

• **Joaquin Hawkes.** Hawkes was another of the seeming hundreds of spies who popped up in five paperback originals in 1965 and 1966 in the wake of James Bond's success. Hawkes, though, was a little different.

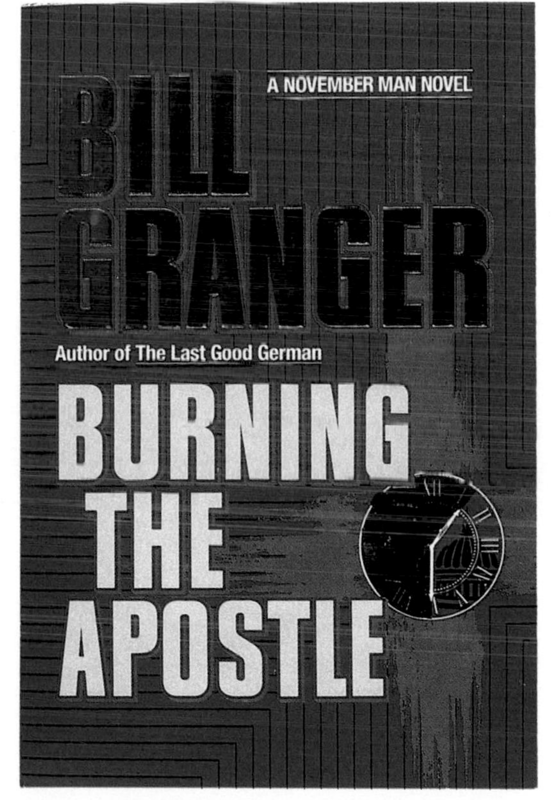

(Courtesy Warner Books)

Creator Bill S. Ballinger did two things that make Hawkes more than a footnote to his era. It certainly isn't the writing, which is average, or the plots, which are the usual spy fiction assortment of thrills and spills. First, Hawkes is part Nez Percé Indian (the same tribe made famous by their dogged resistance to the U.S. Army against overwhelming odds in the last part of the nineteenth century). There have not been a lot of Indian fictional detectives, let alone spies. Second, Hawkes works Southeast Asia for the CIA at the same time the United States is escalating its involvement in Vietnam. He travels Indonesia, China, Laos, Cambodia and Thailand, and he does all of those things the American government was insisting it wasn't doing. Ballinger's foresight is enough to make some readers wonder if he knew something no one else did.

THE THIRD DEGREE: Calling Mr. Moto

The most fascinating American fictional spy was not even an American. In fact, I. A. Moto often worked against American interests, his political philosophy often conflicted with that of the American system, and he once told a colleague that he considered himself a fascist.

Yet the character created by John P. Marquand, who was as American as his Boston background, is not easily dismissed.

In 1935, when the first Mr. Moto, *No Hero,* appeared, the United States and Japan had been diplomatically feuding since 1931 over the Japanese invasion of Manchuria, and Japan's subsequent bullying of China. War between the world's two largest Pacific powers didn't seem inevitable at that time, six years before Pearl Harbor, but it didn't seem far-fetched, either. The two countries, who had been allies in World War I against Germany, disagreed over any number of issues in addition to China during the decade before World War II—the size of each country's navy, Japanese expansion in the Pacific, and Japanese trade policies. Their relationship had deteriorated to such a point that when Amelia Earhart disappeared over the Pacific Ocean during her

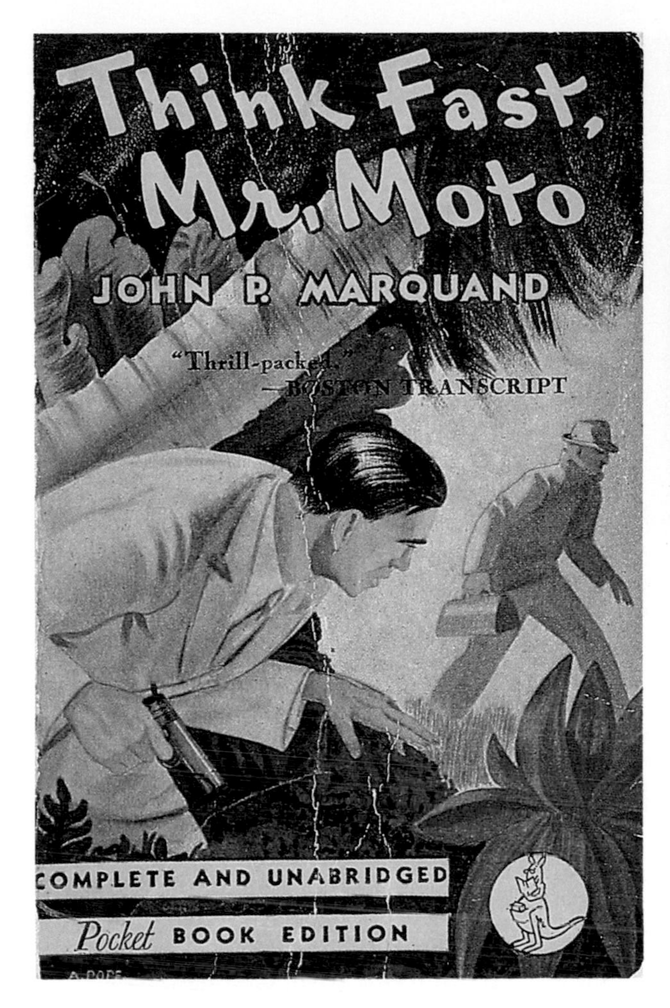

Peter Lorre's Mr. Moto in action on Danger Island *(1939).*

(Courtesy Bob Lakin Books)

around-the-world flight in 1937, some contemporary accounts said the Japanese shot her plane down. Mr. Moto fit, in almost every respect, this U.S. perception of what Japan was like in the 1930s. He was serious, sly, cunning and talented—the newest and most improved version of the Yellow Peril. He was the top intelligence agent for the Japanese government, which meant that he was stirring up trouble in China at the same time that U.S. policy was to get the Japanese out of the country. There is no logical reason, considering the equation six decades later, why Mr. Moto should have been so popular.

Yet he was. Marquand wrote five books in seven years, including four in the 1935–38 period. If the author is remembered today at all, it is not for the Pulitzer Prize he won in 1937 for the novel *The Late George Apley*, but for the Moto books. Hollywood embraced Mr. Moto with even more fervor. It featured the character

John P. Marquand (center) on the set of The Late George Apley, *with Ronald Colman and Vanessa Brown.*
(Photofest)

in eight films between 1937 and 1939, all with first-rate casts and competent direction. The films were powered by the offbeat casting of Hungarian-born Peter Lorre as Mr. Moto, who needed only glasses and slick-backed hair to look insidious.[2] Something was going on here, and it had little to do with the actions of a Japanese detective.

Of course, much of the credit for Mr. Moto's success had little to do with Marquand or Mr. Moto. It had a lot to do with the success of the most famous Oriental detective, Charlie Chan. Chan's first book appearance was in 1925, and the first of the Chan movie series was made in 1931.[3] Chan showed that the American public would accept a hero who wasn't a white, Anglo-Saxon Protestant. This meant that publishers and producers, who always get their best ideas by copying something that was successful, rushed to copy Chan. The Moto character gave them that opportunity. The Mr. Moto stories were serialized in *The Saturday Evening Post,* which also showcased Nero Wolfe, Perry Mason and Chan. The fact that Mr. Moto's political background was not as

---

[2]The Moto of the movies is a more important character than the Moto who appears in the books. The former is the central character, and the plot revolves around him. In the books, Mr. Moto is usually a secondary character who moves in and out of the story, "arranging things" (as he describes it).

[3]This does include other less well-known Oriental heroes such as the Chinese Mr. Wong, who, played by Boris Karloff, was featured in six films between 1938 and 1940, and is almost unknown today. Mr. Wong and his ilk were "B" productions, cheapies made by smaller studios to cash in on Chan.

reputable as Chan's was a small problem that could be overlooked until the shooting started on December 7, 1941. After that, Mr. Moto became as much a relic as Arthur B. Reeve's Professor Craig Kennedy, the Scientific Detective, or Raoul Whitfield's Filipino private eye, Jo Gar. The one book and the one movie that featured Mr. Moto that appeared after World War II vanished quickly.

Although this copying of Chan may account for Mr. Moto's success, it doesn't come close to explaining how and why Marquand came up with a series of books starring a hero who was a spy for a country that was hostile to the United States. This sort of thing certainly didn't happen during the Cold War, when spies like Mickey Spillane's Tiger Mann were shooting Commies instead of joining the party. Part of the rationalization may stem from any writer's desire to make money, and a Chan clone offered Marquand that opportunity. He had spent two decades as a

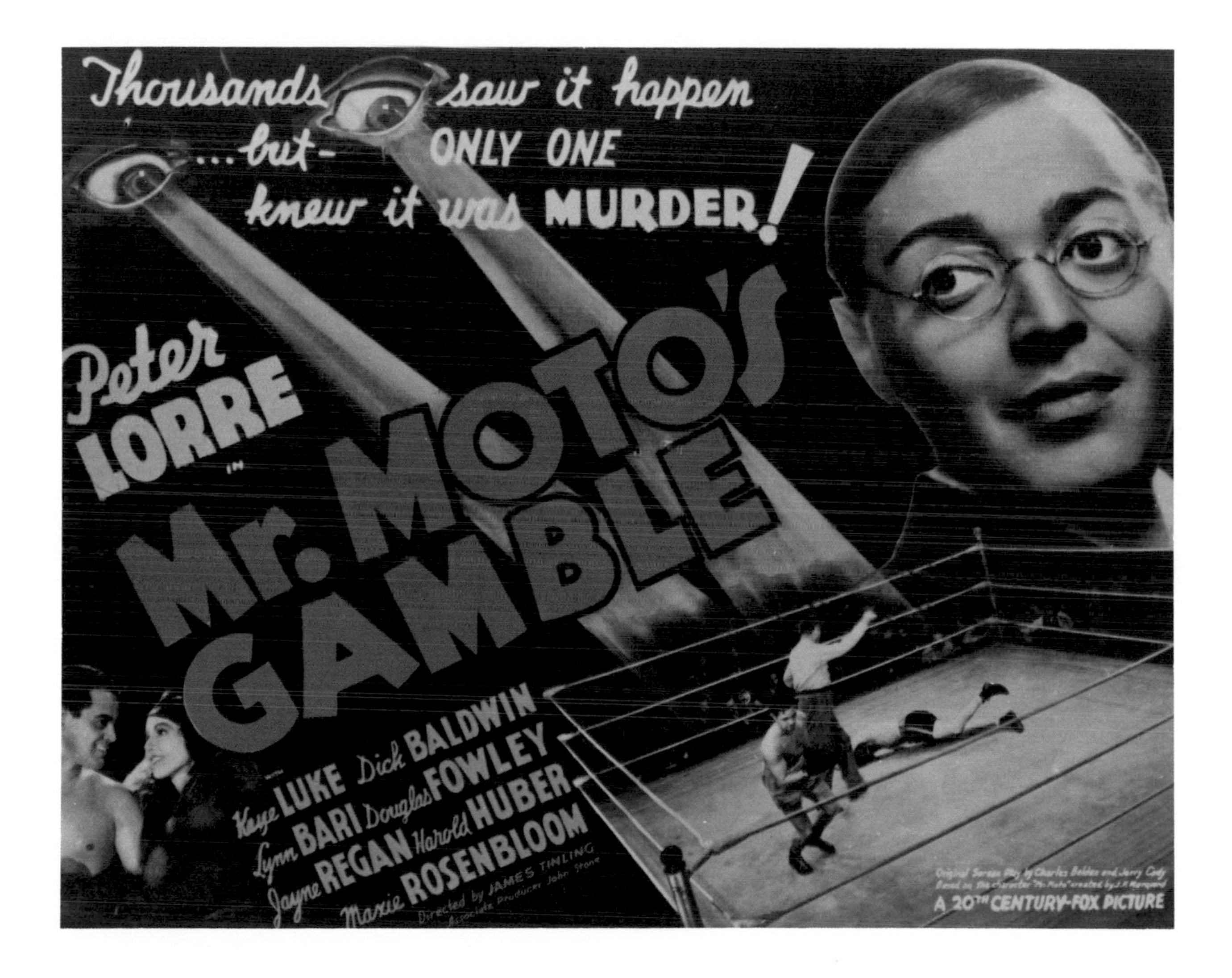

newspaperman and advertising copy writer, hardly the kind of jobs that paid for an early retirement in pre-Depression America (or in post-Depression America, for that matter). He sold dozens of tales to the slick magazines like *The Post* and *Collier's* during that era—not only for the money, says one of his biographers, but to gain revenge on his family. They thought Marquand's slick work was beneath someone of their class (as, Marquand claimed occasionally, he did too). Don't forget, also, it's a common practice for aspiring mainstream writers to try their hand at genre fiction first to learn the intricacies of plotting, characterization and the like.

The key, though, may be in Marquand's approach to all of his fiction. *George Apley*, his Pulitzer winner, is always described as a bitter social commentary about the New England elite. Most of the rest of Marquand's non-Moto work is from this same vein, and there are almost as many similar references in the Moto books. Mr. Moto is always meeting cynical and disillusioned Occidentals who have a change of heart after watching the sage Mr. Moto. It is always difficult to guess at a writer's meaning sixty years after the fact, and it is often not fair to the writer. But there are two ways to look at what Marquand did. The first is that he was playing a joke on his readers, publishers and the movie world. The second was that he was serious, and that Mr. Moto was a warning to the West to get ready for a December 7 that was inevitable.

There is probably some truth to the second explanation. Marqaund traveled extensively in the Far East during the 1930s, and took a trip to China during one of the periodic border disputes between China and Japan in the mid-1930s. But the first reason, though more distasteful, is probably closer to the truth. Mr. Moto was likely nothing more than the creation of a superbly cynical mind, who offered them their Charlie Chan knockoff on two levels. On one level, Mr. Moto was a self-effacing copy of Chan who goes around saying things like "you are so clever and I am so very stupid." This was what Americans wanted to believe. On the other, he was a dangerous, evil man whose obsequiousness hid his decidedly un-American beliefs—the racial superiority of the Japanese and his country's desire to establish its "divine hegemony" over the Pacific Ocean and its territories. This would not have been the first time an American author has mocked his audience, and it's in keeping with Marquand's attitude toward the Moto books. It's also in keeping with Marquand's attitude toward people. His family life was a mess (married several times, with several more affairs), and one biographer says he treated his children as badly as he treated his wives.

It took a bitter, cynical and disillusioned man to write *George Apley*, and it would be expecting too much to think he would have been any less cynical or bitter when writing about Mr. Moto.

THE SOLUTION: The Spy Who Loved Me

There have always been women traditional detectives, and there have recently been a number of women hard-boiled detectives, as well as women lawyers and women police officers.

What there have never been are women spies (as well as spies—with a few exceptions—from ethnic and racial groups other than white, Anglo-Saxon Protestants, but that's a story for a different time and place).

This is unusual, both today—when the hard-boiled women are becoming critical and popular favorites—and in years past, when women were the backbone of the traditional detective subgenre not only in this country, but in Britain. It would have seemed almost inevitable that someone, somewhere, sometime, would have created a women spy. But save for a handful of exceptions, such as television's "Scarecrow and Mrs. King" (which depended as much on its suburban matron theme as it did on espionage) and Dorothy Gilman's pleasantly unbelievable Mrs. Polifax, that hasn't been the case. For instance, in a listing of fictional sleuths from 1878 to 1975 compiled by noted mystery bibliophile Allen J. Hubin, twenty-four American spies had their own book series, and none of them were women.[4]

It's much more difficult to figure out why there haven't been any women spies. Certainly a number of stereotypes seem obvious: Women aren't believable in the rough and tumble world of espionage; the male writers who dominated the spy field wrote about what they knew, and that didn't include women; the social and political climate of the Cold War era, when most U.S. spies first appeared, precluded the appearance of a woman who didn't stay home, raise babies, and cook dinner. But these explanations don't go deep enough. Believability has never been high on the list of required characteristics in spy novels, or James Bond never would have been successful (as would none of the imitators who followed in the shadow of his martini glass). Besides, the spy world isn't, and doesn't need to be, as rough and tumble as most writers make it out to be. Ambler's heroes could as easily have been women as men. The plots don't often demand any physical derring-do that

---

[4]The Hubin List, which appears in *The Mystery Story* (The Mystery Library, 1976), is a work that defies description. It lists more than nine hundred detectives, classed by year of first appearance, character name, type of detective, country of origin, whether paperback or hardcover original, number of books, and author. It is something that only Allen J. Hubin, editor of *The Armchair Detective*, is capable of compiling.

requires a man's upper body strength. There is rarely any shooting in the George Smiley books, and it wouldn't take much imagination to turn George into a woman. Le Carré, to be fair, is one of the few spy authors who realizes that the secret service business isn't for men only. Many of Smiley's colleagues are women, and Smiley's relationship with his estranged wife helps to turn the novels into something more than genre fiction.

Then, too, male writers have always written about women, just as women have always written about men. It's a common practice in other genres (including mainstream, romance and literary fiction) as well as in the detective subgenres. For instance, Dell Shannon (pen name for Elizabeth Linington) wrote about Lt. Luis Mendoza of the Los Angeles Police Department. The British spy Modesty Blaise, who first appeared in a comic book before getting novel and movie lives, was created by a man, Peter O'Donnell. And Blaise was at the height of her popularity during the Cold War, smashing spy rings instead of making meat loaf (although how many remember her today is a good question).

There have been few female American spies because no one ever thought of inventing them, whether writer, publisher or producer. This is not as simple (or as revolutionary) as it sounds. The vagaries of detective fiction run in cycles, no matter what the subgenre. When it was trendy to write hard-boiled fiction, everyone wanted to write hard-boiled fiction. When it was trendy to write techno-thrillers, everyone wrote techno-thrillers. So it's not surprising that women weren't included, since they weren't included in any of the cycles that ran through the spy business, on either side of the Atlantic. The stories written by Ambler and John Buchan didn't include women (save as secondary characters), nor did the Bond and Bond-like thrillers. When those styles were succeeded by the likes of le Carré and Len Deighton, women still weren't included. The current spy writers like Clancy still haven't thought to include women, which is one of the weaknesses of the Jack Ryan books. There is a joke, intentional or not, in one of the Devlin stories, *The British Double Cross* (1983), along these lines. At the end of the novel, Devlin's girlfriend has been marked for death by the Soviets, who can't believe she is only a reporter who only gets mixed up in the spy business only because she happens to be in love with Devlin. It's obvious that the Soviet spymasters know little of American spy fiction. They didn't read James Grady's *Six Days of the Condor* (1974), or see the movie version, *Three Days of the Condor.* Its hero is a man who reads books for the CIA—something that a woman could certainly do, but no one wants to consider one for the job. Somewhere along the line, if a character like Modesty Blaise—who is today an exception—had turned out to be more than that, the publishing and film worlds would have been overrun with female spies. Instead, most female spies have been as quaint as poor Mrs. Polifax, an elderly widow who once got herself thrown in an Albanian jail while in her country's service.

If women detectives have made a success of themselves in the hard-boiled genre in the past decade, there is no reason why they shouldn't be able to do the same thing in the spy genre. It doesn't matter what a person's sex is when that person's job is to interpret satellite photos or to debrief defectors. This, for everyone who insists on plausibility, is much more plausible than Kinsey Millhone or V. I. Warshawski, who are as unreal as Marlowe was. But there is nothing unreal about a spy story featuring an analyst for the CIA whose breasts are larger than her testosterone level, except that the idea hasn't occurred to anyone yet.

Isn't it about time it did?

Faye Dunaway and Robert Redford in Three Days of the Condor.

Tracking the Sources

The most enjoyable part about writing a book like this was reading the books and watching the movies and television shows featuring and explaining the American fictional detective. It's true that most of the novels, movies and television shows aren't memorable—even after allowing for the vagaries of genre fiction—but I never had much of a problem plowing through them. There was always the hope that I would stumble across another Dan Turner or Coffin Ed Johnson and Grave Digger Jones in my research—someone who isn't well known, but who should be. The excerpts from the works quoted here are from the standard U.S. editions, almost always from my paperback collection. In addition, I was privileged to quote from the letters and comments I received from a number of authors about their characters and their genre.

It was even more fun to read the critical literature dealing with the American fictional detective. This has always appealed to my sense of humor, which nice people describe as Pythonesque. The scholarship is surprisingly vast for a subject that so many learned souls go out of their way to scorn. In fact, sometimes it's hard to figure out why, if a particular critic hates Mickey Spillane as much as he says he does, he goes to all of the trouble to write a long, footnoted chapter in a collection of critical essays to explain his distaste.

The books included here are not everything that I consulted, but those that were the most important. The starting point for any project like this is with the four major reference works. Each is equally ambitious and is equally as valuable to anyone who has any interest in this subject. The only problem is that books like these rarely stay in print, and are usually prohibitively expensive when they are in print. Still, don't despair, This is what libraries, remainder catalogues, and secondhand bookstores were invented for.

Typical is Bill Pronzini and Marcia Muller's *1001 Midnights: The Aficionado's Guide to Mystery and Detective Fiction* (New York: Arbor House, 1986). It's a forty-dollar book, but only for the reader lucky enough to find it. *1001 Midnights* is a mammoth undertaking, summarizing the plots of the 1001 titles (from throughout the world) that the editors feel are the most important in the history of the genre. It comes as close to being indispensable as any of these books can. It demonstrates not only that Pronzini is a tireless worker, but that his contributions to the nonfiction portion of the genre are more important than his Nameless Detective. Anyone can write a private eye story, but only Pronzini seems able to produce such outstanding nonfiction. Nameless, in fact, shows up in two of the 1001 entries—more than Ernest Tidyman's John Shaft (0), more than Chester Himes's Coffin Ed and Grave Digger (1), more than Lawrence Treat's Mitch Taylor (1), and more than K. C. Constantine's Mario Balzic (1). If this book has a flaw, it's that it seems weighted in favor of Pronzini and his contemporaries—writers like Max Allan Collins, Michael Collins and Lawrence Block. This does not, however, detract from the book's value.

The other standard works are *A Catalogue of Crime* (New York: Harper & Row, 1974), by Jacques Barzun and Wendell Hertig Taylor, Allen J. Hubin's *Bibliography of Crime Fiction 1749–1980* (New York: Garland, 1984), and Chris Steinbrunner and Otto Penzler's *Encyclopedia of Mystery and Detection* (New York: McGraw-Hill, 1976). The first contains critical evaluations by the authors of some 7,500 works of detective fiction, and is wonderfully idiosyncratic. Barzun is a genuine treat, a Frenchman whose love affair with American culture has lasted since he arrived in this country in 1920. Barzun is perhaps most famous for his oft-quoted statement: "To understand America, you must understand baseball." The next two are pretty much what they seem. The Hubin book is an example of the man's previously mentioned prodigious powers, while the latter is a compilation of characters, plots, and author biographies for film and print. Penzler and Steinbrunner are almost as prolific as Pronzini, with countless books and television programs to their credit (Penzler worked for The Mysterious Press, the New York publisher that does only mysteries, and Steinbrunner is a television producer). They also helped put together *Detectionary* (Woodstock, New York: The Overlook Press, 1977), a similar, but shorter, version of their encyclopedia, while Penzler compiled *The Private Lives of Private Eyes* (New York: Grosset & Dunlap, 1977), which is as much fun to read as it is difficult to find.

Philadelphia mystery bookstore owner Art Bourgeau's *The Mystery Lover's Companion* (New York: Crown, 1986) has, unfortunately, vanished from print. Find this book at all costs. It isn't as thorough or as critically precise as the four standards, but this is not a drawback. It contains capsule summaries of more than 2,500 books, grouped by author and category, and includes a witty description of each of Bourgeau's four categories—American, English, thriller and police procedural. His explanation of the difference between the West Coast and East Coast detective story is so good I wish I had written it.

Of the countless other books dealing with the history, development and form of the genre, it's hard to improve on *The Mystery Story* (Del Mar, California: Publishers, Inc., 1976). It features essays by thirteen detective fiction critics on their specialties as well as an extensive, accurate and annotated bibliography. However, there is no index, and James Sandoe's chapter on the hard-boiled subgenre verges on the infuriating. Sandoe, who should have known better, denigrates Chandler by comparing him unfavorably to the likes of Raoul Whitfield, who never met a cliché he couldn't use. A similar sort of book, complete with similar aggravations, is Dilys Winn's *Murder Ink* (New York: Workman Publishing, 1984). For every outstanding article—Ed McBain on the genesis of the 87th Precinct, Ian Carmichael on how he managed to make Peter Wimsey much more interesting on television than he was in the books—there are just as many silly pieces, usually dealing with the traditional English mystery. Does the world really need one more smarmy article describing how poisons work?

Howard Haycraft's two books, especially *Murder for Pleasure: The Life and Times of the Detective Story* (New York: Carroll & Graf, 1984), are well worth picking up. Do not think that because Haycraft has come in for more than his fair share of criticism in this book that I do not appreciate his work. I do, for it was both pioneering and ground-breaking. *Murder for Pleasure* deals brilliantly with the first one hundred years of the detective's history, and it is thorough, knowledgeable and authoritative. It is marred only by Haycraft's distaste for the hard-boiled hero, which is as understandable as it is unfortunate. Also helpful is H. R. F. Keating's *Crime & Mystery: The Best 100 Books* (New York: Carroll & Graf, 1991). Keating, the author of the Inspector Ghote series, is a British critic who appreciates the importance of the American detective in a way others, both and American and British, don't. Keating, in two paperback-sized pages per book, evaluates one hundred books with a clarity and firmness other critics can only dream about.

In fact, a British critic, T. J. Binyon, is one of the few I've found who has been able to put the eclipse of the hard-boiled detective in perspective. Binyon's *Murder Will Out: The Detective in Fiction* (Oxford, England: Oxford University Press, 1989) is a wonderfully concise history of the entire genre (only 166 pages), where the only drawback is not the length, but the author's insistence in fitting every detective into one of four categories and then into one of thirty-five subcategories. It gets a little confusing keeping the amateur amateurs and the professional amateurs straight. Hillary Waugh's *Guide to Mysteries and Mystery Writing* (Cincinnati: Writer's Digest Books, 1991), by the author of one of the first police procedurals, is a much more personal look at the genre, starting with Poe and concluding with the women hard-boiled private eyes (he has some doubts about their staying power, too). There is also a section on how to write mysteries, as well as Waugh's list of thirty books or authors to be sure to read. The list includes, along with the usual suspects, Mickey Spillane and Sue Grafton.

Two other surveys of the history of the genre are helpful. *An Introduction to the Detective Story* (Bowling Green, Ohio: Bowling Green State University Popular Press, 1987) hits the high points without, as author LeRoy Lad Panek points out, getting into too much academic detail. *The Dimensions of Detective Fiction* (Bowling Green, Ohio: Bowling Green State University Popular Press, 1987), written by Pat Browne, is a touch more academic, but still useful.

Hard-boiled criticism begins with *Which Way Did He Go?* (New York: Holmes & Meier, 1982), by Edward Margolies. This is the most level, evenhanded book that I have found that deals with the contributions of Hammett, Chandler, Macdonald and Himes to the genre. The chapter on Himes is especially valuable, since his work has been as overlooked by the critics as it was by the book-buying public. There is nothing evenhanded about William Ruehlmann's *Saint With a Gun: The Unlawful American Private Eye* (New York: NYU Press, 1974)—starting with the cover photo of a man in a trenchcoat pointing a pistol at the reader. But this does not detract from Ruehlmann's effort. He may not always say things that are easy to hear, but they deserve to be listened to.

More conventional is Robert Baker and Michael Nietzel's *Private Eyes: 101 Knights* (Bowling Green, Ohio: Bowling Green State University Popular Press, 1985). The authors start with Daly and work to the present, rating hard-boiled private eyes in a surprisingly worshipful system (knights, jesters, etcetera) that belies their academic backgrounds. Geoffery O'Brien's *Hard-boiled America* (New York: Van Nostrand Reinhold, 1981) is a more typical academic effort.

Ron Goulart's *The Dime Detectives* (New York: Mysterious Press, 1988) is a good starting place to learn about the pulps. An even better place (though harder to find) is Tony Goodstone's *The*

Pulps (New York: Chelsea House, 1976), which includes a history of all the pulp magazines, a well-annotated collection of stories that appeared in the various pulps, and one hundred color pulp covers. Goodstone's book includes a rare Dan Turner story from *Spicy Detective* in 1940, "Death's Passport"—which features a brunette frail named Lanya Kensington with gorgeous whatchacallems. Pronzini's two "Gun in Cheek" books: *Gun in Cheek* and *Son of Gun in Cheek* (New York: Mysterious Press, 1982 and 1987) are not for all tastes. But anyone who has ever read a wretched paperback in an airport terminal and wondered why anyone printed that junk should read these. Pronzini shows there were much worse efforts.

It is much easier to find collections of hard-boiled stories than collections of anything else, especially traditional stories. In fact, the dearth of traditional anthologies is nothing short of amazing. The best way to keep track of what's what in that field is to check *Ellery Queen's Mystery Magazine* (both current and back issues), which religiously prints and reprints stories about little old ladies, eccentric amateurs and the like. Perhaps the Oxford University Press, whose *Oxford Book of English Detective Stories* is a classic, will decide to do a similar book for the American traditional detective.

The Private Eye Writers of America is just one group that does an annual hard-boiled anthology; American publishers also release any number of volumes each year, usually edited by at least one of three people: Pronzini; Martin Greenberg, a professor at the University of Wisconsin–Green Bay; or Amos Walker creator Loren Estleman. There are entirely too many floating around to note here, and they go out of print too quickly. One, *Hard-Boiled Detectives* (New York: Gramercy Books, 1992) is notable not only for its stories from *Dime Detective* (it has a truly dreadful Erle Stanley Gardner about a palmist who solves a murder featuring a cut-off hand), but also for a disclaimer on the copyright page. The disclaimer warns readers that some of the ethnic and racial terms used fifty years ago may be offensive to people today. Political correctness comes to the pulps.

The Great American Detective (New York: New American Library, 1978), compiled by William Kitteredge and Steven M. Krauzer, is the genre's essential short story collection. It features fifteen stories covering every important fictional detective from every category, and its introductory essay is one of the clearest, most cogent explanations of the development of the American detective to be found. Herbert Ruhm's *The Hard-Boiled Detective: Stories from Black Mask Magazine* (New York: Random House, 1977) was one of the first successful attempts to update Joseph Shaw's landmark collection of *Black Mask* stories, *The Hard-Boiled Omnibus* (New York: Simon & Schuster, 1946). Shaw's book is so rare that even most large libraries don't have a copy. The prolific William F. Nolan's contribution is *The Black Mask Boys* (New York: William Morrow, 1985), and it does Ruhm one better. It includes biographies, a novelette, checklists and sources for Hammett, Chandler, Horace McCoy, Daly, Nebel, Whitfield and Cain. This book, thankfully, is still in print. Two books that bridge the hard-boiled/traditional gap were compiled and annotated by David Willis McCullough. *City Sleuths and Tough Guys* (Boston: Houghton Mifflin, 1989) leans toward the hard-boiled, while *Great Detectives* (New York: Random House, 1984) is more evenly divided (and has British authors). Each book includes hard-to-find gems as well as worthwhile introductory essays. The first has the *Double Indemnity* screenplay; the latter has a William Faulkner detective story. One of the few solid efforts in the field of traditional anthologies is *Murder Impossible* (New York: Carroll & Graf, 1990), edited by Jack Adrian and Robert Adey. Its focus is locked-room murders, which is a British specialty, but it includes a piece featuring Professor S. F. X. Van Dusen—a rare event. The standard spy reference is *The Spy Story* (Chicago: University of Chicago Press, 1987), written by two professors, John Cawelti and Bruce Rosenberg.

Raymond Chandler has not been well-treated by critics and biographers. The authorized work—*The Life of Raymond Chandler* (New York: E. P. Dutton, 1976)—by Frank MacShane is too long-winded and too unfocused. Better is the first (and best), by the late Philip Durham: *Down These Mean Streets a Man Must Go* (Chapel Hill: University of North Carolina Press, 1963), but it is almost impossible to find. Almost all other Chandler biography and criticism is mean-spirited and almost venal, in the vein of *The World of Raymond Chandler* (New York: A & W Publishing, 1978), edited by Miriam Gross. The exception is *Raymond Chandler* by Jerry Speir (New York: Frederick Ungar, 1981). This is an even-handed assessment with a thorough bibliography. Also try to find *Raymond Chandler Speaking* (Boston: Houghton Mifflin, 1962), a collection of Chandler's letters that are as charming and witty as they are informative.

Hammett has been much more fortunate with the critics. There are three excellent biographies. The authorized one is *Dashiell Hammett: A Life* (New York: Random House, 1983), by the novelist Diane Johnson. Its main drawback is that it is written in the present tense, which is annoying to read. William F. Nolan has tackled Hammett in *Hammett: A Life at the Edge* (New York: Congdon & Weed, 1983), a full-scale biography, and in *Dashiell Hammett: A Casebook* (Santa Barbara, California: McNally and Loftin, 1969), a full-scale bibliography of Hammett criticism. Perhaps the best of the efforts is Richard Layman's *Shadow Man:*

The Life of Dashiell Hammett (New York: HBJ, 1981). Valuable, too, is Lillian Hellman's introduction to a collection of Hammett stories, *The Big Knockover* (New York: Random House, 1966).

Poe's biographers don't often spend much time discussing his invention of the detective story. The definitive Poe book may be *Poe Poe Poe Poe Poe Poe Poe* by Daniel Hoffman (Garden City, New York: Doubleday, 1972). *Rex Stout: A Biography* by John McAleer (Boston: Little, Brown, 1977) may not be the definitive effort, but it is certainly the longest—621 pages. Also of interest is *Nero Wolfe of West 35th Street* (New York: Viking Press, 1969), an attempt by William S. Baring-Gould to write Wolfe's biography based on the information in the novels. Stout, reports McAleer, was not impressed, but the book is required reading for anyone with any interest in the world's fattest detective. The authoritative Ellery Queen biography is Francis M. Nevins Jr.'s *Royal Bloodline: Ellery Queen, Author and Detective* (Bowling Green, Ohio: Bowling Green State University Popular Press, 1974). The definitive Gardner is *Erle Stanley Gardner: The Case of the Real Perry Mason* by Dorothy B. Hughes (New York: William Morrow, 1978).

Finally, four books are invaluable for anyone who has an interest in the detective as portrayed on television and in the movies. *The Encyclopedia of Film* (New York: Putnam, 1991) doesn't always include every actor and director it should, but its biographies are thorough and accurate. Leonard Maltin's current edition of his *TV Movies and Video Guide* (New York: New American Library, 1992) is, until something better comes along, the book by which other movie guides should be judged. Third is Ric Meyers's *Murder on the Air: Television's Great Mystery Series* (New York: The Mysterious Press, 1989). Meyers interviewed everyone who was anyone for this book. Although it is often too much about too little (a twenty-two-page chapter on "Hawaii 5-0"?), it is always entertaining and informative.

The fourth book is the most impressive, and that's saying a lot given the quality of the previous three. *The Complete Directory to Prime Time Network TV Shows* (New York: Ballantine, 1991) is such a vast undertaking that it is, in its own way, even more incredible than *1001 Midnights*. Tim Brooks and Earle Marsh list every show, complete with cast lists, air dates and synopses, for every episode to ever appear on network television. Awesome doesn't even begin to describe their achievement.

Mystery Writers of America Edgar Allan Poe Awards*

1946

Best First Novel
Watchful At Night by Julius Fast

Best Motion Picture
Murder, My Sweet, screenplay by John Paxton

Best Radio Drama
"The Adventures of Ellery Queen" by Frederic Dannay and Manfred B. Lee

Outstanding Mystery Criticism
Anthony Boucher

1947

Best First Novel
The Horizontal Man by Helen Eustis

Best Motion Picture
The Killers, screenplay by Anthony Veiller

Best Radio Drama
"The Adventures of Sam Spade" by Bob Tallman, Jason James, and William Spier (director)

Outstanding Mystery Criticism
William Weber

1948

Best First Novel
The Fabulous Clipjoint by Fredric Brown

Best Short Story
Ellery Queen

Best Fact Crime
Twelve Against The Law by Edward D. Radin

Best Motion Picture
Crossfire, screenplay by John Paxton

Best Radio Drama
"Suspense" by William Spier (producer/director)

Outstanding Mystery Criticism
Howard Haycraft

1949

Best First Novel
The Room Upstairs by Mildred Davis

Best Short Story
William Irish (Cornell Woolrich)

Best Fact Crime
Regional Murder Series: Boston Murders edited by Marie Rodell

Best Motion Picture
Call Northside 777, screenplay by Quentin Reynolds, Leonard Hoffman, and Jay Dratler

Best Radio Drama
"Inner Sanctum" by John Roeburt (principal writer) and Himan Brown (producer/director)

Outstanding Mystery Criticism
James Sandoe

Special Edgar
Best foreign-made film, *Jenny LaMour*

Special Edgar
Clayton Rawson for *Clue*

Special Edgar
Arthur A. Stoughton, President of the Bronx Society of Arts and Sciences, custodian of Poe Cottage, Fordham

1950

Best First Novel
What A Body by Alan Green

Best Short Story
Ellery Queen

* *Awards presented for works and contributions of the previous year.*

Best Fact Crime
Bad Company by Joseph Henry Jackson

Best Motion Picture
The Window, based on a Cornell Woolrich story

Best Radio Drama
"Murder By Experts" by Robert Arthur and David Kogan (producers)

Oustanding Mystery Criticism
Anthony Boucher

Special Edgar
Sidney Kingsley for *Detective Story*

Special Edgar
John Dickson Carr for *The Life of Sir Arthur Conan Doyle*

1951

Best First Novel
Nightmare In Manhattan by Thomas Walsh

Best Short Story
"Diagnosis: Homicide" by Lawrence G. Hochman

Best Fact Crime
Twelve Against Crime by Edward D. Radin

Best Motion Picture
The Asphalt Jungle, screenplay by Ben Maddow

Best Radio Drama
"Dragnet" by James Moser and Jack Webb

Outstanding Mystery Criticism
Dorothy B. Hughes

Special Edgar
Franklin Heller, producer-director of *The Web*

1952

Best First Novel
Strangle Hold by Mary McMullen

Best Short Story
"Fancies and Goodnights" by John Collier

Best Fact Crime
True Tales from the Annals of Crime and Rascality by St. Clair McKelway

Best Motion Picture
Detective Story, screenplay by Philip Yordan and Robert Wyler

Best Episode In A Television Series
"The Web"

Best Radio Drama
"Dragnet" by James Moser and Jack Webb

Outstanding Mystery Criticism
Lenore Glen Offord

Special Edgar
Ellery Queen for *Queen's Quorum*

1953

Best First Novel
Don't Cry For Me by William Campbell Gault

Best Short Story
"Something To Hide" by Philip MacDonald

Best Fact Crime
Court of Last Resort by Erle Stanley Gardner

Best Motion Picture
Five Fingers, screenplay by Michael Wilson

Best Episode in a Television Series
"Dragnet"

Best Radio Drama
"The Mysterious Traveler" by Robert Arthur and David Kogan

Outstanding Mystery Criticism
Anthony Boucher

Raven
E. T. Guymon, Jr.

Special Edgar
Frederick Knott for *Dial "M" for Murder*

1954

Best Novel
Beat Not The Bones by Charlotte Jay

Best First Novel
A Kiss Before Dying by Ira Levin

Best Short Story
"Someone Like You" by Roald Dahl

Best Fact Crime
Why Did They Kill? by John Bartlow Martin

Best Motion Picture
The Big Heat, screenplay by Sidney Boehm

Best Episode in a Television Series
"Crime At Blossoms" ("Studio One") by Jerome Ross

Best Radio Drama
"The Shot" ("Suspense") by E. Jack Neuman

Outstanding Mystery Criticism
Brett Halliday and Helen McCloy

Raven
Dr. Thomas A. Gonzales, Chief Medical Examiner, New York City

Raven
Dr. Harrison Martland, Chief Medical Examiner, Essex County, New Jersey

Raven
Tom Lehrer for songs and poems parodying mystery and crime

Special Edgar
Mary Roberts Rinehart

1955

Best Novel
The Long Goodbye by Raymond Chandler

Best First Novel
Go, Lovely Rose by Jean Potts

Best Short Story
"The House Party" by Stanley Ellin

Best Fact Crime
The Girl With The Scarlet Brand by Charles Boswell and Lewis Thompson

Best Motion Picture
Rear Window, screenplay by John Michael Hays

Best Episode in a Television Series
"Smoke" ("Suspense") by Gore Vidal

Best Radio Drama
"The Tree" ("21st Precinct") by Stanley Niss

Outstanding Mystery Criticism
Drexel Drake

Raven
Berton Roueche for *11 Blue Men*

Raven
Best Hardcover Book Jacket Illustration: Dell

Special Edgar
Agatha Chrisite for *Witness for the Prosecution*

Grand Master
Agatha Christie

1956

Best Novel
Beast In View by Margaret Millar

Best First Novel
The Perfectionist by Lane Kauffman

Best Short Story
"Dream No More" by Philip MacDonald

Best Fact Crime
Dead And Gone by Manly Wade Wellman

Best Motion Picture
The Desperate Hours, screenplay by Joseph Hayes

Best Episode in a Television Series
"A Taste Of Honey" ("Elgin Hour") by Alvin Sapinsley

Raven
Best Hardcover Book Jacket Illustration: Charles Scribner's Sons

Special Edgar
Henri-Georges Clouzot for writing and directing *Diabolique*

1957

Best Novel
A Dram Of Poison by Charlotte Armstrong

Best First Novel
Rebecca's Pride by Donald McNutt Douglas

Best Short Story
"The Blessington Method" by Stanley Ellin

Best Fact Crime
Night Fell on Georgia by Charles and Louise Samuels

Best Episode in a Television Series
"The Fine Art Of Murder" ("Omnibus") by Sidney Carroll

Outstanding Mystery Criticism
Curtis Casewit

Raven
Best Hardcover Book Jacket Illustration: Doubleday Crime Club's *Inspector Maigret and the Burglar's Wife*, designed by Tony Palladino

Special Edgar
Meyer Levin for outstanding novel related to the mystery field, *Compulsion*

1958

Best Novel
Room To Swing by Ed Lacy

Best First Novel
Knock And Wait A While by William Rawle Weeks

Best Short Story
"The Secret Of The Bottle" by Gerald Kersh

Best Fact Crime
The D.A.'s Man by Harold R. Danforth and James D. Horan

Best Motion Picture
Twelve Angry Men, screenplay by Reginald Rose

Best Episode in a Television Series
"Mechanical Manhunt" by Harold Swanton

Best Radio Drama
"The Galdincz-Murphy Case" by Jay McMullen

Raven
Best Hardcover Book Jacket Illustration: Harper

Grand Master
Vincent Starrett

1959

Best Novel
The Eighth Circle by Stanley Ellin

Best First Novel
The Bright Road To Fear by Richard Martin Stern

Best Short Story
"Over There, Darkness" by William O'Farrell

Best Fact Crime
They Died in the Chair by Wenzell Brown

Best Motion Picture
The Defiant Ones, screenplay by Nathan E. Douglas and Harold Jacob Smith

Best Episode in a Television Series
"Edge of Truth" by Adrian Spies ("Studio One")

Best Radio Drama
"Suspense" by William Robson

Best Foreign Film
Inspector Maigret

Raven
Lawrence G. Blockman for editing *The Third Degree*

Raven
Frederic G. Melcher for 35 years with *Publisher's Weekly*

Raven
Western Printing for general excellence of Dell jackets

Special Edgar
Alice Woolley Burt for *American Murder Ballads*

Special Scroll
Eleanor Roosevelt as a posthumous award to her late husband, Franklin Delano Roosevelt, as Mystery Reader of the Year

Grand Master
Rex Stout

1960

Best Novel
The Hours Before Dawn by Celia Fremlin

Best First Novel
The Grey Flannel Shroud by Henry Slesar

Best Short Story
"The Landlady" by Roald Dahl

Best Fact Crime
Fire at Sea by Thomas Gallager

Best Motion Picture
North by Northwest, screenplay by Ernest Lehman

Best Episode in a Television Series
"The Empty Chair" by David Karp

Best Foreign Film
Sapphire, screenplay by Janet Green

Raven
Gail Jackson, producer of "Perry Mason"

Raven
Lucille Fletcher for the radio play "Sorry, Wrong Number"

Raven
Ray Brennan for crime reporting

Raven
David C. Cooke for editing *Best Detective Stories of the Year*

Raven
Phyllis McGinley as mystery fan of the year

Raven
Alfred Hitchcock for his contributions to the mystery genre

Raven
Best Hardcover Jacket Illustration: Simon & Schuster

1961

Best Novel
Progress of a Crime by Julian Symons

Best First Novel
The Man In The Cage by John Holbrook Vance

Best Short Story
"Tiger" by John Durham

Best Fact Crime
The Overbury Affair by Miriam Allen deFord

Best Juvenile Novel
The Mystery of the Haunted Pool by Phyllis A. Whitney

Best Motion Picture
Psycho, screenplay by Joseph Stefano (also a Scroll to Robert Bloch as novel author)

Best Episode in a Television Series
"The Case of the Burning Court" by Kelly Roos and "The Day Of The Bullet" by Bill Ballinger

Outstanding Mystery Criticism
James Sandoe

Raven
Charles Addams

Raven
Philip Wittenberg

Raven
Best Hardcover Jacket Illustration: Charles Scribner's Sons (*A Mark of Displeasure*)

Raven
Best Paperback Book Cover Illustration: Dell (*The Three Coffins*)

Special Edgar
Elizabeth Daly

Grand Master
Ellery Queen

1962

Best Novel
Gideon's Fire by J. J. Marric

Best First Novel
The Green Stone by Suzanne Blanc

Best Short Story
"Affair of Lahore Contomnent" by Avram Davidson

Best Fact Crime
Death and the Supreme Court by Barrett Prettyman

Best Juvenile Novel
The Phantom of Walkaway Hill by Edward Fenton

Best Motion Picture
The Innocents, screenplay by William Archibald and Truman Capote

Best Episode in a Television Series
"Witness in the Dark" by Leigh Vance and John Lemont

Best Foreign Film
Purple Noon, screenplay by Paul Degauff and Rene Clement

Raven
Herbert Brodkin

Raven
Best Hardcover Book Jacket Illustration: Random House

Raven
Best Paperback Book Cover Illustration: Bantam

Special Edgar
Frederick Knott for play, *Write Me A Murder*

Special Edgar
Thomas McDade for *Annals of Murder*

Grand Master
Erle Stanley Gardner

1963

Best Novel
Death of the Joyful Woman by Ellis Peters

Best First Novel
The Fugitive by Robert L. Fish

Best Short Story
"The Sailing Club" by David Ely

Best Fact Crime
Tragedy in Dedham by Francis Russell

Best Juvenile Novel
Cutlass Island by Scott Sorbett

Best Episode in a Television Series
"The Problem of Cell 13" by A. A. Roberts

Raven
Best Hardcover Book Jacket Illustration: Doubleday Crime Club

Raven
Best Paperback Book Cover Illustration: Collier

Special Edgar
Frances and Richard Lockridge on the publication of their 50th thriller, *The Ticking Clock*

Special Edgar
Philip Reisman for *Cops and Robbers*

Special Edgar
E. Spencer Shew for *Companion to Murder*

Special Edgar
Patrick Quentin for *The Ordeal of Mrs. Snow*

Grand Master
John Dickson Carr

1964

Best Novel
The Light of Day by Eric Ambler

Best First Novel
The Florentine Finish by Cornelius Hirschberg

Best Short Story
"Man Gehorcht" by Leslie Ann Brownrigg

Best Fact Crime
The Deed by Gerold Frank

Best Juvenile Novel
Mystery Of The Hidden Hand by Phyllis A. Whitney

Best Motion Picture
Charade, screenplay by Peter Stone

Best Episode in a Television Series
"End of the World Baby" ("Kraft Suspense Hour") by Luther Davis

Best Foreign Film
Any Number Can Play, screenplay by Simonin, Andiard, and Verneuil

Outstanding Mystery Critcism
Hans Stefan Santesson

Raven
Best Hardcover Book Jacket Illustration: Random House

Raven
Best Paperback Book Cover Illustration: Bantam

Special Edgar
Hans Stefan Santesson

Special Edgar
Phillip Durham for *Down These Mean Streets*

Grand Master
George Harmon Coxe

1965

Best Novel
The Spy Who Came in from the Cold by John Le Carre

Best First Novel
Friday the Rabbi Slept Late by Harry Kemelman

Best Short Story
"H as in Homicide" by Lawrence Treat

Best Fact Crime
Gideon's Trumpet by Anthony Lewis

Best Juvenile Novel
Mystery of Crans Landing by Marcella Thum

Best Motion Picture
Hush, Hush Sweet Charlotte, screenplay by Henry Farrell and Lukas Heller

Best Episode in a Television Series
"The Fugitive" by Alan Armer

Best Foreign Film
Seance on a Wet Afternoon, screenplay by Brian Forbes

Raven
Best Hardcover Book Jacket Illustration: Doubleday

Raven
Best Paperback Book Cover Illustration: Bantom

Raven
Dr. Milton Helpern

1966

Best Novel
The Quiller Memorandum by Adam Hall

Best First Novel
In the Heat of the Night by John Ball

Best Short Story
"The Possibility of Evil" by Shirley Jackson

Best Fact Crime
In Cold Blood by Truman Capote

Best Juvenile Novel
The Mystery of 22 East by Leon Ware

Best Motion Picture
The Spy Who Came In from the Cold, screenplay by Paul Dehn and Guy Trosper

Best Episode in a Television Series
"An Unlocked Window" ("Alfred Hitchcock Hour") by James Bridges

Best Foreign Film
The Ipcress File, screenplay by Bill Canaway and James Doran

Raven
Best Hardcover Book Jacket Illustration: Random House

Raven
Beat Paperback Book Cover Illustration: Bantam

Raven
Rev. O. C. Edwards for "The Gospel According to 007" in *The Living Church*

Grand Master
Georges Simenon

1967

Best Novel
King of the Rainy Country by Nicolas Freeling

Best First Novel
The Cold War Swap by Ross Thomas

Best Short Story
"The Chosen One" by Rhys Davies

Best Fact Crime
The Boston Strangler by Gerold Frank

Best Juvenile Novel
Sinbad and Me by Kin Platt

Best Motion Picture
Harper, screenplay by William Goldman

Best Episode in a Television Series
"Operation Rogesh" ("Mission: Impossible") by Jerome Ross

Outstanding Mystery Criticism
John T. Winterich

Raven
Ellery Queen's Mystery Magazine

Raven
Clayton Rawson

Raven
Best Hardcover Book Jacket Illustration: Morrow

Raven
Best Paperback Book Cover Illustration: Collier

Special Award
Richard Watts, Jr., Mystery Reader of the Year

Grand Master
Baynard Kendrick

1968

Best Novel
God Save the Mark by Donald E. Westlake

Best First Novel
Act of Fear by Michael Collins

Best Short Story
"The Oblong Room" by Edward D. Hoch

Best Fact Crime
A Private Disgrace by Victoria Lincoln

Best Juvenile Novel
Signpost to Terror by Gretchen Sprague

Best Motion Picture
In the Heat of the Night, screenplay by Stirling Silliphant

Best Episode in a Television Series
"Tempest in a Texas Town" ("Judd for the Defense") by Harold Gast and Leon Tokatyan, based on a story by Paul Monash

Raven
Best Hardcover Book Jacket Illustration: Doubleday Crime Club (*Perturbing Spirit*)

Raven
Best Paperback Book Cover Illustration: Ballantine (*Johnny Underground*)

Special Blunt Instrument
Joey Adams, Mystery Reader of the Year

1969

Best Novel
A Case of Need by Jeffery Hudson

Best First Novel
Silver Street by E. Richard Johnson and *The Bait* by Dorothy Uhnak

Best Short Story
"The Man Who Fooled the World" by Warner Law

Best Fact Crime
Poe, the Detective by John Walsh

Best Juvenile Novel
The House of Dies Drear by Virginia Hamilton

Best Motion Picture
Bullitt, screenplay by Alan R. Trustman and Harry Kleiner

Best Episode in a Television Series
"The Strange Case of Dr. Jekyll and Mr. Hyde" by Ian Hunter

Raven
Best Hardcover Book Jacket Illustration: Charles Scribner's Sons (*God Speed the Night*)

Special Award
Ellery Queen on the 40th anniversary of *The Roman Hat Mystery*

Grand Master
John Creasey

1970

Best Novel
Forfeit by Dick Francis

Best First Novel
A Time of Predators by Joe Gores

Best Short Story
"Goodbye, Pops" by Joe Gores

Best Fact Crime
The Case That Will Not Die by Herbert B. Ehrmann

Best Juvenile Novel
Danger in Black Dyke by Winifred Finlay

Best Motion Picture
Z, screenplay by Jorge Semprun and Costa-Gavras

Best Episode in a Television Series
"Daughter of the Mind" by Luther Davis

Raven
Best Hardcover Book Jacket Illustration: Dutton (*The Spanish Prisoner*)

Raven
Best Paperback Book Cover Illustration: Avon (*Classic Crime Collection*)

Special Award
John Dickson Carr for 40 years as a mystery writer

Grand Master
James M. Cain

1971

Best Novel
The Laughing Policeman by Maj Sjowall and Per Wahloo

Best First Novel
The Anderson Tapes by Lawrence Sanders

Best Paperback Original
Flashpoint by Dan J. Marlowe

Best Short Story
"In the Forests of Riga the Beasts Are Very Wild Indeed" by Margery Finn Brown

Best Fact Crime
A Great Fall by Mildred Savage

Best Juvenile Novel
The Intruder by John Rowe Townsend

Best Motion Picture
Investigation of a Citizen Above Suspicion, screenplay by Elio Petri and Ugo Pirro

Best Episode in a Television Series
"Berlin Affair" by Richard Alan Simmons

Raven
Best Hardcover Book Jacket Illustration: Doubleday Crime Club (*If Laurel Shot Hardy the World Would End*)

Raven
Best Paperback Book Cover Illustration: Popular Library (*Picture Miss Seeton*)

Grand Master
Mignon G. Eberhart

1972

Best Novel
The Day of the Jackal by Frederick Forsyth

Best First Novel
Finding Maubee by A. H. Z. Carr

Best Paperback Original
For Murder I Charge More by Frank McAuliffe

Best Short Story
"Moonlight Gardener" by Robert L. Fish

Best Fact Crime
Beyond a Reasonable Doubt by Sandor Frankel

Best Juvenile Novel
Nightfall by Joan Aiken

Best Motion Picture
The French Connection, screenplay by Ernest Tidyman

Best Episode in a Television Series
"A Step in Time" ("Mannix") by Mann Rubin and "Thief" by John D. F. Black

Raven
Best Hardcover Book Jacket Illustration: Putnam (*If You Want to See Your Wife Again*)

Raven
Best Paperback Book Cover Illustration: Ace (*Black Man, White Man, Dead Man*)

Special Award
Jacques Barzun and Wendell Hertig Taylor for *A Catalog of Crime*

Grand Master
John D. MacDonald

1973

Best Novel
The Lingala Code by Warren Kiefer

Best First Novel
Squaw Point by R. H. Shimer

Best Paperback Original
The Invader by Richard Wormser

Best Short Story
"The Purple Shroud" by Joyce Harrington

Best Fact Crime
Hoax by Stephen Fay, Lewis Chester, and Magnus Linkletter

Best Juvenile Novel
Deathwatch by Robb White

Best Motion Picture
Sleuth, screenplay by Anthony Shaffer

Best Episode in a Television Series
"The New Mexico Connection" ("McCloud") by Glenn A. Larson and "The Nightstalker" by Richard Matheson

Raven
Best Hardcover Book Jacket Illustration: Random House (*Dead Skip*)

Raven
Best Paperback Book Cover Illustration: Ace (*Fetish Murders*)

Special Award
Julian Symons

Special Award
Jeanne Larmoth

Special Award
Charlotte Turgeon

Grand Master
Judson Philips

1974

Best Novel
Dance Hall of the Dead by Tony Hillerman

Best First Novel
The Billion Dollar Sure Thing by Paul E. Erdman

Best Paperback Original
Death of an Informer by Will Perry

Best Short Story
"The Whimper of Whipped Dogs" by Harlan Ellison

Best Fact Crime
Legacy of Violence by Barbara Levy

Best Juvenile Novel
The Long Black Coat by Jay Bennett

Best Motion Picture
The Last of Sheila, screenplay by Stephen Sondheim and Anthony Perkins

Best Episode in a Television Series
"Requiem for an Informer" ("Police Story") by Sy Salkiwitz and "Isn't It Shocking" by Lane Slate

Raven
Best Hardcover Book Jacket Illustration: Simon & Schuster (*The Cold Ones*)

Special Edgar
Joseph Wambaugh

Grand Master
Ross Macdonald

1975

Best Novel
Peter's Pence by Jon Cleary

Best First Novel
Fletch by Gregory McDonald

Best Paperback Original
The Corpse that Walked by Roy Winsor

Best Short Story
"The Fallen Curtain" by Ruth Rendell

Best Fact Crime
Helter Skelter by Vincent Bugliosi and Curt Gentry

Best Juvenile Novel
The Dangling Witness by Jay Bennett

Best Motion Picture
Chinatown, screenplay by Robert Towne

Best Episode in a Television Series
"Requiem for C. Z. Smith" ("Police Story") by Robert Collins and "The Law" by Loel Oliansky

Raven
The Royal Shakespeare Company for its revival of *Sherlock Holmes*

Raven
CBS Radio Mystery Theatre

Raven
ABC for the "Wide World of Mystery" series

Special Award
Howard Haycraft

Special Award
Francis M. Nevins for *Royal Bloodline: Ellery Queen, Author and Detective*

1976

Best Novel
Hopscotch by Brian Garfield

Best First Novel
The Alvarez Journal by Rex Burns

Best Paperback Original
Autopsy by John R. Feegal

Best Short Story
"The Jail" by Jesse Hill Ford

Best Fact Crime
A Time To Die by Tom Wicker

Best Juvenile Novel
Z for Zachariah by Robert C. O'Brien

Best Motion Picture
Three Days of the Condor, screenplay by Lorenzo Semple, Jr. and David Rayfiel

Best Episode in a Television Series
"No Immunity for Murder" ("Kojak") by Joe Gores and "The Legend of Lizzie Borden" by William Baxt

Raven
Leo Margolies, editor of *Mike Shane Mystery Magazine*

Special Edgar
Jorge Luis Borges for his distinguished contributions to the mystery genre

Special Edgar
Donald J. Sobol for his Encyclopedia Brown books.

Grand Master
Eric Ambler

1977

Best Novel
Promised Land by Robert Parker

Best First Novel
The Thomas Berryman Number by James Patterson

Best Paperback Original
Confess, Fletch by Gregory Mcdonald

Best Short Story
"Like a Terrible Scream" by Etta Revecz

Best Fact Crime
Blood and Money by Thomas Thompson

Best Critical/Biographical Study
Encyclopedia of Mystery and Detection by Chris Steinbrunner,
Otto Penzler, Marvin Lachman, and Charles Shibuk

Best Juvenile Novel
Are You in the House Alone? by Richard Peck

Best Motion Picture
Family Plot, screenplay by Ernest Lehman

Best Episode in a Television Series
"Requiem for Murder" ("The Streets of San Francisco") by James J. Sweeney and "Helter Skelter by J. P. Miller

Raven
"The Edge of Night"

Grand Master
Graham Greene

1978

Best Novel
Catch Me: Kill Me by William Hallahan

Best First novel
A French Finish by Robert Ross

Best Paperback Original
The Quark Maneuver by Mike Jahn

Best Short Story
"Chance After Chance" by Thomas Walsh

Best Fact Crime
By Persons Unknown by George Jonas and Barbara Amiel

Best Critical/Biographical Study
Rex Stout by John J. McAleer

Best Juvenile Novel
A Really Weird Summer by Eloise Jarvis McGraw

Best Motion Picture
The Late Show, screenplay by Robert Benton

Best Episode in a Television Series
"The Thigh Bone Connected to the Knee Bone" ("Quincy") by Tony Lawrence and Lou Shaw and "Men Who Love Women" George Cotler and Don M. Mankiewicz

Raven
Edward Gorey

Special Edgar
Allen J. Hubin for a decade as editor of *Armchair Detective*.

Special Edgar
Dilys Winn for *Murder Ink*.

Special Award
Lawrence Treat as editor of *The Mystery Writer's Handbook*

Special Award
"Barney Miller," Danny Arnold (executive producer)

Special Award
"I Am My Brother's Keeper," Richard N. Hughes (executive producer)

Grand Masters
Daphne du Maurier, Dorothy B. Hughes, Ngaio Marsh

1979

Best Novel
The Eye of the Needle by Ken Follett

Best First Novel
Killed in the Ratings by William L. DeAndrea

Best Paperback Original
Deceit and Deadly Lies by Frank Bandy

Best Short Story
"The Cloud Beneath the Eaves" by Barbara Owens

Best Fact Crime
Til Death Do Us Part by Vincent Bugliosi and Ken Hurwitz

Best Critical/Biographical Study
The Mystery of Agatha Christie by Gwen Robins

Best Juvenile Novel
Alone in Wolf Hollow by Dana Brookins

Best Motion Picture
Magic, screenplay by William Goldman

Best Television Feature
"Dashiell Hammett's The Dain Curse," Robert Lenski

Best Episode in a Television Series
"Murder Under Glass" ("Columbo") by Robert Van Scoyk

Raven
Alberto Tedeschi of Mondadori, publisher of the most successful Italian series of mysteries

Special Award
Frederic Dannay and Mignon G. Eberhart on the 50th anniversaries of their first novels

Special Award
Richard Levinson and William Link, producers of "Ellery Queen" and "Columbo"

Grand Master
Aaron Marc Stein

1980

Best Novel
The Rheingold Route by Arthur Maling

Best First Novel
The Lasko Tangent by Richard North Patterson

Best Paperback Original
The Hog Murders by William L. DeAndrea

Best Short Story
"Armed and Dangerous" by Geoffrey Norman

Best Fact Crime
The Falcon and the Snowman by Robert Lindsey

Best Critical/Biography Study
Dorothy L. Sayers, A Literary Biography by Ralph E. Hone

Best Juvenile Novel
The Kidnapping of Christian Lattimore by Joan Lowery Nixon

Best Motion Picture
The Great Trian Robbery, screenplay by Michael Crichton

Best Television Feature
"Murder by Natural Causes," Richard Levinson and William Link

Best Episode in a Television Series
"Skin" ("Roald Dahl's Tales of the Unexpected") by Robin Chapman and Roald Dahl

Raven
"Muppet Murders" ("Muppet Show")

Special Edgar
Chester Gould, creator of Dick Tracy

Special Edgar
The Murderer's Who's Who, J. H. H. Gaute and Robin Odell

Special Play Award
Death Trap by Ira Levin

Grand Master
W. R. Burnett

1981

Best Novel
Whip Hand by Dick Francis

Best First Novel
The Watcher by Kay Nolte Smith

Best Paperback Original
Public Murders by Bill Granger

Best Short Story
"Horn Man" by Clark Howard

Best Fact Crime
A True Deliverance by Fred Harwell

Best Critical/Biography Study
Twentieth Century Crime and Mystery Writers by John Reilly

Best Juvenile Novel
The Seance by Joan Lowery Nixon

Best Motion Picture
The Black Marble, screenplay by Joseph Wambaugh

Best Television Feature
"City in Fear," by Albert Rubin

Best Episode in a Television Series
"China Doll" ("Magnum P.I.") by Donald P. Bellisario and Glen A. Larson

Special Edgar
The Edge of Night, celebrating its 25th year

Special Edgar
Joan Evans of the PBS series *Mystery!* for best international mystery programming

Special Edgar
Lawrence Spivak, founding publisher of *Ellery Queen's Mystery Magazine*, celebrating its 40th year

Special Edgar
Paul Nathan for his play *Ricochet*

Grand Master
Stanley Ellin

1982

Best Novel
Peregrine by William Bayer

Best First Novel
Chiefs by Stuart Woods

Best Paperback Original
The Old Dick by L. A. Morse

Best Short Story
"The Absence of Emily" by Jack Ritchie

Best Fact Crime
The Sting Man by Robert W. Greene

Best Critical/Biography Study
What About Murder? by John L. Breen

Best Juvenile Novel
Taking Terri Mueller by Norma Fox Mazer

Best Motion Picture
Cutter's Way, screenplay by Jeffrey Alan Fiskin

Best Television Feature
"Killjoy" by Sam H. Rolfe

Best Episode in a Television Series
"Hill Street Station" ("Hill Street Blues") by Steven Bochco and Michael Kozoll

Special Edgar
HBO for *Sherlock Holmes*, the William Gillette play

Special Play Award
A *Talent For Murder* by Jerome Chodorov and Norman Panama

Special Award
William Vivian Butler for *The Young Detective's Handbook*

Grand Master
Julian Symons

1983

Best Novel
Billingsgate Shoal by Rick Boyer

Best First Novel
The Butcher's Boy by Thomas Perry

Best Paperback Original
Triangle by Teri White

Best Short Story
"There Are No Snakes in Ireland" by Frederick Forsyth

Best Fact Crime
The Vatican Connection by Richard Hammer

Best Critical/Biographical Study
Cain by Roy Hoopes

Best Juvenile Novel
The Murder of Hound Dog Bates by Robbie Branscum

Best Motion Picture
The Long Good Friday, screenplay by Barrie Keeffe

Best Television Feature
"Rehearsal for Murder" by Richard Levinson and William Link

Best Episode in a Television Series
"In the Steele of the Night" ("Remington Steele") Joel Steiger

Special Edgar
The Case of Dashiell Hammett by Stephen Talbot

Ellery Queen Award
Emma Lathen

Special Reader's Award
Issac Bashevis Singer

Grand Master
Margaret Millar

1984

Best Novel
LaBrava by Elmore Leonard

Best First Novel
The Bay Psalm Book Murder by Will Harriss

Best Paperback Original
Mrs. White by Margaret Tracy

Best Short Story
"The New Girlfriend" by Ruth Rendell

Best Fact Crime
Very Much a Lady by Shana Alexander

Best Critical/Biography Study
The Dark Side of Genius: The Life of Alfred Hitchcock by Donald Spoto

Best Juvenile Novel
The Callender Papers by Cynthia Voigt

Best Motion Picture
Gorky Park, screenplay by Dennis Potter

Best Television Feature
"Mickey Spillane's Murder Me, Murder You," by Bill Stratton

Best Episode in a Television Series
"The Pencil" ("Phillip Marlowe") by Jo Eisenger

Special Edgar
The Bibliography of A. Conan Doyle by Richard Lancelyn Green and John Michael Gibson

Robert L. Fish Award
"Locked Doors" by Lilly Carlson

Special Reader's Award
Sylvia Porter

Grand Master
John le Carré

1985

Best Novel
Briarpatch by Ross Thomas

Best First Novel
Strike Three, You're Dead by R. D. Rosen

Best Paperback Original
Grandmaster by Warren Murphy and Molly Cochran

Best Short Story
"By the Dawn's Early Light" by Lawrence Block

Best Fact Crime
Double Play: The San Francisco City Hall Killings by Mike Weiss

Best Critical/Biography Study
Novel Verdicts: A Guide To Courtroom Fiction by Jon L. Breen

Best Juvenile Novel
Night Cry by Phyllis Reynolds Naylor

Best Motion Picture
A Soldier's Story, screenplay by Charles Fuller

Best Television Feature
"The Glitter Dome" by Stanley Kallis, from the book by Joseph Wambaugh

Best Episode in a Television Series
"Deadly Lady" ("Murder, She Wrote") by Peter S. Fischer

Special Edgar
The Silent Shame, NBC news report on child abuse crimes, Mark Nykanen

Ellery Queen Award
Joan Kahn

Robert L. Fish Award
"Poor, Dumb Mouths" by Bill Crenshaw

Reader of the Year
Eudora Welty

Grand Master
Dorothy Salisbury Davis

1986

Best Novel
The Suspect by L. R. Wright

Best First Novel
When the Bough Breaks by Jonathan Kellerman

Best Paperback Original
Pigs Get Fat by Warren Murphy

Best Short Story
"Ride the Lightning" by John Lutz

Best Fact Crime
Savage Disgrace by Natalie Robins and Steven M. L. Aronson

Best Critical/Biography Study
John Le Carre by Peter Lewis

Best Juvenile Novel
The Sandman's Eyes by Patricia Windsor

Best Motion Picture
Witness, screenplay by Earl W. Wallace and William Kelley, from a story by Wiliam Kelley, Pamela Wallace, and Earl W. Wallace

Best Television Feature
"Guilty Conscience" by Richard Levinson and William Link

Best Episode in a Television Series
"The Amazing Falsworth" ("Amazing Stories") by Mick Garris, story by Steven Speilberg

Special Edgar
Detective and Mystery Fiction: An International Bibliography of Secondary Sources by Walter Albert

Robert L. Fish Award
"Final Rites" by Doug Allyn

Special Play Award
The Mystery of Edwin Drood by Rupert Holmes

Reader of the Year
State Senator Suzi Oppenheimer

Grand Master
Ed McBain

1987

Best Novel
A Dark-Adapted Eye by Barbara Vine

Best First Novel
No One Rides for Free by Larry Beinhart

Best Paperback Original
The Junkyard Dog by Robert Campbell

Best Short Story
"Rain in Pinton County" by Robert Sampson

Best Fact Crime
Careless Whispers: The True Story of a Triple Murder and the Determined Lawman Who Wouldn't Give Up by Carlton Stowers

Best Critical/Biography Study
Here Lies: An Autobiography by Eric Ambler

Best Juvenile Novel
The Other Side of Dark by Joan Lowery Nixon

Best Motion Picture
Something Wild, screenplay by E. Max Frye

Best Television Feature
"When the Bough Breaks," teleplay by Phil Penningroth, from the novel by Jonathan Kellerman

Best Episode in a Television Series
"The Cup" ("The Equalizer") by David Jackson and Carleton Eastlake, story by Andrew Sipes and Carleton Eastlake

Ellery Queen Award
Eleanor Sullivan

Robert L. Fish Award
"Father to the Man" by Mary Kittredge

Grand Master
Michael Gilbert

1988

Best Novel
Old Bones by Aaron Elkins

Best First Novel
Death among Strangers by Deidre S. Laiken

Best Paperback Original
Bimbos of the Death Sun by Sharyn McCrumb

Best Short Story
"Soft Monkey" by Harlan Ellison

Best Fact Crime
CBS Murders by Richard Hammer

Best Critical/Biographical Study
Introduction to the Detecive Story by Leroy Lad Panek

Best Juvenile Novel
Lucy Forever and Miss Rosetree, Shrinks by Susan Shreve

Best Motion Picture
Stakeout, screenplay by Jim Kouf

Best Television Feature
"Nutcracker: Money, Murder and Madness" by William Hanley

Best Episode in a Television Series
"The Musgrave Ritual" ("The Return of Sherlock Holmes") dramatized by Jeremy Paul

Ellery Queen Award
Ruth Cavin

Robert L. Fish Award
"Roger, Mr. Whilkie!" by Eric M. Heideman

Grand Master
Phyllis A. Whitney

1989

Best Novel
A Cold Red Sunrise by Stuart M. Kaminsky

Best First Novel
Carolina Skeletons by David Stout

Best Paperback Original
The Telling of Lies by Timothy Findley

Best Short Story
"Flicks" by Bill Crenshaw

Best Fact Crime
In Broad Daylight by Harry N. MacLean

Best Critical/Biographical Study
Cornell Woolrich: First You Dream, Then You Die by Francis M. Nevins, Jr.

Best Juvenile Novel
Megan's Island by Willo Davis Roberts

Best Young Adult Novel
Incident at Loring Groves by Sonia Levitin

Best Motion Picture
The Thin Blue Line, directed by Errol Morris

Best Television Feature
"Man Against the Mob" by David J. Kinghorn

Best Episode in a Television Series
"The Devil's Foot" ("The Return of Sherlock Holmes"), adapted by Gary Hopkins

Raven
Bouchercon

Raven
Special Theater Award to Bruce Jordan and Marilyn Abrams for their production of "Shear Madness"

Special Edgar
Joan Kahn

Ellery Queen Award
Richard Levinson and William Link

Robert L. Fish Award
"Different Drummers" by Linda O. Johnston

Grand Master
Hillary Waugh

1990

Best Novel
Black Cherry Blues by James Lee Burke

Best First Novel
The Last Billable Hour by Susan Wolfe

Best Paperback Original
The Rain by Keith Peterson

Best Short Story
"Too Many Crooks" by Donald E. Westlake

Best Fact Crime
Doc: The Rape of the Town of Lovell by Jack Olsen

Best Critical/Biographical Study
The Life of Graham Greene: Volume I: 1904-1939 by Norman Sherry

Best Young Adult Novel
Show Me the Evidence by Alane Ferguson

Best Motion Picture
Heathers, screenplay by Daniel Waters

Best Television Feature
"Shannon's Deal" by John Sayles

Best Episode in a Television Series
"White Noise" ("Wiseguy") by David J. Burke and Alfonse Ruggiero, Jr.

Best Play
City of Angels, book by Larry Gelbart, music by Cy Coleman, and lyrics by Davis Zippel

Raven
Carol Brener

Ellery Queen Award
Joel Davis

Robert L. Fish Award
"Hawks" by Connie Holt

Reader of the Year
Sarah Booth Conroy

Grand Master
Helen McCloy

1991

Best Novel
New Orleans Mourning by Julie Smith

Best First Novel
Post Mortem by Patricia Daniels Cornwell

Best Paperback Original
The Man Who Would Be F. Scott Fitzgerald by David Handler

Best Short Story
"Elvis Lives" by Lynne Barrett

Best Fact Crime
In A Child's Name by Peter Maas

Best Critical/Biographical Study
Trouble Is Their Business: Private Eyes in Fiction, Film and Television, 1927-1988 by John Conquest

Best Juvenile Novel
Stonewords by Pam Conrad

Best Young Adult Novel
Mote by Chap Reaver

Best Motion Picture
The Grifters, screenplay by Donald E. Westlake

Best Television Feature
"Killing in a Small Town" by Cynthia Cidre

Best Episode in a Television Series
"Goodnight, Dear Heart" ("Quantum Leap") by Paul Brown

Special Edgar
The Encyclopedia of World Crime by Jay Robert Nash

Robert L. Fish Award
"Willie's Story" by Jerry F. Skarky

Grand Master
Tony Hillerman

1992

Best Novel
A Dance at the Slaughterhouse by Lawrence Block

Best First Novel
Slow Motion Riot by Peter Blauner

Best Paperback Original
Dark Maze by Thomas Adcock

Best Short Story
"Nine Sons" by Wendy Hornsby

Best Fact Crime
Homicide: A Year on the Killing Streets by David Simon

Best Critical/Biographical Study
Edgar A. Poe: Mournful and Never-Ending Remembrance by Kenneth Silverman

Best Juvenile Novel
Wanted . . . Mud Blossom by Betsy Byars

Best Young Adult Novel
The Weirdo by Theodore Taylor

Best Motion Picture
Silence of the Lambs, screenplay by Ted Tally

Best Television Feature
"Murder 101" by Bill Condon and Roy Johansen

Best Episode in a Television Series
"Poirot: The Lost Mine" ("Mystery!"), dramatized by Michael Baker and David Renwick

Raven
Harold Q. Masur

Ellery Queen Award
Margaret Norton

Grand Master
Elmore Leonard

1993

Best Novel
Bootlegger's Daughter by Margaret Maron

Best First Novel
The Black Echo by Michael Connelly

Best Paperback Original
A Cold Day for Murder by Dana Stabenow

Best Short Story
"Mary, Mary, Shut the Door" by Benjamin J. Schutz

Best Fact Crime
Swift Justice by Harry Farrell

Best Critical/Biographical Study
Alias S.S. Van Dine by John Loughery

Best Juvenile Novel
Coffin on a Case by Eve Bunting

Best Young Adult Novel
A Little Bit Dead by Chap Reaver

Best Motion Picture
The Player, screenplay by Michael Tolkin

Best Television Feature
Prime Suspect by Lynda La Plant

Best Episode in a Television Series
"Conspiracy" ("Law & Order"), teleplay by Michael S. Chernuchin and Rene Balcer

Robert L. Fish Memorial Award
"A Will Is A Way" by Steven Saylor

Reader of the Year
President Bill Clinton

Grand Master
Donald E. Westlake

Index

C

D

E

F

A GUMSHOE TIMELINE

1829 François Eugène Vidocq writes his memoirs, *Memoires de Vidocq,* considered the first detective nonfiction.

1841 Edgar Allan Poe publishes "Murders in the Rue Morgue," the first detective fiction.

1872 Old Sleuth, first dime novel series detective.

1886 Nick Carter, the quintessential dime novel detective, debuts in *New York Weekly.*

1891 *Nick Carter*

1896 Shyster Ra
his first clie
of Randolp
Melville Da

1907 Jacques Fu
Machine, fe
Van Dusen

1908 Mary Rober
Circular Sta
but known"

1918 Uncle Abne
Davisson P
of short sto

1922 *Black Mask*
Daly's "The
first hard-b

1923 The first C
Plus," appe

1925 Charlie Ch
in Earl Der
a Key.

1926 S. S. Van Dine's introductory Philo Vance book, *The Benson Murder Case,* is published.

1927–28 *Red Harvest,* featuring the Continental Op, is serialized in *Black Mask.*

1929 Ellery Queen's inaugural appearance is chronicled in *The Roman Hat Mystery.*

1930 Sam Spade solves the case of *The Maltese Falcon.*

1931 Warner Oland is the first film Charlie Chan in *Charlie Chan Carries On.*

1933 Perry Mason clears his first client in *The Case of the Velvet Claws.*

st Raymond Chandler
oiled detective story,
nailers Don't Shoot," is
ed.

out's Nero Wolfe makes his
pearance in *Fer-de-Lance.*

Marlowe walks down Los
' mean streets for the first time
mond Chandler's *The Big Sleep.*

uston turns Hammett's novel
novie, *The Maltese Falcon,*
Humphrey Bogart.

Queen's Mystery Magazine
publication.

ce Treat writes the first police
ral, *V as in Victim.*

mmer debuts in Mickey
s *I, The Jury.*

ob premieres the "Dragnet"
gram.